SOUND RISING

Long Island Sound at the Forefront of
America's Struggle for Independence

Richard A. Radune

Research in Time Publications
Branford, Connecticut

*Maps, illustrations and cover art
for this book were produced
by Michael Herda.*

Copyright © 2011 by Research in Time Publications

ISBN: 978-0-9764341-1-5

LCCN: 2010919404

CONTENTS

Preface   v
Acknowledgments   ix
Maps and Illustrations   x
    Eastern United States   x
    Long Island Sound   xi
    West Indies   xii
    Ships   69

PART I: SOUND RISING   1

Chapter 1   The Strategic Maritime Power of Long
             Island Sound   3
Chapter 2   Ingredients for Maritime Independence   13
Chapter 3   Testing the Waters   28
Chapter 4   Prelude to Revolution: A Conflict of Interests   42

PART II: WAR COMES TO
LONG ISLAND SOUND   53

Chapter 5   Action and Reaction: 1775–1776   55
Chapter 6   Battle Lines Are Formed: 1775–1776   86
Chapter 7   A Swarm of Privateers: 1777–1783   108
Chapter 8   Connecticut and Continental
             Navies: 1777–1779   129

Chapter 9   Between and Behind the Lines: 1777–1779   146
Chapter 10   The Tide Turns: 1780–1783   171

                      PART III: THE BURDEN
                         OF INDEPENDENCE   199

Chapter 11   The Struggle Between Wars   201
Chapter 12   The War of 1812: America's Second War
             of Independence   227
Chapter 13   Free at Last   256

             Bibliography   265
             Notes   275
             Index   299

PREFACE

The importance of Long Island Sound cannot be attributed to any one specific port but rather the aggregate power of its multitude of harbors. Together, these had a substantial impact on history. In many endeavors, the Sound lacked large scale maritime operations but made up for this by its vast number of smaller ports and individual enterprises; Yankee ingenuity and creativity; and the daring, relentless pursuit of independence and economic gain by its people. Long Island Sound enterprises and seamen were strong proponents of maritime independence as well as political freedom.

The true power of Long Island Sound has been hidden for centuries and little has been written about it. Much of this was due to the Revolutionary War attack led by Benedict Arnold on New London and Groton in 1781 after he had switched to the British side. New London was burned and its maritime records were destroyed. The Port of New London was important because it was a primary customs clearing house for ships entering and leaving Long Island Sound.

Emerging facts indicate a burgeoning maritime trade from Long Island Sound. Connecticut was the fifth largest trader to the West Indies and was ahead of both New York and Rhode Island, its neighboring colonies. Connecticut farms were highly productive and generated enough surplus to provide much of the needs of Boston, New York and the British West Indies islands. In fact, there was enough New England produce left over to generate a thriving illegal trade with the French, Dutch and Spanish West Indies islands. Illicit trade not only originated in Long Island Sound but the Sound also served as an important conduit for New York merchants seeking to circumvent customs enforcement in that port.

During wars with France, Great Britain branded this illicit trade as treasonous. Americans simply viewed it as an assertion of their right of maritime independence. British attempts to stop illegal trade after 1763 would provide impetus for the growing political independence movement in America.

During the Revolutionary War, Long Island Sound was a thorn in Britain's side that became an open wound which refused to heal. Its privateers, whaleboat forces and the Connecticut State Navy interdicted vital British and Loyalist supply lines; captured or destroyed many ships; struck at will targets on British held Long Island; tied down military forces necessary for defense and threatened British offensive operations by reducing the flow of military supplies to troops in the field. The choking of supplies such as firewood into New York also undermined Loyalist civilian morale and turned many against the abusive, overbearing and demeaning British marshal law that governed them.

Barnet Schecter, in his book *The Battle for New York*, convincingly argues that "New York was the centerpiece of England's plan for suppressing the American rebellion" and that it then became "an albatross that helped strangle the British war effort." *Sound Rising* supports that view and argues that Long Island Sound, through its maritime and whaleboat forces, played an important role in this process. It was also a major factor behind Great Britain's decision to abandon its naval base at Newport and move its military focus to the southern states at the end of 1779.

Events between the Revolutionary War and War of 1812 provided short periods of maritime prosperity but also, longer periods of high risk and chance of failure. The loss of many ships to French and British forces sparked growth in the ship building industry around Long Island Sound in order to replace these losses. Advancements in ship design propelled America into a world class maritime power after 1815 and the long struggle for independence was finally achieved. Significant credit for this achievement must go to Long Island Sound.

After 1800, the merchant economic power and maritime expertise accumulated over a period of many years, by Connecticut in particular, was used to develop the Port of New York and to fund the transformation of Connecticut into an industrial economy. It will be shown that the most significant source of finance, leadership and seamen resources enabling the rapid growth in the Port of New York came not from New York or New Jersey but from Connecticut. Connecticut's future became industrial and its products could easily be sent to New York where worldwide, scheduled shipping was readily available.

I used a liberal definition of Long Island Sound with respect to its influence on the course of history. This included maritime enterprises emanating from all of its bays, ports, coves and navigable rivers feeding into and out of the Sound. Any river port that was reached by ocean tides was therefore considered a seaport. The Port of New York City had (and still has) a unique geographical position in relation to Long Island Sound. Its front door opened directly to the Atlantic Ocean while its back door opened into the Sound. For purposes of this book, the Port of New York City was included only to the extent of its back door interests and involvement.

The time frame focus for my book was the period between 1750 and 1820. The influence of Long Island Sound and its immediate environs in support of both maritime and political independence deserves more credit than it has been given. I had no esoteric academic agenda for writing *Sound Rising*. My goal was to blend a multitude of resources into a comprehensive view which showed the importance of the Sound and was also enjoyable to read.

# ACKNOWLEDGMENTS

I would like to thank my wife, Eleanor, for supporting my writing projects, reading my drafts and providing helpful comments and suggestions. Also, William Peterson, retired Senior Curator at Mystic Seaport, gave me insightful advice and recommended important additional resources for my review. Finally, I am grateful to Michael Herda for creating the wonderful maps, illustration and cover artwork.

Richard Radune is also the author of *Pequot Plantation*, The Story of an Early Colonial Settlement, which was published in 2005.

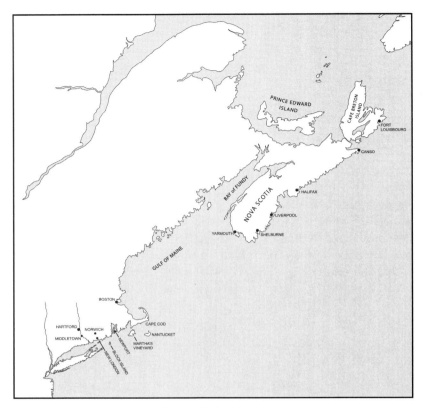

Eastern United States

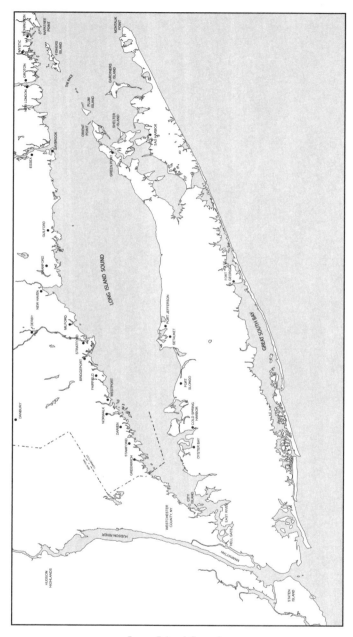

Long Island Sound

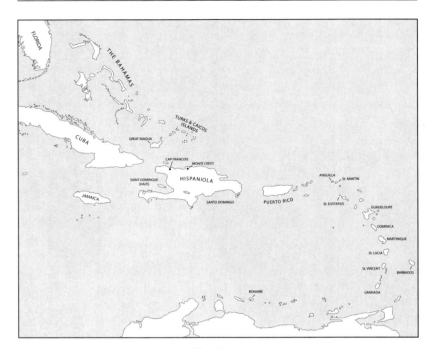

West Indies

Part I

Sound Rising

Chapter One

The Strategic Maritime Power of Long Island Sound

The struggle for American maritime independence from Great Britain began long before the Revolutionary War. A strong foundation for independence was established in the 1600s as New England sailors and merchants ignored British imposed trade restrictions and enforcement provisions that were enumerated in a series of Navigation Acts. Between 1684 and 1687, England, frustrated by the flagrant disregard of its mandates, seized direct control of all the New England colonies. In order to enforce British mandates, King James II appointed Sir Edmund Andros as Royal Governor of New England as well as the Governor of the Royal Colony of New York. The crisis soon passed however, when King James was overthrown by William and Mary in 1689 and Governor Andros was thrown in prison.

Sailors and merchants continued to do what they had always done but the pace quickened during the middle of the next century with the additional element of sea warfare adding great drama as North America became a focus of critical international events. Long Island Sound's geographic location and geological features placed it in position to influence the course of history. Its burgeoning produce and maritime commercial enterprise increasingly conflicted with British interests and set the stage for conflict.

Long Island Sound developed strategic significance for several reasons. First, it was ideally situated between New York and Boston and ships had easy access to the produce of highly productive farms all around its periphery and inland waterways. Connecticut, as well as Westchester County and Long Island in New York, provided much of the food and livestock requirements of these two cities for their domestic consumption and for transshipment to other destinations as well. Still, plenty was left over for direct trade with the British West Indies and Canadian maritime territories. Surplus produce from New England farms eventually exceeded the needs of all the British Caribbean islands so Yankee sailors also began trading with French and Dutch islands, ignoring and circumventing British trade regulations.[1]

Secondly, the strength of Long Island Sound lay not in its large ports but in the multitude of ideal, smaller locations. By some accounts there were at least ninety-three harbors around Long Island Sound and many additional in the Connecticut, Housatonic, Thames and Pawcatuck Rivers capable of being considered a home port for at least a few ships of the era. This was a great strategic advantage for the Sound. The British concentrated their enforcement of trade restrictions on the larger ports such as New York, New London, Newport, Boston and Salem. They either underestimated the amount of trade emanating from Long Island Sound or found it too difficult to monitor its myriad of smaller ports. As a result, some merchants even moved their operations from larger port cities into the hinterlands of Long Island Sound in order to circumvent British controls. The enforcement difficulty prompted one frustrated British official in New Haven to report that "The harbors, rivers and creeks along the coast are many and commodious for smuggling."[2]

The small, family operated maritime enterprises of Long Island Sound provided for relentless individual initiative, energy and creation of entrepreneurial spirit. The array of small ports also thwarted British control of the Sound during the Revolutionary War when it was the eye of the storm. It was a constant source of frustration to England and Connecticut would pay a price for this obstinacy during the Revolutionary War and the War of 1812.

Finally, the many coves, harbors, inlets and other protected waterways of Long Island Sound produced a huge shipbuilding capability from 1750–1820 and beyond. Thousands of ships were built for owners both internal and external to the Sound. This activity occurred predominantly in Connecticut and Westchester County on the north side of the Sound. Most of the south, or Long Island side, remained agrarian and sparsely populated during this time frame. While there were magnificent harbors on Long Island's eastern and western ends, they would not be fully utilized commercially until later.

By the mid 1700s, the maritime power of Long Island Sound was poised to make an impact on the world stage. This would include the West Indies, Nova Scotia, five wars and the advancement of ship design, technology and commercial shipping lines.

Most ships in the West Indies trade were sloops but some schooners and brigs were also involved. Ship sizes ran from 20–150 tons or more but the average size was around 50 tons and less than 100 feet in length. Smaller ships actually had an advantage because they were less costly to operate and were competitive on West Indies routes.[3] Crews were smaller and turnaround time was quicker. It took less time both to assemble a cargo from locations around Long Island Sound and distribute this produce in the West Indies. Multiple stops at different islands often had to be made in order to sell the produce for the best price. The proximity of farmers to ports also reduced shipping costs. The Connecticut River in particular tapped into the interior heartland of Connecticut where strong partnerships developed between farmers and merchants.

The smallest but most common ship was the sloop. These were single mast vessels with fore and aft sail rigging. They often had several jib sails in front with a long bowsprit for jib attachment. Occasionally, they also had a square topsail in addition to the main. Depending on configuration, the sloop only needed a crew of three–six people and often one or two of the crewmen were boys serving as apprentices. Sloops were highly maneuverable and could sail closer to the wind than other ship designs. Schooners were similar, but generally larger, with two masts, each of which had fore and aft rigged sails. Brigs were generally the largest and required a crew of eight–ten or more because the sails could not all be managed from the deck and required sailors to go aloft. The brig had two or more masts, at least one of which was square rigged.

A strong relationship was also forged with Nova Scotia after the British expelled the Acadians during the French and Indian War (Seven Years War in Europe). Thousands of New Englanders, including many from Connecticut, responded to British recruitment efforts and moved to Nova Scotia to replace the depleted population. Maritime trade between there and Long Island Sound soon increased thanks in part to the planting of family business agents in Nova Scotia such as Simeon Perkins who moved there in 1762 from Norwich, Connecticut.

Long Island Sound, with its expanding maritime presence, made strong contributions during several wars. Connecticut ships and troops participated in the capture of Fort Louisbourg from the French on Cape Breton in 1745. During the Revolutionary War, Connecticut established one of the more effective State Navies. Five of its vessels participated in commerce raiding and captured forty-three enemy ships. It's smallest but speediest ship succeeded in carrying across the Atlantic the ratified treaty establishing an alliance with France. While its submarine invention failed to sink a ship, it still captured the imagination of a young nation. The development of floating mines and booby trapped ships also created a sensation. As many as 300 privateer voyages were made during the Revolutionary War by Long Island Sound Patriots and many others by Loyalists on Long Island.

Finally, Long Island Sound functioned as a seedbed for development of seamen, ship captains, technological advancement, larger merchant operations and shipping lines. Many of its men sailed on Continental Navy warships. Nathaniel Palmer of Stonington discovered Antarctica in 1820. Subsequently, he designed the prototype of the famed clipper ship. Steamship service within the Sound was initiated in 1815 and the first transatlantic steamship voyage was made in 1819 by Moses Rogers, a native of New London, sailing out of Savannah. As America's maritime power began to migrate in the early 1800s to large seaports such as New York City, Long Island Sound entrepreneurs helped to make that happen.

Long Island Sound was created by a complex series of geologic events. Initially, the area was a broad river valley. During various ice ages a large quantity of sand and stone was deposited on Long Island in the form of terminal moraines. The basin that was created when the ice retreated became a fresh water lake for several thousand years. Eventually this lake overflowed at the eastern end. Deep channels sliced through the moraine reducing the size of the lake. At the same time, sea level rose as glaciers continued to melt. Ocean water began flowing into the lake from the east side about 8,000 years ago. Later, the western end at New York City was also breached as sea level continued to rise. The creation of Long Island Sound was therefore a progression from river valley to ice gouged basin to glacial lake then saltwater bay and finally a sound.

Long Island Sound is 110 miles long and twenty-one miles across at its widest point. It has a surface area of 787,000 acres with 577 miles of shoreline. The average depth is 65 feet but is 350 feet deep at the Race between Fishers Island and Plum Island.[4] There is a significant tidal variation between eastern and western portions of the Sound. Mean tide ranges from 2.5 feet at New London and Orient Point on the eastern side to 7.3 feet at New Rochelle and Oyster Bay near the western side. Fierce tidal currents exist at both ends of the Sound, particularly at The Race and in Plum Gut on the east and at Hell Gate on the western side.

The preferred approach for most ships entering the east end of the Sound was through The Race between Plum Island and Fishers Island due to the wide width of this passage and minimal obstructions. A secondary entrance between Fishers Island and Napatree Point required intimate knowledge of the numerous reefs, rocks and shoals that cluttered both the entrance to and the length of Fishers Island Sound which was a sound within a sound. Ship captains entering here had to thread their way through one of several passages identified as Watch Hill Passage, Sugar Reef Passage, Catumb Passage, Lords Passage or Wicopesset Passage.

Entering or leaving Long Island Sound was a hazard that all sea captains faced if they wanted to ply the waters of the "devil's belt." On a clear day or night with a favorable wind and tide, this could be a pleasant experience. A missionary by the name of George Fox records a far different experience in his journal during a trip in 1672.[5] He related that his ship cast of from the protection of Fisher's Island, bound for Long Island, but found the water too rough for their ship and had to return. They tried again the next day and passed over waters called the Two Horse Races where the elements combined to push their vessel further east than intended, towards Gardiner's Island. They were forced to tack back out past Gull Island where they could finally tack once more in towards Shelter Island, just a short distance off Long Island. The straight line distance was only a few miles but the trip took three days due to wind and tide.

Fox's adventure was far from over. The voyagers then attempted to travel further west into Long Island Sound but had a very rough time of it. The tide was stronger than anything they had ever seen and, despite having a gale force favoring wind, they could make little progress for several hours while the tide was against them. They struggled all day and the next night but, to their dismay, found themselves being driven back towards Fisher's Island, their original starting place several days before. Towards daybreak it remained very dark as a heavy fog settled in and they could not determine their heading. To make matters worse, it started raining and a great storm arose but at last the fog lifted and the winds shifted to favor them. Finally into the heart of Long Island Sound, they sailed past Faulkner's Island and headed into the Connecticut mainland, probably at Guilford or Branford to ride out the storm.

This was quite a harrowing adventure. Today, the body of water George Fox called the Two Horse Races is simply known as The Race.

The East River at the western entrance to Long Island Sound presented another set of challenges. Technically a straight, this narrow, sixteen mile passage connected the Sound to the Atlantic Ocean through New York Harbor. The straight was as much as 110 feet deep but at Hell Gate its narrow confines, hazardous rock outcroppings, swift tidal current and swirling eddies required skillful maneuvering during the age of sail. Originally named Helegat (bright, open or beautiful passage) by Adriaen Block, its Anglicized name, Hell Gate, seemed eminently more appropriate. As many as 1,000 ships wrecked within the treacherous Hell Gate passage and thousands more went aground.

One of the most notorious ship wrecks occurred in November of 1780 when the British frigate of war, HMS Hussar, sailing from New York into Long Island Sound, was swept onto Pot Rock and sank. There are so many versions of the aftermath that the truth may never be known. Most versions believe this ship was carrying a large amount of gold and silver; payroll for Britain's Naval and Army forces during the Revolutionary War.[6] The British have denied this. Others believe the money was stolen by members of the crew and the ship wrecked to cover-up the theft.

Today, the Hell Gate rocks are gone. Work began in 1850 and continued for another seventy years to reduce these obstructions by dynamite.[7] In 1923, additional dynamiting was done in an attempt to widen the channel. Still, salvagers continue to be intrigued by the prospect of finding the warship's sunken treasure.

Despite the challenges of entering and exiting, the potential of Long Island Sound was clearly evident by the end of the seventeenth century. The south shoreline was sandy with few hazards. The excellent harbors and inlets on its southwestern shore were formed by ancient streams now flooded by higher sea level. The north shoreline was a mixture of rocky headland cut by coves and inlets, sandy beaches, tidal marshes, drowned stream beds, river estuaries and other features. This side contained a plethora of good harbors and anchorages but also contained many hazards such as shoals, reefs, rocks, sandbars and small islands.

Several of the best harbors and anchorages were situated on the eastern end of the Sound. On the Long Island side, Gardiners Bay provided a safe anchorage for large ships. This reality would be detrimental to American interests during both the Revolutionary War and War of 1812 when Britain used it as an anchorage for warships patrolling the area. Within this bay, good harbors would develop at Sag Harbor, Greenport and Shelter Island. Across the Sound the best port locations on Connecticut's eastern side were Stonington, Mystic, the Thames River and the Connecticut River. One negative aspect to Stonington was its vulnerability to enemy attack because of its exposed location. It would be attacked by the British in both the Revolutionary War and the War of 1812 but came through both ordeals with colors flying.

The best harbor on Long Island Sound and among the best on the eastern seaboard was the Thames River. It was deep, wide and mostly unobstructed. Even at the lowest tide there was at least twenty-five feet of depth for about seven miles. In fact most ships of the day had no difficulty traveling twelve miles upriver all the way to Norwich. Geologically, the Thames River was a drowned river valley but much deeper near the coast than other major rivers emptying into the Sound. This feature minimized swift tidal currents which bedeviled other rivers such as the Connecticut River and made access easier at all tides and times. Finally, Fisher's Island formed a natural wave barrier when wind and waves were driven into Long Island Sound from the open ocean. It was estimated that from 300–500 sailing vessels could anchor in New London Harbor at the same time.[8] Norwich, at the head of navigation on the Thames River, could accommodate many more. Due to its distance inland, Norwich was safe from enemy attack. New London was also thought to be safe because it was the most heavily fortified harbor in the Sound. Tragically, that was proven wrong in 1781.

The Connecticut River was a natural wonder that succored many seaports and ship yards. At a length of 410 miles, it was the longest river in New England, extending through Massachusetts and forming the border of Vermont and New Hampshire. It was navigable to Windsor, a distance of about sixty miles, and had tidal impact up to Hartford. Furthermore, it provided immediate access to Connecticut hinterlands which produced a large quantity of farm and forest products for the West Indies trade and lumber for ship building. It was considered completely safe from enemy attack; a belief that proved incorrect in 1814 when a daring British raid penetrated almost seven miles to burn twenty-eight ships in Essex.

The central portion of Long Island Sound extended from the Connecticut River to Bridgeport. Small ports existed in Westbrook, Clinton, Guilford and Branford. New Haven Harbor was slow to develop until the eighteenth century. This harbor, while large, was shallow, not well protected and prone to silting which hampered its maritime development. Despite its drawbacks, New Haven Harbor supported coastal trading and some West Indies trade by the first half of the eighteenth century.[9] Longer wharfs were built improving access to deep water which allowed merchant activity to increase significantly, keeping pace with other harbors.

Milford Harbor was small but comfortable. It was deep enough to handle good size vessels but finding room to maneuver was a challenge. The Housatonic River had a shallow entrance with sandbars yet still supported ships and ship building upstream to Derby. Black Rock Harbor in Fairfield (now Bridgeport) was another excellent but small deep water port. Its small fort with twenty-three defenders protecting the harbor successfully held off a British attack in 1779 although the nearby town of Fairfield was destroyed.

Both shores on the western end of Long Island Sound contained many harbors and inlets. Coastal trade predominated from this area and market boats carrying produce supplied most of the needs of a growing population in New York City. The western end also became the focus of incessant whaleboat warfare and a prime pathway for espionage after the British occupied Long Island during the Revolutionary War.

Ports on the western Long Island side included Setauket, Huntington Bay, Lloyd Harbor, Cold Springs Harbor, Oyster Bay, Hempstead and Port Washington. These were all excellent harbors but population was sparse and maritime development proceeded slowly. During the Revolutionary War, Loyalists established four forts among these harbors. The strongest was Fort Franklin on Lloyd Neck established by the Board of Associated Loyalists under William Franklin, son of Benjamin Franklin. All of these forts were attacked by Patriots from Connecticut. The French Army even tried their hand against Fort Franklin in 1781 when Rochambeau's troops marched through Connecticut. On their way to link up with General Washington's Continental Army north of New York City, a French detachment crossed the Sound but was routed in an ill advised frontal assault on the fort in full daylight.

Ports on the northwestern side of the Sound included Southport, Westport, Norwalk, Stamford, Greenwich, Mamaroneck, City Island and many others. City Island in the town of Pelham, Bronx, New York became particularly important due to its position near the Hell Gate Channel into New York Harbor. The location between City Island and Hart Island provided an excellent, protected, deep water anchorage for ships waiting for optimum conditions of wind, tide and visibility to sail through the hazardous channel. Controlled by the British during the Revolutionary War, this area would be the scene of daring whaleboat raids staged by Connecticut Patriots.

Norwalk Harbor was restricted because it could only accommodate small ships, generally around forty tons, but not more than sixty tons. Still, these small ships proved troublesome to the British during the Revolutionary War prompting them in 1779 to destroy the town and seventeen ships in the harbor. Two years before this, British troops were landed with a mission to destroy military supplies further inland that were destined for the Continental Army. These troops were almost cut off from their ships while returning on the third day. After this, British troops would never again spend more than one night ashore on the Connecticut portion of Long Island Sound, nor venture too far inland.

Chapter Two

Ingredients for Maritime Independence

Three other elements were necessary for maritime independence in addition to seaports detailed in the previous chapter. These consisted of the availability of produce that was in demand, merchant entrepreneurs to establish and maintain trade and maritime related industry such as shipbuilding.

Trade and related custom duties were the most important underlying cause of the growing friction between Great Britain and America. In particular, the burgeoning ability of Long Island Sound area farmers to produce surplus product above subsistence fueled this escalating conflict of interests. Connecticut farms in particular were more productive than has been previously acknowledged, especially in central Connecticut.[10] These products found a ready market in the West Indies and farmers were crucial participants in this trade. When access to this market was reduced during the Revolutionary War, farming surplus was not wasted. It was used to supply General Washington's Continental Army and Connecticut consequently became known as "the provision state." In a similar vein, Connecticut merchant ships were easily converted to privateer duty where they wrecked havoc on British shipping.

The West Indies trade was a significant force driving the North American economy and British policies fostered its growth. Trade by the American colonies was heavily restricted for all areas and products that competed with the products or interests of Great Britain. However, since Great Britain was unable to easily provide products needed in the West Indies, Americans where given the green light at first for unrestricted trade with islands under British control. Profits were generally used to purchase English goods so everyone benefited. Increasingly however, Long Island Sound sailors and merchants evaded payment of duties on legal trade and also traded illegally with non-British islands where prices were more favorable. British mandates to curtail these practices were simply ignored or circumvented. Long Island Sound merchants were in a better position to do this than their counterparts in either Boston or New York where the British concentrated their enforcement efforts.

It was relatively easy for ship Captains to evade restrictions and there were many ways to do this. One method was to simply not clear through customs at New London or one of the other designated ports of clearance. An example of this is evidenced by an affidavit signed by John Blackstone and William Hoadley of Branford, Connecticut on August 9, 1734. These men brought in 671 gallons of Antigua Island rum and sold it to Gurdon Saltonstall. Duty on the rum had not been paid and the two men pledged to reimburse Saltonstall from the proceeds of sale if he should decide to pay the duty at the Customs Office in New London.[11] Most likely this was never done. By 1764, the British stationed a naval ship of war in New London Harbor in order to maintain surveillance on shipping in and out of Long Island Sound. This and other efforts to reduce violations were futile and only increased hostility during the years leading up to the Revolutionary War.

A robust merchant economy developed which was ideally suited to small Long Island Sound ports supported by nearby farms. In the 1720s, Connecticut merchants owned only 41 ships engaged in off shore trade with an average of just 35 tons. This small fleet of ships grew rapidly after 1750 and by 1773 there were 180.[12] In 1730, the Connecticut River town of Middletown was home port to only two seagoing vessels. By 1789 this had grown to twenty and Hartford, just a short distance north, had the same number.

At the Port of New London, newspaper shipping records indicate that sixty-two outbound ships cleared in 1748.[13] This number increased to 100 annually in the 1760s with ships now averaging approximately fifty tons with a deck length of about sixty feet. About fifty-seven percent were coastal traders primarily to Boston and New York and the remaining forty-three percent were voyages primarily to the West Indies.[14] By 1770, it was common for the Port of New

London to receive as many as 100 ox drawn carts full of produce per day during warmer months of the year.[15] In 1756, New Haven was officially added by the British as a designated port for clearing customs. By 1774, there were a total of 108 outbound clearances primarily to the West Indies.[16]

In 1773, Boston Harbor records showed that the greatest number of arriving ships were from Connecticut.[17] Connecticut however, was determined to spur the growth of direct offshore trade and reduce its dependence on trade through Boston and New York. As an incentive, the Legislature established a tax system favoring goods brought in directly from the ports of their origin or making.[18] Further maritime growth was aided by Great Britain's decision to more rigidly enforce its trade restrictions and duties after 1750. They concentrated their efforts on larger ports but were unable to effectively control activity in the many smaller ports of Long Island Sound. Some New York and Boston merchants, exasperated by these restraints, moved their operations into the hinterlands of Long Island Sound in places such as Middletown on the Connecticut River.[19]

Trade with the West Indies was prodigious. So many ships were engaged in this trade that a Captain usually had to visit several islands in order to obtain a good price for his produce onboard and a good price at which to buy commodities for the return trip. A captain would often reach his primary destination only to find that three or four ships had just arrived and had sold quantities of the same cargo, temporarily depressing the price. Insurance policies purchased for each trip ordinarily identified the specific destination and then gave liberty for the ship to visit several other islands without naming them. Ship owners gave the captain considerable latitude and discretionary power to obtain the best deal he could find. Sometimes, when cargo was damaged or degraded from a storm, the voyage would be unprofitable.

In the West Indies, all available acreage was put into sugar cane production so the islands had to import everything necessary to sustain them. The cargos in greatest demand were horses, mules, other livestock (cows, sheep and swine), salted fish, onions, dairy products (cheese and butter), barreled meat, lumber, barrels and staves. Other products included peas, pear brandy, cider, Connecticut River shad cured with salt, tobacco grown in the Connecticut River Valley north of Hartford and unassembled house frames.[20]

Connecticut was the fifth largest trader to the West Indies and was ahead of both New York and Rhode Island, its neighboring colonies.[21] The average number of vessels entering and clearing Connecticut ports dramatically increased from about 100 annually in 1750 to 1,200 annually in 1770.[22]

Increasingly, trade from Long Island Sound and the rest of New England gravitated towards French rather than British islands. There were two reasons for this. The first was surplus produce. Farm and forest production exceeded both domestic consumption and requirements of the British islands. Second, the French islands overtook and then greatly out-produced the British islands and offered molasses at a much cheaper price.[23] By 1775, at least forty percent of Connecticut's West Indies trade was with French and Dutch islands, much of which was considered illicit by England.[24] Some merchants, such as Nathaniel Shaw of New London, traded almost exclusively with the French. Great Britain tried to suppress American trade with non-British islands but they were not successful. This growing conflict of interest would be a major factor leading to the American Revolution.

While sugar was in demand, the real driving force of West Indies trade was rum or the molasses to produce rum in northern distilleries. One of the reasons for rum's popularity was that it was considerably cheaper than other comparable alcoholic beverages. Undoubtedly, this was because of the slave labor used in the West Indies to grow and harvest sugar cane and produce molasses. The average American colonist over the age of fifteen consumed between five and seven shots of rum a day.[25] This was in addition to other beverages such as beer, hard cider and wine that may have been consumed.

Salt was also a critical commodity and enormous amounts were required. It was important for preserving meat, fish and vegetables used for both local consumption or to sell in the coastal or West Indies trade. Salt cured meat and was used with pickling vegetables. Other preservative methods involved smoking, drying or packing in sugar syrup but salt was the most commonly used. It took forty pounds of salt per year to support the food preservation requirements of the average person. Two pounds of salt was required just to preserve one pound of cod fish.[26]

Salt was produced in salt ponds or salinas utilizing evaporation methods. There were three primary and three secondary locations in the West Indies producing salt. First, was the island of St. Martins which contained three large salt pans. Although the island was divided between the Dutch and French, both jurisdictions produced salt. In the 1700s, approximately 200,000 barrels were exported annually. The production capacity could support 400 ship loads annually. Second, was the island of Bonaire just off the coast of South America which was owned by the Dutch. The third primary location was British owned Turks & Caicos Islands. Production on Grand Turk and Salt Cay supplied about one sixth of the salt used in British North America.[27] The three secondary locations with lesser production were British controlled Great Inagua and Anguilla and Spanish owned Tortuga near the Venezuela coast.[28]

Merchant entrepreneurs, another critical ingredient of successful maritime operations, incurred many expenses in order to mount a trading voyage. Normally the merchant was owner or part owner of the vessel and had to acquire and pay a captain and crew, purchase a cargo to carry and purchase provisions for the crew and any livestock carried. If insurance was obtained it could cost several hundred pounds for the ship and a similar amount for the cargo being carried. The merchant then had to consider port fees, tariffs and customs expenses and what instructions to give the ship captain for attempting to avoid or minimize these costs.

Port fees were generally established to provide services and fortifications for defense. The Port of New London first started charging port fees in 1694. In order to supply the harbor's fort with powder and ammunition, the colony imposed a tax on ships over eight tons that loaded or unloaded in the Port of New London. The fee for each ton above eight was one quarter of a pound of ammunition and half a pound of powder or else one schilling.[29] Passes certifying compliance had to be obtained by the ship's captain from the office of the port and given to the fort's gunner. The gunner was empowered and required to fire on those ships that had not provided him with a pass.[30] The first shot would be over the mast, the second, near the front of the ship and the third, at the mast and ship itself if it did not stop to anchor.

Harbor fees for landing in the West Indies were considerable but did not discourage Captains from visiting more than one island to obtain the best trading opportunity. In 1766, for example, the sloop *Delight* from Stratford paid fees of nearly twenty pounds in Barbados. These consisted of nearly six pounds to the collector, five pounds to the fort, an additional five pounds for gunpowder, three pounds for customhouse stamps, money for the searchers office, naval office and liquor office plus "toss in cash for an officer."[31] The ship brought a cargo of horses and other goods and traded at more than one island for salt, sugar and 1,825 gallons of rum.

Merchant protocols were firmly established by 1750 and the perils of maritime trade were well known. Some prospered and others failed through no fault of their own. Their endeavors were heroic but all too often ended in tragic fashion. Long Island Sound merchants were shrewd competitors and Yankee traders would, at the same time, be admired and castigated throughout the world. Every opportunity was taken to achieve a competitive advantage and trade at the best price. One way to do this was to insert a family member at the trade destination to represent the family's merchant interests. Daniel Stanton was an early example of this concept.

In the spring of 1678, thirty-year-old Daniel Stanton made preparations for another voyage from Stonington, Connecticut to Barbados. This time was different however, as he would not be coming back. Daniel's father, Thomas had died the previous December and the five Stanton sons gathered to discuss the future of the family's trade and merchant operations. Their father had been an original founder of Stonington, a merchant all of his life and a pioneer of the early West Indies trade.

The Stantons decided it was time to improve their competitive position by placing a family representative on Barbados to function as local business agent and broker. A local agent on the island could better negotiate the sale of goods shipped down from Long Island Sound and obtain better prices for rum, sugar and molasses carried back on the return trip. The ship captain would no longer have to make trade arrangements after reaching port or be at the mercy of un-scrupulous dealers. Moreover, deals could be lined up in advance thereby reducing the time that a ship would have to remain in port.

The decision to select Daniel for this role was not difficult. Daniel's wife, Sarah Wheeler, had died previously and there was lit-tle holding him back. On Sunday, March 31, the Reverend James Noyes led the church congregation in prayers to Daniel for a safe journey and successful venture.[32] He accepted the good wishes and tearful fair wells of family and friends and headed out to sea. With him was fifteen-year-old James Fanning, a servant indentured to Daniel for a year to help establish his new residence and business.

Daniel remarried and had two children in Barbados where he died just nine years later, probably from a tropical disease. He helped establish the protocol of having local family business agents at trade destinations. Others from Long Island Sound seaports would follow this practice.

Risk was the common element binding merchant and sailor. For the merchant the risk was severe financial loss and for the sailor it was his very life. Storms at sea were an unpredictable hazard that could sink a ship or push it off course for a thousand or more miles. Masts were often broken, sails ripped and seams opened on the hull admit-ting sea water. Horses and other livestock or merchandise carried on deck were at risk of being washed overboard during a storm. If not ac-cidentally lost, these cargos were often thrown overboard to save a ship made top heavy by the extra weight on deck. Produce carried below deck was in jeopardy of contamination when leaks opened in the hull.

The twenty-one ton sloop, *Sarah* out of Norwalk was the victim of such a storm in 1759. Bound for Halifax, Nova Scotia, the storm blew this tiny vessel most of the way to the West Indies and forced Captain Thaddeus Raymond to seek the safety of a port in Barbados instead. Along the way, he was forced to pitch much of his merchan-dise overboard in order to save his crew and the badly damaged ship. With what little merchandise he had left, Captain Raymond was able to obtain a small quantity of rum in Barbados and return to Norwalk, lucky to be alive. The ship's disappointed investors or owners were not so charitable and quickly pursued litigation against him. Captain Raymond countersued blaming the misfortune on the *Sarah* which he said was an old, unseaworthy ship with worn out sails.[33]

Shipwrecks or sinking were also common risks. Overdue ships caused anguish and a craving for information from anyone who may have seen the ship. Daily visits to the docks would be made to obtain any news from arriving ship captains who were always good about collecting and disseminating information on every ship and sailor they knew at every port they visited. They frequently carried letters hastily written by sailors on other ships addressed to people at the captain's destination port. Gradually however, hope would diminish and the crew would be listed as lost at sea and eventually declared dead.

The experience of Joseph Pendleton and his son of Westerly, Rhode Island illustrate this concern. The year was 1750 and it was the dawn of Long Island Sound's Golden Age. Prospects for a successful voyage couldn't have been better. The pirate menace had been largely quelled and there was no threat from privateers since England and France were between wars thus temporarily at peace. Joseph Pendleton had just completed construction of a brig on his property beside the Pawcatuck River between Westerly and Watch Hill. When cargo was loaded, his vessel was ready to sail.

With high hopes, Pendleton sent his ship out under command of his son, Joseph, Jr. The elder Pendleton must have been so confident of success that he decided to assume the whole financial risk and he also decided to waive insurance for the voyage. This trip would make him a wealthy man. The brig eased through Little Narragansett Bay, negotiated the narrows near Stonington Point and passed out of Long Island Sound between Napatree Point and Fishers Island. It reached Anguilla in the West Indies without incident where a profitable trade was made for rum, molasses and probably salt as well.[34]

On its homeward journey, the ship disappeared and was never seen again. The loss was devastating to Pendleton. The most distressing peril to a sailor's family, friends and loved ones at home was the disappearance of a ship at sea. Hundreds of ships put out to sea and were never heard from again. They met with disaster and went down alone with no survivors and no one to witness or learn of their demise. Waiting for information often lasted years before hope faded.

Not only had Pendleton lost a son but his ship and cargo were uninsured. Unable to pay his debts, Pendleton was forced to sell much of his property in small parcels through a lottery established in Rhode

Island.[35] A new town was created by this called Lotteryville (now known as Avondale). Most ship owners avoided a catastrophic event of this nature by either selling shares in the voyage or purchasing insurance. On a risk sharing basis, the ship and its cargo were valued and the owner would sell shares to as many as ten or twenty people who would then share proportionately in the profit or loss for that voyage. The alternative was to purchase insurance for the voyage which might cost five to ten percent of the value, and twenty percent or more during times of war. The insurance industry was born due to necessities of maritime trade.

Occasionally, shipwrecks had happy endings. Jabez Perkins of Norwich experienced a more fortunate outcome in 1775. He sailed under a business consortium owned by the Perkins and Backus families. Outward bound from Norwich to the West Indies, his ship was wrecked, probably striking a reef in southern latitudes. Jabez was near death by the time a passing ship spotted the wreckage six days later. His tongue was so swollen from severe dehydration that he was unable to speak.[36] Upon arrival in the West Indies, a number of ship captains chipped in to give Jabez fifty dollars so he could buy some clothing and other necessities.

One person's misfortune could be another's fortune. Shipwrecks on or near shore presented salvage opportunities and they occurred all around Long Island Sound. Some areas were particularly hazardous. One such location was Watch Hill, Rhode Island, a strategic point situated at the entrance to Long Island Sound with views to Block Island, Long Island and Fishers Island. Many ships were lost on the reefs off of Watch Hill Point. Periodically the point was manned by lookouts and fortified with cannon.

Long Island Sound was occasionally the recipient of storm battered ships seeking safety. In most cases these ships struggled into New London for repairs. One instance involved a distressed Spanish ship, the 200 ton *St. Joseph and St. Helena*, bound from Honduras to Cadiz, Spain by way of Havana. This ship, which had been captured from the British some years earlier during King George's War, was blown far off course to the north of Cuba. Leaking and in distress, the Spaniards hailed a passing ship which happened to be the *Susannah* out of New London. The *Susannah* agreed to place a pilot onboard and both ships made for New London on November 24, 1752.

What appeared to be a simple matter soon became an ugly, international incident rife with allegations of purposeful destruction, theft and collusion. England ultimately sent the warship *Triton* to New London in order to monitor and attempt to resolve the confused state of affairs.[37] The cargo of the *St. Joseph and St. Helena* included valuable indigo, thirty-nine chests of silver dollars and three chests of gold doubloons and was worth $400,000 Spanish dollars or about $4,000,000 in today's money. By the time the ship was finally repaired and allowed to depart more than two years later, most of the gold was gone along with nine chests of silver and forty bags of indigo.[38]

Despite the considerable increase in maritime commerce there were virtually no navigation aids in Long Island Sound to guide sailors and prevent shipwrecks. The only lighthouse in the Sound until the end of the eighteenth century was at the entrance to New London Harbor. This was a clear indication of the vital significance of this port. In most cases, safe passage rested primarily on the experience and skill of the ship captain. A key factor was the apprentice system where young men were taught the art of sailing, were trained in navigation and learned the position of hazards and safe channels in areas they frequently sailed.

A less than successful effort was made to place and maintain buoys in the Connecticut River to mark the channel. The effort was financed by lotteries run by the colony. By the beginning of the Revolutionary War however, depth charts of the river's mouth were made to assist larger ships in and out of this vital waterway.

Maritime related industries developed in great numbers around Long Island Sound. These included shipbuilding, rope making, sail making, cooperage, tannery, slaughter house and saw mill operations. Ship building provided the main non farm employment. On the Connecticut side of the Sound, virtually every harbor, cove and navigable river had at least one shipyard. On the Long Island side of the Sound, major ship building did not start until after the Revolutionary War. A small but important exception was Sag Harbor. This village was minimally settled prior to 1730 and had only thirty-two families by 1775 but it did support three wharves, a try works, warehouses, a shipyard and a ropewalk.

By 1750, the premier ship building location became the Connecticut River. About fifty shipyards operated on the navigable portion between the mouth of the river and Windsor where at least 4,000 vessels were built prior to 1850.

The area encompassing Portland and Middletown, which then included Upper House (now the town of Cromwell), had ten shipyards by the time of the American Revolution and was considered one of the leading commercial areas between New York and Boston.[39] During the Revolutionary War, two ships were built here for the Continental Navy. These were the *Trumbull* at 700 tons, carrying thirty-six guns and the *Bourbon* at 900 tons, carrying forty guns.

The Essex and Deep River areas were known as Potapaug. Six large shipyards were in operation and supported seven saw mills and five blacksmith shops. The largest and most famous of the shipyards was started just before the Revolutionary War by Uriah Hayden. During the War of 1812 the British raided Essex and burned twenty-eight ships including five sleek privateers. Both this area and the Middletown area upstream each had the capacity to construct thirty vessels at the same time.[40]

The dramatic growth in ship building that took place after 1750 on the Connecticut River was due in part to easier access to timber supplies farther inland as these resources disappeared from shoreline harbor areas. The river itself was used to float large quantities of forest products downstream. Logs were floated to saw mills close to the ship building site and shingles and barrel staves were floated to a river port for loading onto ships. If necessary, rafts of logs were floated all the way from Massachusetts, New Hampshire and Vermont.[41] By 1752, theft and clandestine disposal of these products floating down the river became a serious problem. The Connecticut General Court was forced to pass "An Act to prevent secret Trespasses in taking up and disposing of Saw Mill Logs and other Timber, Shingles and Staves, floating or floated down Connecticut River."[42]

Slave labor was an increasingly important element of merchant operations around Long Island Sound during the eighteenth century. Many slaves and free blacks worked as ship crew members, dock hands, in shipyards and in other maritime related industries. In 1690, Connecticut had only 200 black inhabitants representing about one percent of the population. By 1775, the number had increased to about 6,400 or three percent of the population. This was the highest percentage for any colony in New England but still much smaller than that of New York. The black inhabitants of Manhattan and its four surrounding counties were seventeen percent of the population on the eve of the Revolutionary War. Further out on Long Island, the black population in Suffolk County was about eleven percent. The total numbers for New York increased from about 2,000 black inhabitants in 1698 to about 20,000 in 1775.

While the overall black population in Connecticut was about three percent, it was much higher in major maritime communities. It was nine percent in New London, seven percent in Fairfield and almost four percent in Middletown.[43] While inland, Middletown was a major maritime port and ship building center. The percentage figures suggest that slave and free black labor provided useful value in activities supporting maritime trade, ship building and merchant businesses. Slaves were often shopped out on a contract basis with wages payable to the owner. They often performed tasks others didn't want to do but also worked in skilled positions as well. By 1737, free coopers in New York City were complaining about the great number of slaves working in their trade.

The production of rope was another industry that utilized slave labor and required a rope walk in order to twist hemp or flax yarn into rope. As shipyards multiplied, rope walks also sprouted in those communities. In the late 1750s for example, Middletown was a major and still growing, maritime and ship building center that did not have a rope walk. Merchants were at a competitive disadvantage because they had to buy all of their rope for ship rigging from as far away as New London, New York or Boston. Philip Mortimer, a Boston entrepreneur, came to Middletown and soon identified rope making as a great business opportunity.[44] He constructed his rope walk on the west side of Main Street just north of Washington Street. His building was one thousand feet long and about twenty-five feet wide. The one thousand feet length was necessary to start the process because spinning the yarn into rope eventually reduced its length to 600 feet which was the size desired for a ship's cable.

Typically, a rope walk might employ skilled, unskilled, apprentice and slave labor. There were a number of processes and jobs involved in rope making and the most skilled position was that of spinner or master spinner. The hard, mundane, manual labor of rope making however, was tedious and unrewarding. Because few were willing to work in this trade, it was well suited for employment of slaves since they could be forcibly utilized.

The life of slave Prince Mortimer was intimately connected to that of rope making. Prince arrived in Middletown in the 1730s and probably lived and worked initially in a farm environment. He was handicapped by painful yaws disease, an infection which produced lesions, bumps, ulcerations and disfigurement. This plagued him for his entire life which spanned approximately 110 years. Prince was purchased by Philip Mortimer after Mortimer constructed his rope walk in the late 1750s.[45] He was put to work there probably with other slaves as well. Eventually, he apprenticed as a spinner and continued the trade of master spinner for many years. Upon Philip Mortimer's death in 1794, Prince was bequeathed to George Starr but, in 1811, was convicted and sent to prison for attempting to poison Starr. He was released after a few years but generally refused to leave, voluntarily spending most of his remaining years living in prison until his death in 1834.[46] It was just too difficult for him to survive outside of prison with his disability and advanced age.

There were many instances of slaves being allowed to purchase their freedom. One such person was Venture Smith. Born in 1729, Venture purchased his freedom for fifty-one pounds in 1765 at the age of thirty-six.[47] He then worked in the New London and Stonington area to purchase the freedom of his two sons for two hundred pounds each and his wife for forty pounds. Maritime opportunities often provided the initial employment for newly freed slaves. Venture's son Solomon almost immediately signed on for a whaling voyage where he died of scurvy. After his own freedom, Venture chartered a thirty ton sloop for one year and used it for coastal trade, primarily hauling cordwood and lumber from Long Island to Rhode Island. He hired a navigator to assist and cleared one hundred dollars over his costs at the end of the year.[48] He also fished with nets, set lobster and eel pots and hired out on a seven month whaling cruise. Eventually, Venture purchased a farm in Haddam Neck near the Connecticut River where he also had a landing and shipyard.

Maritime service during the Revolutionary War afforded some slaves with an opportunity to purchase their freedom. Prince Brown, a slave owned by Captain Joseph Mather of Lyme, negotiated an arrangement with his owner that allowed him to participate in several privateering expeditions. His share of the spoils went to Captain Mather and proved so lucrative that Mather emancipated Prince in September 1779.[49]

Acquiring and transporting slaves was also a business of sailing. Full treatment of this subject as applied to Long Island Sound would require a separate book beyond the scope of *Sound Rising*. Therefore, only a brief overview is provided. Readers who are interested in this subject are encouraged to review other sources for detailed information.[50]

It has been estimated that less than one percent of the millions of slaves brought across the Atlantic were carried in ships sailing from all northern colonies combined.[51] The overwhelming majority of slaves were carried across the Atlantic in foreign country vessels with Great Britain having the largest role. There is documentation to support about 1100 voyages from New England to Africa with 934 of these being made by Rhode Island vessels that carried a total of 106,000 slaves.[52] There are records of only four ships going to Africa from Long Island Sound.[53] One of these was the sloop *Good Hope* which picked up 169 slaves in Sierra Leone and transported them to St. Christopher's (St. Kitts today) in 1757. It is likely that more than four voyages were made, however the true total will probably never be known. As previously mentioned, shipping records at New London, the primary customs clearing port for ships entering and leaving Long Island Sound, were burned by Benedict Arnold during an attack on the town in 1781.

While the total participation of Long Island and Connecticut in the direct slave trade is not fully known, they were far from innocent bystanders and fully supported the institution of slavery in the West Indies. The complicity of Long Island Sound involved providing supplies and sustenance to the West Indies and buying the commodities that these islands produced. This helped to maintain the system of plantations based on slave labor. It also generated wealth for maritime entrepreneurs and farmers around Long Island Sound. While most Long Island Sound area, slave driven enterprises were small, significant exceptions have recently been identified in Salem, Brooklyn and Lebanon, Connecticut.[54] In Salem for example, a large agribusiness was developed utilizing slave labor to provide food and barrel staves for West Indies trade markets. The farm may have encompassed as many as 13,000 acres that were worked by more than 100 slaves.

Slaves were imported into Long Island Sound communities from the West Indies but were not brought in on vessels where the sole cargo was a hold crammed with slaves to be put on an auction block. They were generally transported singly or in small groups. Although some were speculative, most slaves were purchased on a contract basis and brought back individually on consignment to the purchaser. The slave or slaves would only be an incidental part of the trade conducted and cargo carried. Often, a resident wishing to acquire a slave would place an order directly with a sea captain sailing to the West Indies. Otherwise, a slave dealer might be utilized to line up the transaction.

Slave dealers were known to exist in New London and Middletown and were probably located in most major port communities. Dealers would handle those slaves brought in on speculation and these were probably sold through placement of ads in newspapers rather than via an auction block. Slave dealers would also handle the sale of slaves from one owner to another and might also handle the contracting of slaves to perform temporary work for others. The slave's wages would be paid back to the owner.

The New York City area, due to its size and larger slave population, had a more formalized system. In 1711, a slave market was established on Wall Street that served as a central focus for all slave dealer functions and this might have included slave auctions as well. One of its primary purposes however, was to facilitate job contracting of slave labor. The market was a gathering place for slaves available to work and for employers to contract for that labor.

Chapter Three

Testing the Waters

Despite the immense importance of the West Indies, emerging New England sea power was first demonstrated in the Canadian maritime territories in support of British international interests. From the beginning, both French and English Canadian maritime areas were important trading partners for Long Island Sound merchants. Prior to 1760, the primary commodity was salted fish which was carried to the West Indies. The fish cargoes were purchased with salt, rum, molasses and sugar obtained in the West Indies and with apple cider, corn and other supplies from farms around Long Island Sound. After 1760, lumber became increasingly important and fur pelts were also added.

During intermittent periods of war between France and Great Britain, Nova Scotia became a haven for French privateers and warships preying on American commerce along the northeast seaboard. In the second of the wars (Queen Anne's War or the War of Spanish Succession) which ended in the Treaty of Utrecht in 1713, France lost much of Nova Scotia but retained Cape Breton Island and Prince Edward Island. Over a period of thirty years the French constructed Fort Louisbourg which was to be their bastion for defense of French Canadian territory. English communities along the Atlantic seaboard also had reason to fear its potential as a launching point for raids and disruption of commerce.

In March 1744, France declared war on Great Britain and began attacking New England fisheries and commercial shipping before the American colonies were even aware of the resumption of warfare. Within a few months however, authorized colonial privateers fought back and quickly managed to contain and push back French shipping in the North Atlantic by trapping it within the harbor at Fort Louisbourg. While this was happening, Governor Shirley of Massachusetts began lobbying for a home grown invasion of Fort Louisbourg to wipe out the menace once and for all.

British officials and regular military personnel scoffed at the idea. They were convinced that the undisciplined colonials could never succeed. English military officers had such contempt for colonial militias that the word "American" was considered a derogatory term.[55] This contempt originated in 1689 during King William's War and steadily hardened over the years. It became increasingly evident with the brutality of the Royal Navy's impressments of American sailors. British attitude crystallized during the Louisbourg invasion and was often officially expressed.

In the face of this humiliating derision, an all New England invasion force was quickly put together. During the winter of 1745 approximately 100 ships and 4,100 ground troops were committed to the attack. Massachusetts contributed the bulk of these forces with about 3,300 troops while Connecticut contributed 500 and New Hampshire 300. Rhode Island promised 150 but these troops did not arrive at Cape Breton until after Fort Louisbourg surrendered.[56]

In early April, the Connecticut troops gathered in New London where six ships were assembled for transportation and supply. The sloop *Defense*, under command of Captain John Prentice, was owned by Connecticut Colony but the other five ships were chartered for the mission. Fortunately, the small convoy was joined for protection by the *Tartar*, an armed Rhode Island vessel with ninety men and fourteen guns.

The vulnerable Connecticut troop convoy did not anticipate any trouble from French warships that early in the season but the French were more vigilant in 1745 due to the war. They sent the 32 gun frigate, *Renommee* over from France early to keep an eye on things. Louisbourg harbor was not yet free of ice so the ship continued on down the coast where it soon blundered into a hornet's nest of activity on April 18. Massachusetts forces were already ashore at the rendezvous port of Canso in Nova Scotia and nine armed vessels with more than 100 guns between them swarmed out after the *Renommee*.[57]

A running battle lasting thirty hours ensued, but the fast sailing *Renommee* managed to escape. The chase however, pushed the French Frigate right into the path of the arriving Connecticut troop convoy.

Fortunately, Captain Fones on the fourteen gun *Tartar* was in advance of the fleet and had the courage to immediately challenge the superior French ship and draw it away from the convoy. After initiating fire from his bow gun and receiving four broadsides in return, Captain Fones struggled to escape as the *Tartar* clawed its way upwind.[58] The pursued was now the pursuer but the *Tartar* managed to slip away under cover of darkness. Captain Fones' actions allowed the Connecticut troop convoy to arrive safely at Canso on April 24. Meanwhile, the *Renommee* sped directly back to France and arrived at Brest on June 19 to report its discovery of the impending invasion of Cape Breton by New England colonial forces.

Although England did not sanction the American campaign to capture Fort Louisbourg, the British Navy sent a number of ships which began arriving on April 22. This additional naval support was welcomed but would prove to be more detrimental to American interests than helpful. The New Englanders landed on May 1 to begin the siege of Fort Louisbourg and the French capitulated on June 17 after their ramparts were breached by constant bombardment.

Two major events paved the way for this amazing outcome. First, was the capture of the Grand Battery in a fortress located outside of the walls of the main fortification. Two of the captured forty-two pounder cannons and two eighteen pounders were then repositioned to fire on fortress Louisbourg. It took a herculean effort by the soldiers to drag these huge guns the two miles needed to bring them into range. The second event occurred on June 11 when all of the defenders' major cannons were knocked out of action on the Island Battery. Again, it took a heroic effort by the Americans to establish a gun battery at a nearby lighthouse capable of striking the Island Battery. With access to the harbor now available to British warships and the fortress walls breached, the French had little hope of sustaining their defense and surrender terms were then negotiated.

Throughout the siege, Commodore Warren of the British Navy constantly interfered with operational planning, made contemptuous statements and claimed credit for the victory even though the Royal Navy's contribution was little more than a show of force.[59] He also deprived the American Army of any plunder and spirited away most of the spoils of war. The arrogant behavior of Commodore Warren, his officers and sailors left the Americans with a bitter feeling. The continuation of this demeaning legacy, begun the previous century, would fester and grow in the years leading up to the Revolution. It would also be a primary cause for the War of 1812.

Two Connecticut ships were lost in support of operations at Fort Louisbourg. The *Jane* owned by four Norwalk, Connecticut residents was "cast away" at Louisbourg. Apparently the ship was either wrecked or damaged and abandoned. The owners were reimbursed by the Colony for their loss.[60] The other ship was the *Diamond* which was sent to Louisbourg in November 1745 with supplies and garrison troops.[61] It was released to make its return voyage in February 1746 but was never heard from again.

During the siege and afterwards, other French communities on Cape Breton were plundered by raiding parties. The Connecticut sloop *Defense*, under command of Captain John Prentice of New London, attacked St. Ann's and came away with a rich supply of plunder. Captain Prentice hailed from a long line of ship captains from New London.[62] The plunder he acquired at St. Ann's was estimated at £1,200 in old tenor currency. Captain Prentice sold the merchandise in Boston to William Bowdoin for more than £5,000, probably in new tenor notes.[63] Both Connecticut and Massachusetts revaluated their currency in the 1740s, Connecticut at three and a half times and Massachusetts at four times old tenor.

Apparently an agreement had been reached onboard the *Defense* that the value of the plunder would be shared equally between captain and crew regardless of rank or position. Subsequent to that however, Captain Prentice maintained a position that under British Navy mandates he was entitled to retain three eighths for himself and the commissioned officers under him, shared proportionately.[64]

In addition to this money, the British Admiralty later agreed to share other plunder obtained in the Louisbourg expedition. In 1750, the Admiralty Court of Appeals agreed to allow prize shares only to those ships that had directly participated in the capture of a French ship. The *Defence* of Connecticut was one of only three American ships to qualify for prize money.[65] Captain Prentice bought up the claim shares of his crew and sailed for England in April 1746 to collect what was due. While in England, he contracted smallpox and died.[66]

Subsequent to the death of Captain Prentice, dispute over the £5,000 resulted in prolonged litigation against Sarah Prentice, executrix of the estate. By 1749, the court ruled in favor of the ship's crew but the money had vanished. Sarah Prentice was issued an order to appear in court and show cause why the order should not be enforced. The record ends in 1750 with an indication that none of the plaintiffs ever received any money due them. A bill from one of the plaintiffs' attorneys, Christopher Palmer, also went unpaid. As for the money owed by the British Admiralty, it was finally paid over to the six Prentice children many years later.[67]

This episode of war between France and Great Britain ended in the spring of 1748 with the Treaty of Aix-la-Chapelle. To the great dismay and disgust of New Englanders, Cape Breton and Louisbourg were returned to French control. Their magnificent effort, financial expenses and casualties sustained during the siege and as occupying forces seemed to be in vain. They felt like pawns in a global conflict with no say in the outcome.[68] The British government did offer limited compensation in order to quell the outrage but procrastinated in delivery until the fall of 1749. Massachusetts received £183,649; Connecticut £28,863; New Hampshire £16,355; and Rhode Island £16,322.

In 1755, two events occurred that would eventually have significant impact on Long Island Sound maritime enterprise through the natural progression of actions that followed. First was the renewal of hostilities between France and Great Britain; part of the long series of wars loosely known in America as the French and Indian Wars. During this final phase known also as The Seven Years War, France would loose her North American possessions. The second event was the commencement of a policy to expel French residents of Nova Scotia.

With the resumption of warfare, England established a new colony in Nova Scotia. This new colony would provide substantial trade opportunities for Long Island Sound merchants but would also pose a significant threat during the Revolutionary War and War of 1812. Halifax became a base for British North American naval operations and privateers eventually sailed out of its harbors to attack American interests.

Nova Scotia's colonial governor, Charles Lawrence, initiated action to round up and deport the Acadians in August 1755 because, even though they pleaded neutrality, they refused to take an unconditional oath of allegiance to England. The expulsion of 10,000 Acadians entirely changed the dynamics of life in Nova Scotia. Their eviction commenced a sad and long suffering odyssey for one group of people and produced great opportunity for another. Without the Acadians, Nova Scotia was no longer able to generate trade goods and continue as a trade partner. In order to overcome this calamity, a recruiting effort was mounted to entice New Englanders to come to Nova Scotia and replace the Acadians. The recruiting effort succeeded in attracting 8,000 to emigrate by the lure of free land and great opportunity. During and after the Revolutionary War, thousands of Loyalists also fled to Nova Scotia, adding to the population.

On October 27 the first groups of Acadians were expelled with disbursement destinations to nine of the American colonies. Little specific information was provided to these colonies in advance of ship arrivals so the response to arriving ships was erratic with each colony treating them differently. Virginia even refused to accept its allotment of 1,100 passengers and these unfortunate souls were forced to continue on to England where they were made prisoners of war. Connecticut was allotted 744 Acadians and 344 were sent to New York.

Connecticut was the only colony to anticipate and officially recognize the possibility of receiving an allotment or refugees.[69] This recognition however, was little more than a resolution by the Legislature in October that, if any Acadians should arrive, further orders would then be issued for their care and dispersion. It wasn't until after the first two ships arrived in New London on January 21 and 22, 1756 that orders were actually issued.[70] A committee of four people was charged with responsibility to handle the details and disburse the families into fifty separate towns. Each town was responsible for the support of their allotted number of people to the same extent as they would for any other member of that community and in accordance with the laws of the colony. The first three ships arrived in New London in late January 1756 but the fourth ship did not arrive until

May 22 because it was blown off course by a storm and landed in Antigua before continuing on to Connecticut.[71]

Although the Acadians were dispersed to all areas of Connecticut, this was done primarily to spread the cost of maintaining the people so that the economic burden would not fall entirely on a just a few towns. Connecticut however was the only colony to issue orders keeping families together by prohibiting the placement of family members in two or more towns.[72] New York, by contrast, received only about 344 Acadians and separated the children from their parents by placing them in other homes as indentured servants. This New York mandate applied to everyone under age twenty-one.[73]

The Acadians that were consigned to remain in New London were put to work building a stone house in 1756 for Nathaniel Shaw, Sr. The French refugees quarried all of the stone needed to build the house from the property on which it was constructed. Ironically, this house would play a significant role in defeating the British during the American Revolutionary War. During that war, Shaw's son, Nathaniel Shaw, Jr., was appointed by the Continental Congress as Connecticut's Naval Agent and the Shaw Mansion became Connecticut's Naval War Office.[74] Because of its stone construction, this house was one of the few that survived the burning of New London by Benedict Arnold in 1781. The flames were twice extinguished before serious damage was done.

After the end of the French and Indian War in 1763, England allowed the Acadians to relocate. Most who returned to Nova Scotia found their land occupied by New Englanders and others who had been recruited to come in their absence. Most Acadians were forced to move on with final destinations including Quebec, Louisiana, the French Caribbean islands and France.

Many of the Acadians who chose to leave New York went to Martinique, Louisiana or Santo Domingo. Some of the Acadians residing in Connecticut requested to go to France but this petition was denied. In August 1767, 240 Acadians chartered the brig *Pitt* out of Norwich, captained by Richard Leffingwell, and departed for Quebec.[75] On his return trip, Capt. Leffingwell stopped at Liverpool, Nova Scotia on August 31 to visit and trade with Simeon Perkins, a Norwich merchant who had moved to this new community in 1762. Leffingwell sold a supply of pork and then departed for the return to Norwich on

September 5.[76] Simeon Perkins was becoming an important connection for trade between Long Island Sound and Nova Scotia.

A few Acadians remained considerably longer in Connecticut. Records indicate that a large Acadian family lived in Guilford, Connecticut until at least 1772. Upon their arrival in 1756, the town voted to put as many of the family to work as possible in order to minimize welfare expenses to the town. The family must have had a difficult time making ends meet for in 1763 the town voted to pay the rent on their home. Finally, in 1772, the town approved the French family's petition for twenty-five dollars in order to help pay the cost of ship transportation to Albany.[77] From there the family may have continued on to Quebec.

The Nova Scotia population replacement effort began in October 1758 when Governor Lawrence issued his first proclamation specifically inviting New England farmers to the colony. Free, prior cultivated land was offered with no property tax for ten years. A similar arrangement was soon made to attract merchants and mariners with land being offered along harbors and waterways. These locations were along the southwest coast of Nova Scotia where good harbors and coves abounded but the land was not generally farmable. This was virgin land not previously occupied by Acadians.

Four of the first five land agents to arrive in Nova Scotia in the spring of 1759 were from Connecticut and many more would follow. Among them were Major Robert Denison of Montville and Samuel Starr of Norwich.[78] Their task was to select large tracts of the best land for their representative contingents back home and make arrangements for their arrival. The agents were taken into the Bay of Fundy and shown land around the Annapolis River valley and the Minas Basin. The Connecticut agents selected a large area along the southwest shore of the Minas Basin and Avon River between what is today Canard on the north and St. Croix on the south. This contained the finest acreage previously tilled by the Acadians.[79]

The advertising and recruitment campaign was successful. It is not hard to imagine the anguish this brought to those Acadians exiled in Connecticut or elsewhere knowing their land would now be taken irrevocably. In 1760, a flood of settlers left Connecticut to take up the land grants provided. Among them was sixty-three-year-old Major Robert Denison, his second wife, Prudence Sherman and the youngest of his eleven children. They settled in Horton. Samuel Starr and his brother David settled at what is now Starr's Point.

Similarly, an advertisement campaign elicited excitement in Southern New England maritime communities. New settlements were being created specifically to develop and support maritime trade with Great Britain, Newfoundland, the thirteen American colonies and the West Indies. People were needed in order to generate products to sell, provide merchant services and handle trade arrangements and serve as mariners to transport goods. The expectation was that Nova Scotia would develop a robust economy fueled by exploitation of its natural resources.

The influx of New England farmers to replace Acadians was soon followed by merchants, ship builders, sawyers and seamen. These were people from coastal areas of Massachusetts, Rhode Island and Connecticut. Fishing fleets grew rapidly, water powered saw mills sprouted up everywhere and ship building commenced immediately. The lynchpin for all of this enterprise was the merchant who could buy or sell and make arrangements for consummation of trade deals. The most effective expression of this endeavor was for an American merchant or maritime family to permanently place a family member in Nova Scotia. This person would then act as an agent for the family's commercial interests back in Long Island Sound and would also assist other merchant families from the same or neighboring homeports. Cargoes would be obtained for arriving ships or the ships would be redirected to other ports where cargoes were available.

By 1760, recruitment of merchant and maritime tradesmen to the southwest shore of Nova Scotia was in full swing. The practice of placing a family agent on site at the trade destination started in the seventeenth century involving trade with the West Indies. It was not a new idea but little research exists as to how many Long Island Sound merchant families made use of this system.

The Perkins and Backus families, who lived in the bustling seaport town of Norwich Connecticut, were among those considering the prospect of inserting an agent onshore in Nova Scotia. Norwich, at the head of the Thames river had grown to rival the Port of New

London fourteen miles downstream at the mouth of the river. Both families had multiple branches living in the Norwich and New London area and both families were large. Jacob and Jemima Leonard Perkins had fifteen children, several of whom were sea captains. Ebenezer Backus was a businessman, legislator and Justice of the Peace. He had twelve children born to three wives. Two of the three wives, Abigail Trumbull and Eunice Dyer, died previously from complications of childbirth.

On June 12, 1759, an alliance between the Backus and Perkins families occurred when Jacob Perkins' fourth child Simeon, married Abigail Backus. Just eighteen years old, Abigail died on December 22, 1760 with the birth of their son.[80] This shattering event may have been the catalyst for Simeon's decision to take on the Nova Scotia challenge. He formed a business arrangement with his father-in-law, Ebenezer Backus and Captain Jabez Perkins from a different branch of his family.[81] Simeon departed for Liverpool, Nova Scotia in May 1762 leaving his young son, Roger, in Norwich for the next ten years.[82] He was probably in the care of Sarah Clark Backus, his father-in-law's third wife. For much of the time up to the Revolutionary War however, he had a younger brother with him and often one or two additional young men from Norwich or New London families under an apprenticeship arrangement.

Simeon was not among the initial land grant holders but many of these became discouraged by the poor prospects, returned home and forfeited their land grants. He decided to take one of the available Liverpool grants and set to work developing all sorts of trade opportunities. By 1766, Liverpool had five sawmills, 23 fishing boats and fifteen schooners and sloops. The primary commodities that Perkins became familiar with were lumber, fish, beaver pelts and feathers. He also engaged in ship building and held part interest in a saw mill and several vessels.[83] Ships from many Long Island Sound ports made visits to Liverpool but those from Norwich and New London were the most frequent. Simeon Perkins kept a diary which is often referred to as a resource because it helps to understand exactly how trade was conducted with Canadian maritime areas.

Fish were in continual demand and this was an important commodity that could be acquired from Nova Scotia and Newfoundland. The dried fish were either taken directly to the West Indies or transferred to other ships which came from Long Island Sound or Boston that were bound to the West Indies. Perkins tried to maintain a stockpile of dried fish that could be transported on ships of his business partners or sold to others. Sometimes he sent one of his own ships, such as the *Jolly Fisherman,* out to fish. In these cases he claimed half of the fish and oil brought in as his share. In return, he provided the ship, all of the provisions and paid a portion of the shore men's wages and other fees.[84] When his fish stockpile was insufficient, he might buy from others if any could be had.

On June 12, 1766, the Norwich sloop *Liberty* owned by Perkins and his Norwich business partnership arrived with provisions that could be marketed within the Liverpool community. There were no fish available anywhere at the time to load for the return trip. Perkins therefore decided to send the *Liberty* itself out on a fishing trip and rounded up additional crew members needed for such an expedition. It was the end of August before enough fish were obtained after which the ship was sent on to Boston.

Demand for lumber grew steadily and became a significant Nova Scotia trade item with Long Island Sound merchants up until the Revolutionary War. Convenient resources along the shoreline of Long Island Sound were diminished by 1760 forcing logging operations further and further into the interior. The increasing difficulty getting logs or lumber to market made the purchase of lumber from Nova Scotia competitive with local sources.

Simeon Perkins' diary reflects two large lumber contracts in 1766. On August 25, two ships arrived from Norwich with orders for lumber to be delivered to Trumbull & Company. Perkins' second order came from the Briggen Company of London England via Captain Doggett on the *William and Mary* which arrived September 23. An agent for Briggen came to inspect the sixty oak trees selected and then Perkins put ten men to work felling the trees and bringing them to the saw mill for cutting according to specification.[85] On May 8, 1773, two New London ships sent by Thomas Mumford arrived with a large lumber order. While waiting for Perkins to fill the requisition, the two ships ventured out on a fishing expedition off the Gaspe Peninsula.[86]

Another trade item was beaver pelts although availability was inconsistent and the supply eventually dried up as it had at every other previous location where fur was traded. The greatest chance for success each year was to accomplish this trade as early in the season as possible. Simeon's schooner, *Jolly Fisherman* and his business consortium sloop, *Liberty* sailed into Liverpool Harbor on March 26, 1767. Both ships had spent the winter in Norwich. The *Liberty* had orders to continue on to Chaleur Bay between New Brunswick and the Gaspe Peninsula to trade with the Indians for pelts. It was Perkins responsibility to round up a local crew and a person with knowledge of Indian trade. He hired Captain Howes Stewart at £4 per month, Samuel Crowell at fifty schillings per month and also placed his own apprentice, John Knowles, onboard at forty schillings per month. The Indian trader was Robert Plaiceway.

The *Liberty* sailed on April 3 with £360 worth of merchandise onboard and stopped in Halifax to purchase another £50 of merchandise before continuing northward.[87] The mission resulted in a very successful exchange of this merchandise for beaver pelts in Chaleur Bay around the beginning of June. The *Liberty* returned to Liverpool, Nova Scotia on July 2, discharged the local crew members and set sail for Norwich on July 6 under command of Benjamin Arnold.[88]

In spite of Simeon's energy and creativity, he had difficulty making ends meet and the new community of Liverpool struggled to survive. Many people, including those in New York and New England, did not pay debts owed to him. In October, 1766, he was forced to place an advertisement in a New York newspaper demanding payment and threatening to sue those who did not do so.[89]

Simeon also harbored some ambivalence about his allegiance. He returned home to Norwich three times between 1762 and 1775. The duration of his second visit was a year and a half. His last visit was between March 20 and May 28, 1775. American resolve to separate from England was growing but Nova Scotia, vulnerable and isolated, had no recourse but to remain within the British realm in spite of its ties with New England and its sympathy for the American cause. On this last visit to Norwich, Simeon held critical discussions with family and business associates. A decision was reached; Simeon Perkins would become a Nova Scotian.

Trade restrictions and duties were not the only factors in contention. Impressment of American sailors into the British Navy was also a growing cause for concern. One of the earliest records of forced conscription of a colonist into the British Navy was that of Thomas Wheeler of Black Rock Harbor in Fairfield, Connecticut (now Bridgeport). Thomas Wheeler was the son of John Wheeler and grandson of Thomas Wheeler, an original settler to this harbor in 1644. During times of war, England had an insatiable need for sailors. In 1696, Britain had been at war with France for six years in what would be the first of a series of wars known loosely in America as the French and Indian Wars. In Europe this first episode was known as King William's War.

Young Wheeler's ill-fated saga began as a crewman aboard a merchant vessel bound from Black Rock Harbor to Barbados. It was an excellent opportunity for him to earn wages to supplement his small farming enterprise. His spring crop had just been planted so he was available. Their trade mission was successful and Thomas was even allowed to personally acquire three barrels of rum to bring home. However, before he could board ship for the return voyage to Connecticut, he was seized by a British impressment squad and forcibly placed onboard a man-of-war called the *Play* that was in the harbor.

Thomas Wheeler was an ideal candidate for forced conscription since he was young, unmarried and had no family to support. Thomas was allowed to send his personal effects home from Barbados along with a letter to his brother John. In his letter dated July 19, 1696, he told John that his three barrels of rum and three months wages consisting of ten pounds, ten shillings were being carried by Captain Nicklas Inglesbee aboard the Rhode Island vessel, *Dimon* bound for New London, Connecticut.[90] Thomas must have had a premonition that he would never see Black Rock Harbor again. His cruel fate is further revealed in the following excerpt from his letter.

> I hope you will take care of it [the rum and money] and let my honored mother have what she has occasion for and let my honored mother have half the crop of wheat which I have.
>
> As for my lands, I desire that my five brothers may divide them if I do not return again. I know not whether I shall be so happy as to see any of you again but I trust in God who is our presence.

Let us watch and pray one for another. No more at present but your loving brother,

Thomas Wheeler[91]

This was Thomas' last communication with home. He probably died a sailor's death from disease, scurvy or battle wounds. Eight years later he was declared dead. His letter of July 19, 1696 was accepted as his last will and testament and was admitted to probate in Fairfield. Unfortunately, thousands of Long Island Sound sailors would follow in Wheeler's path and suffer a similar fate. The system of impressment did not end with American victory in the Revolutionary War and actually became much worse. It took another war (The War of 1812) plus conclusion of the Napoleonic Wars to end the practice.

Chapter Four

Prelude to Revolution: A Conflict of Interests

The burgeoning American maritime capability increasingly conflicted with British interests. From the earliest New England settlements in the 1600s, colonists wanted to trade freely with anyone providing the best price. England however, with its long established mercantile system, wished to protect its own industries and attempted to coerce its colonies to not compete with English products and to not buy similar products from other countries. This conflict escalated dangerously with the West Indies trade and was a major cause of friction and growing sentiment around Long Island Sound supporting separation from Great Britain.

Generally, illicit trade, which was a violation or circumvention of various British Acts of Trade and Navigation, fell into four categories. First, was trade involving European goods that did not transit to North America through an English port. Second, was trade with non British West Indies islands where the prohibited cargo was disguised as British. Third, was the avoidance of duties on otherwise legally permitted cargo. Fourth, was any trade with the French when Britain and France were at war.

In the first instance, illicit trade in European goods was known as the Dutch Trade and the favorite location was the tiny Dutch neutral island of St. Eustatius. It fulfilled this function by becoming a transshipment center rather than a producer and for the intermingling of goods from many countries, particularly European nations. There were hundreds of warehouses stored with goods that were ready to fill the cargo holds of American merchant ships. This trade was facilitated by Thomas Allen of New London who established himself as a resident agent on St. Eustatius. He provided brokerage services not only to New London merchants but to merchants of the American ports of Salem, Newburyport, Boston, Newport, New York, Philadelphia and Savannah as well.[92] The Dutch island of Curacao was another important location for this trade.

With regards to the second and third types of illicit trade, methods of circumvention were often similar. Much of this activity stemmed from British trade acts. The Molasses Act of 1733 was implemented at the request of British planters who had lost most of their American trade markets to the French and Dutch islands due to much lower product prices. It was aimed at recovering the American trade by placing heavy duties on the purchase of any French or Dutch molasses, rum and sugar. The Molasses Act was replaced in 1764 by the even more onerous Sugar Act which increased existing duties and placed new duties on additional items. This act also placed an outright ban on the importation of French wines and all foreign rum.

Two additional acts were passed in 1764 which would impact future relations between Britain and America. One of these reorganized the customs inspection process in order to reduce violations. The other established a Vice-Admiralty Court in Halifax, Nova Scotia with jurisdiction over all the American colonies. Halifax was becoming Britain's major North American administrative base and military bastion.

In spite of British attempts to restrict American trade, Long Island Sound merchants continued and even increased their trade with non British islands due to the lower cost of rum, sugar and molasses. Many methods were quickly devised to circumvent the restrictions and avoid heavy duties payable at the New London customs house. Ships leaving and entering the Sound were required to stop in New London to obtain clearance documents. Later, New Haven and a few other ports were added to help Britain enforce these provisions.

First of all, customs officials in New England were notoriously lax and routinely looked the other way with regards to collecting taxes under the Molasses Act.[93] Often the ship's captain only declared the legal or non taxable portion of their cargo and was not challenged by the officials. Another way was to quickly unload taxable cargo before clearing customs or simply bypass New London altogether and unload at another port within Long Island Sound where there was no custom house. In a one year period between March 1748 and March 1749, New London records reflect that there were sixty-two ships clearing outbound but only thirty-seven clearing inbound on the return trip.[94] The significantly fewer number of inbound clearances (forty percent less) reflects the tendency of Long Island Sound merchants to ignore and avoid British trade restrictions and tariffs on imports. Cargos were simply delivered to destinations without clearing customs.

Lax officials in the British West Indies also routinely gave fictitious clearances when the cargo was to be obtained at another location on the island that did not have a customs office.[95] Once the documents were secured, the ship would then proceed to a French or Dutch island instead of the declared British port location. Upon arriving in New London, the captain could breeze through customs tax free since his paperwork declared the produce to be British.

Other methods of evasion were devised. Ships would often put into French ports under an alleged emergency and declare that their vessel was in danger of foundering from leaks, cracks in the mast or other damage. The French were only too willing to certify that the repairs could only be made if the costs were defrayed by selling cargo.[96] Instead of using subterfuge, some ships simply sailed with no clearance documents and took their chances of being stopped and asked to produce them. A safer method was to produce forged documents.

Evasion was rampant in western Long Island Sound as well. Britain attempted to control off shore trade from this end of the Sound by establishing another customs house in New Haven. They also inserted a prevention officer in Stamford. This official complained that during the summer months, ten ships per week from towns west of Fairfield made trips into New York City, none of which bothered to obtain required clearance from him.[97] He further noted that many ships from the district also ventured to the West Indies without clearances in either direction. If that wasn't enough, counterfeit clearance certificates were easy to come by. Two prominent Norwalk businessmen, John Cannon and John Pintard, furnished many of these forged documents.[98]

Americans not only disregarded West Indies trade mandates during peacetime, they found ways to circumvent them during the years

England and France were at war. From 1740–1748, this involved the War of Austrian Succession which blended into King George's War, the American phase of the conflict (1744–1748). Next came the Seven Years War (French and Indian War) from 1755–1763.

During these two wars, England banned all trade with the French islands. This didn't stop either Long Island Sound merchants or French islanders, both of whom desired to continue trade during the conflicts. The safest and most widespread way to conduct trade was to sail under a flag of truce. This signified that the ship carried prisoners to exchange. Except for a portion of the Seven Years War when Great Britain attempted to stop the practice, it was honored by French and British military vessels as well as privateers from both nations. The tradition continued until half way through the American Revolution when it was replaced by specially designated "cartel" ships.

Ships exchanging prisoners under a flag of truce also carried produce in order to support and finance the trip. A supply of French prisoners could be obtained by capturing French vessels. When a merchant didn't have any French prisoners it was often possible to purchase some in order to justify the flag of truce.[99] Usually, it was only necessary to carry one or two prisoners. So strong was the desire to continue trade that American merchants devised a deception that was readily agreed to by French islanders. Frenchmen were hired to serve as fictitious prisoners on the voyage down and then brought back again to North America. The process was then repeated again while the welfare of the Frenchmen's families were taken care of by the ship owners during their absence.[100]

Another method of direct trade with the French and avoiding capture by the British Navy was for an American privateer to arrange for the capture of a merchant ship. This "collusive capture" then involved placement of a prize crew on the "captured" merchant vessel or vessels.[101] The vessels would then be convoyed back to North America. If stopped by the British Navy, the Captain could assert his rights to the prizes taken as well as passage to a Maritime Court for condemnation proceedings.

In addition to this direct trade with the enemy, there was a substantial indirect trade thru Dutch, Danish and Spanish merchant intermediaries. The favorite location for this trade was through the

Spanish Neutral port of Monte Cristi on the island of Hispaniola. Here the cargos were either transferred to Spanish ships or else Spanish crews were placed on the American ships and sailed to the French port of Cape Francois, Saint Dominque which was another portion of the same island of Hispaniola.[102] The British Navy intermittently tried to stop this trade with ships stationed near ports in the West Indies and patrolling the islands or approaches to Long Island Sound and New York harbor.

Meanwhile, in Long Island Sound, Connecticut customs officials helped facilitate this illegal trade.[103] They could also be easily bribed to look the other way or to produce false documents. This benefited not only Long Island Sound merchants but also those from the Port of New York when they were forced to utilize their back door transit. This would occur periodically when British and New York government officials attempted to crack down on the illegal trade of that port. Incoming merchandise could also be off loaded in other places within Long Island Sound such as Fishers Island and transferred to smaller sloops or market boats for the run into New York. Outgoing ships could also pick up forged or falsified clearances and proceed out the eastern end.

Joseph Chew, an important customs official, cargo surveyor and searcher and Stamp Act agent for the Port of New London, was a primary source of false documentation and other assistance on the eastern end of the Sound. John Lloyd of Stamford was the most important provider of similar services on the western end.[104] As previously mentioned, another source was John Pintard and John Cannon, owners of a Norwalk Connecticut merchant house, who were particularly adept at procuring and providing forged documents for shippers. Ironically, produce from Western Long Island Sound that was sent into New York for transshipment to the West Indies often found itself funneled back out through the Sound because it was the best way to circumvent the stricter enforcement that was in effect at the Port of New York.

It was not long after France declared war on England in 1756 that allegations were raised of Americans trading with the enemy. The British Board of Trade initiated an investigation which reported alarming abuse and defiance of British mandates. All of the North American colonies were criticized but Connecticut and Rhode Island were singled out as the most blatant abusers.[105] These two colonies were cited for subverting British law and for the corruption of their customs officials which undermined enforcement of the Acts of Trade and Navigation.

Thomas Truxes, in his book *Defying Empire*, cites numerous examples where New London customs officials assisted New York owned ships trading with the enemy. These particular records are available because most of the ships were captured by the British but there would have been many more that were not.[106]

By way of example, between April 26 and May 2, 1762, the British Navy captured four New York vessels as they approached New London on their return voyages loaded with illicit goods from Saint Domingue. Each of the ship captains had instructions to pick up false clearances or other covering documents from Joseph Chew, the customs inspector, before proceeding through the Sound to New York. One of these was the sloop *Prosper* owned by New York merchant, James Thompson. Thompson had given very specific orders to his ship's captain on how he was to proceed with the illegal cargo of fine white sugar from Saint Domingue.[107] Captain Dishington was instructed to sail for New London and make direct contact with Joseph Chew who would take immediate action to clear the vessel into New York. He was then directed to proceed to Cruger's Wharf in New York where Thompson's wife, Catherine would provide further instructions for immediately unloading and selling the sugar.

In the years leading up to the Revolutionary War, the letters of Nathaniel Shaw illustrate other methods of evasion.[108] He was a prominent New London merchant who owned many vessels and was destined to become Connecticut's Naval Agent during the Revolutionary War. In 1766, for example, Captain William Packwood returned from the French island of Martinique in a brig owned by Nathaniel Shaw. He advised Shaw that he had little risk of seizure because he had obtained a crew of mostly Frenchmen, was sailing under French colors and managed to obtain documents which qualified the vessel as French. Another of Shaw's letters in 1766 reveals his intention of smuggling rum from St. Croix into New London in order to avoid the new 1764 Sugar Act taxes. This is evident from the fact that he requested an all risks insurance quote identifying how much it would cost to underwrite such a voyage from St. Croix if the British warship *Cygnet* was patrolling the waters around New London.

Two more of Shaw's letters reveal other schemes in 1766. In June, he devised a plan to avoid some of the duties he would be required to pay. He obtained a clearance in New London for a cargo of molasses and proposed unloading it in New York without entering through customs. The ship would then return to New London and transport another cargo of molasses to New York utilizing the same clearance. He would then carry American produce back to New London which did not require entering or clearing at either port. In the other scheme, Shaw transported some very large casks of molasses to New York but portrayed them as much smaller when he cleared outbound from New London. He instructed his agent in New York to remove them before the ship reached dock because the custom house inspector would undoubtedly notice they were much larger than he had portrayed and was likely to have them measured.

In 1774, the sloop *Sally*, another Shaw vessel, was in Guadeloupe and wanted to load sugar from one of the Spanish West Indies islands (probably Hispaniola). It had to wait for the Spanish Coast Guard to clear out of the area before going there.[109] Shaw also brought sugar from Hispaniola in March of 1775. He did not report it to customs in New London but instead, diverted the vessel to the Boston market. The ship was directed to land at Cohasset, south of Boston, because Shaw had received information that it was easier to elude duties there than in Boston or Salem.[110] Shaw requested that the captain attempt to avoid paying duties or pay as little as possible. If the agent was successful, additional sugar shipments would be sent that way. Nathaniel Shaw would not be able to establish an ongoing Cohasset trade connection. Little did he know, the skirmishes at Lexington and Concord were less than a month away and everything would change after those actions.

After the end of the Seven Years War, Britain instituted a stronger enforcement role with respect to its trade restrictions. The

Molasses Act had largely been a failure. Records show that very little tariff payment was ever made by Americans.[111] It was replaced by the even more unpopular Sugar Act in 1764. Part of this was taxation to pay off debts incurred by the British during the French and Indian War which had just ended. Relations between Great Britain and America began to deteriorate and enforcement measures only quickened the development of irreconcilable differences.

Along with increasing the number of inspectors and strengthening the inspection process, military forces were inserted into the colonies. In 1764, British troops and later, Hessians, were placed in some New England ports and in the Port of New York at the expense of the colonies. This threat of military force was made to support England's right to tax its American colonies. Also that year, the British warship *Cygnet* was stationed in New London Harbor where it remained for four years in order to maintain surveillance on shipping in and out of Long Island Sound and seize violators.

Captain Charles Leslie, commander of the *Cygnet*, did not vigorously pursue his duties and his ship gained the reputation of being a party ship.[112] The crew gave parties onboard, attended parties, frequented taverns, hunted, fished and enjoyed sleighing in the winter snow. While in New London, quite a few of the *Cygnet's* crew members deserted and melted into Connecticut colonial society.[113] Desertion from the British Navy was a general and prolonged problem for England. After the end of the Revolutionary War it would provide them with an excuse for stopping American ships to look for deserters and to impress many others who were not. The practice would lead to America's second war for independence.

When the *Cygnet* returned to England in 1768 matters took a turn for the worse. It was replaced by the *Liberty* whose captain was much more diligent in his duty of inspecting and seizing violators. Cruising between New London and Newport, Rhode Island, the *Liberty* seized and condemned many ships belonging to local merchants. Nathaniel Shaw called it a pirate ship after several of his vessels were confiscated.[114] The *New London Gazette* derisively renamed the ship by calling it the *Slavery*. The demise of the *Liberty* came in 1769 after arriving in Newport with several seized vessels including one owned by Nathaniel Shaw. The residents of Newport, Rhode Island were so outraged that an angry mob went onboard the

Liberty while it was in the harbor, burned the ship and released the captured vessels.[115]

Great Britain grew increasingly annoyed by American subterfuge and disdain for its trade policies. Conversely, Americans felt that it was their right to exercise Yankee ingenuity and creativity in order to compete successfully and obtain the best deals. They took an opportunistic approach and were willing to take risks. Trade and taxes weren't the only points of contention. Great Britain also took measures to protect certain domestic industries and prevent American competition. These included the Wool Act of 1699, the Hat Act of 1732, the more critical sailcloth provisions of 1746 and the Iron Act of 1750.

Most sailcloth, also known as canvas or duck, was imported from European countries such as the Netherlands or Russia rather than from Great Britain. In 1734, Connecticut determined to become more self sufficient in supplies of rope, sailcloth and fine linen. In order to reduce importation of these strategic commodities, the General Court passed an act to encourage more domestic production of hemp and flax and the manufacture of canvas or duck.[116] A subsidy of four pence was provided for every pound of good, well dressed, water rotted hemp and twenty shillings was provided for every bolt or piece of well wrought canvas or duck made from hemp or flax.

Similarly, England was concerned about its own supplies of rope and sailcloth and it also provided a subsidy to encourage domestic production. Furthermore, England wanted to generate export capability, so it wasn't long before Britain moved to further support its industry and reduce competition from the American colonies. In 1746, England expanded its tariff on imports and also established the requirement that all new ships built in America or Great Britain must use British made sailcloth for their first set of sails.[117] These measures served to cripple Connecticut's production efforts until the Revolutionary War.

The Iron Act of 1750 would have even more serious consequences for America. While the Act encouraged mining and the export of pig iron to England, it prohibited manufacturing processes which used iron. The colonies were barred from establishing any new mills for rolling or slitting iron and were prohibited from using plating forges or any other furnaces. In 1764, England specified that iron ore could only be exported to England and also prohibited the colonies from making any cast iron products.[118] As a result, the colonies would be deficient in industrial capability at the outset of the Revolutionary War. No facilities would exist for the manufacture of cannons essential to the army and also critical for waging war at sea. Connecticut would play an important role in remedying that deficiency and would provide many cannons for the Continental Army and for Connecticut's Navy, coastal defenses and privateering vessels.

The gap between British and American interests continued to widen after 1770 and each side had increasing difficulty understanding or accepting the others point of view. Still, after the first shots were fired at Lexington and Concord, merchants, seamen and seaport communities were uncertain as to how widespread the rebellion would become and how they should conduct their activities. It would become a time of change; of action and reaction.

Part II

War Comes to Long Island Sound

Chapter Five

Action and Reaction: 1775–1776

The battles at Lexington and Concord occurred on April 18 and 19, 1775 and then Bunker Hill on June 17. Militias from all over New England organized and marched to Boston. Among them were many able bodied seamen from Connecticut port towns. Siege lines were formed around the perimeter of Boston to contain British military forces and limit their ability to obtain supplies from the surrounding countryside. Later, after George Washington decided to form his own Navy, some of the sailors would be pulled out of the siege lines to man these vessels in an attempt to prevent supplies from reaching the British via the sea.

Even though war had begun, there was considerable uncertainty regarding its impact, how far it would spread and who had control over customs issues in various ports. Nathaniel Shaw no longer had access to Boston markets via Cohasset. In July, he shifted his attention to Philadelphia and sent his sloop *Black Joke* there with sugar, coffee and molasses. No duties had been paid on these goods but he did not know what the status would be in Philadelphia. He decided to take no chances. He ordered the captain to avoid duty if possible by landing at Point Gloucester across the river from Philadelphia, notifying the local business agent and off loading the cargo at this location which was away from the main wharfs.[119]

The first British warship to venture into Long Island Sound after the battle of Lexington and Concord was the sixty-four gun, man-of-war, *Asia* in late April. Because it was the first one to do so after the start of hostilities, nobody knew what to expect or how to react to the situation. For example, Captain John Brooks, Sr. spotted the *Asia* approaching his vessel and decided to run into the safety of port on the Housatonic River. The *Asia* was not after shipping however and began to haul down its sails and then dropped anchor near the mouth of the river off of Stratford Point. Uncertain as to its intentions, the townspeople organized a committee to row out to the Asia under a flag of truce. The British were also uncertain about what kind of reception they might receive on the shores of Connecticut but were definitely interested in refreshing their food supplies and obtaining loyalist recruits. Within a short time, several of the truce committee members actually signed on to serve with the British and one fellow by the name of Chapman was even commissioned on the spot as a lieutenant.[120] Back on shore, many farmers enjoyed lucrative sales of food supplies to British representatives who had come ashore to purchase these items.

The *Asia* returned to Boston but was then ordered to New York City in May to protect British interests and intimidate the residents. Finding that the rebels were in control, negotiations were conducted to evacuate the British military garrison. The garrison troops were allowed to board the *Asia* and merchants were allowed to sell supplies to provision the ship.[121]

The *Asia* appeared again in Long Island Sound at the end of November, 1775 when it delivered a large quantity of arms, powder and ammunition to Loyalists in Queens County, Long Island. Loyalist sympathizers constituted about half of the people in that county. This thwarted the efforts of New York's Provisional Congress which had previously ordered disarmament of Queens County residents, using force if necessary to confiscate weapons. Not only were these efforts unsuccessful, Loyalists actually increased their arsenal thanks to the *Asia*.

The *Asia* appeared one more time. In January 1776, it made a recruiting stop in Stamford, Connecticut. While the war had progressed, it was still largely confined to Boston. Long Island Sound had virtually no coastal defenses at that point and little capability to challenge a British warship. The *Asia* was successful in attracting some recruits including Jesse and Joseph Hoyt who assisted with the recruitment effort and were destined to become active Loyalist participants after the British shifted their forces from Boston to New York.[122]

Nova Scotians were bemused by the growing strife between Great Britain and her New England colonies. With close family and economic ties to New England, the people were sympathetic to their grievances. Their isolated position and weakness as a new colony however, meant that Nova Scotia would remain under the thumb of Great Britain and its overwhelming military presence in Halifax.

On July 5, 1775, the Governor of Nova Scotia issued a proclamation forbidding all intercourse with New England rebels. The proclamation was largely ignored however, and considerable trade with Long Island Sound continued for almost another year. Simeon Perkins' diary reflects numerous visits by Connecticut and other New England ships during this period.[123] Trade even continued after a British Admiral issued an order in September 1775 for naval ships in Halifax "to take, burn, sink and destroy all cities, towns, vessels and boats belonging to the Continent, except Quebec and Nova Scotia."[124]

When the American Continental Congress finally authorized privateering in March 1776, it did not exempt Nova Scotian merchant vessels even though the colony was sympathetic to American interests. One reason for this was the fact that Great Britain had turned Halifax Harbor into a major base for its North American military operations. In March 1776, they began massing troops and ships in this harbor in preparation for its attack and occupation of New York City and Long Island. Nova Scotian food supplies, timber and fish were being utilized by the British thus their commerce was fair game.

In spite of the realities of war, most Nova Scotians were shocked and dismayed by the mounting losses they suffered and had trouble understanding the actions of American privateers whom they considered friends and countrymen. On October 16, 1776, the schooner *Betsey*, part owned by Simeon Perkins and partially loaded with boards, staves and fish, was cut loose from its mooring near his own wharf and taken away by a privateer. His diary entry on this date stated that "this is the fourth loss I have met with by my countrymen, and are altogether so heavy upon me I do not know how to go on with much more business, especially as every kind of property is so uncertain, and no protection afforded as yet, from Government."[125]

Considerable confusion existed as to what constituted a legitimate target. Privateers would often make captures without trying to discern the validity, leaving that decision to a prize court. One such victim was Simeon Perkin's brother, Jabez of Norwich, Connecticut. After trading for salt, rum and sugar in Antigua and Anguilla, he sailed for Liverpool, Nova Scotia and arrived at his brother, Simeon's dock on September 1, 1776. Jabez settled his accounts, departed on September 13 and, shortly after, was captured by an American privateer.[126] Subsequently, Simeon learned that his brother had been released and was back in Norwich. Probably, the American prize court ruled that the capture of Jabez' vessel did not meet the requirements for seizure.

Trade also continued with the West Indies, including the British islands, but the risk was high and the volume of trade greatly diminished as time passed. Salt became scarce during the early days of the War and there was not even enough for residents to put up their own provisions to see them through the winter. Connecticut would send several of its armed or convoyed naval supply vessels to the West Indies to acquire salt, augmented occasionally by captured British merchant vessels containing cargos of salt. A supply of this strategic commodity was stored in Norwich under the strict control and authority of Jabez Perkins for equitable distribution to the populace.[127]

Because the risk of seizure was so high, it became difficult to obtain insurance for voyages to the West Indies. By April of 1776, the availability of marine insurance pretty much disappeared. None could be obtained in Norwich or New London. New London merchant Andrew Huntington wrote to his brother stationed with militia troops in New York City requesting that he inquire as to availability of insurance in New York City. The response was that none was available there but might be in Philadelphia but at prohibitive rates of more than fifty percent of the value of ship and cargo.[128] At these rates, most merchants decided to either discontinue trade or send their ships without insurance.

The difficulties of trade at this time were reported by Captain Waterous of New London, on the sloop, *Commerce*. He was captured by the British on July 15, 1776 between Montserrat and St. Eustatius. He arrived home on July 23, 1776 by way of Nantucket and reported that "very few northern vessels escaped the vigilance of the British cruisers."[129] More and more, trade voyages to the West Indies would be conducted in armed vessels that also carried privateering commissions.

The British military forces and Tories in Boston had restricted access to food and other supplies because they were contained inside a perimeter of colonial militia. They resorted to seaborne costal raids in order to supplement what they received directly from Britain. Several Narragansett Bay communities were the first to be plundered. The British then sent Captain James Wallace with three warships, the *Rose, Swan* and *King-Fisher,* to patrol the waters of Long Island Sound. On July 26, 1775 these vessels and eight other smaller ships initiated a series of raids within eastern Long Island Sound. First, they blockaded New London Harbor and damaged the harbor lighthouse which, at the time, was the only lighthouse within Long Island Sound. Next, they pillaged Fishers Island, taking 1100 sheep, many cattle and other provisions but did offer compensation.

An attempt was made to prevent the British from plundering food supplies across the Sound at the east end of Long Island. An appeal was made to Brigadier General David Wooster for Continental Army troops then stationed in New York. The fledgling Army had only just been authorized on May 10 by the Continental Congress. Wooster, born March 2, 1711 in Stratford, Connecticut, saw important service during the French and Indian Wars. It was Wooster who masterminded the strategy leading to the capture of Fort Ticonderoga three months earlier.

With incredible speed, General Wooster loaded 450 troops onto ships and reached Oyster Ponds (Orient Point, Long Island) on August 9. Finding no gunpowder available, an emergency dispatch was sent by ship across Long Island Sound to Connecticut Governor Trumbull. Sailing within sight of British warships, the American vessel managed the tricky passage through Plum Gut, the crossing to New London and return trip with twelve kegs of powder within a couple of days.[130]

On August 11, a British warship and twelve transports sailed around Plum Island. After they passed through the Gut, General

Wooster sent some of his troops over to the island to remove the livestock. The effort had to be aborted when several British ships, including the warship, reversed their course and returned to the Gut. Shots were traded between the two forces but no injuries were reported. On Plum and Gardiners Islands, the British confiscated 1000 sheep, thirty hogs, thirteen geese, three calves, 1000 pounds of cheese and seven tons of hay. As an insult they left payment of half a guinea and one old Spanish silver piece.

Captain Wallace then shifted his attention back to Rhode Island during August but was not very successful in his attempts to confiscate additional livestock. Several communities took precautionary measures by moving their animals and food supplies to the interior, away from potential British landing parties along the coast. In the meantime, a small force of militia was called out to protect Stonington and New London but officials realized the islands were defenseless to British plundering. Block Island was particularly isolated. Realizing their vulnerability, the Islanders made arrangements to move all of their livestock to Stonington, Connecticut.[131] Near the end of the month a fleet of small boats filled with cattle made the journey from Block Island and unloaded their animals to pasture in the vicinity of Quanaduck Cove, Stonington's inner harbor.

Captain Wallace was furious about this maneuver which was intended to thwart his plans for taking possession of additional food supplies. On August 28, he proclaimed the Block Islanders' action "treasonable" and vowed to destroy any vessels he caught on the water that were engaged in this ferry operation.[132] He departed Newport immediately on the H.M.S. *Rose* along with a small sloop and three tenders. His destination was Stonington with the intention of punishing the inhabitants and confiscating the cattle they were sheltering.

Captain Wallace's demeanor had been arrogant throughout his mission and his unbridled hatred of the colonists was evident in most of his communications. The residents of Stonington would not be cowed. They had established a long history of fierce independence dating back to the very first person to arrive in the area. In 1649, William Chesebrough occupied land as an unauthorized squatter in what was then known as Pequot Plantation. In 1658 the residents seceded from Connecticut Colony to join the Massachusetts Bay

Colony for a period of four years. Subsequent withholding of tax payments to Connecticut Colony brought censure to the community.

The small British sloop was the first to arrive in Stonington Harbor at 7 AM on August 30 followed by the three tenders. Torrential rain fell most of the day and the small Company of militia on duty at Stonington Point had difficulty identifying the arriving ships. Warily, they hailed the approaching vessels to determine their disposition and intentions. The response was a barrage from the ships' cannons and swivel guns. The few defenders had no equivalent weapons but were able to drive the ships farther away from shore with small arms fire.

Both sides were then augmented by additional forces. First, the British frigate, *Rose* came into view after rounding Napatree Point, Watch Hill, Rhode Island. This ship carried twenty guns and a crew of 130. At about the same time, an additional contingent of patriot militia arrived bringing the total to about forty men but still without cannons. These forces were led by Major Oliver Smith and included Captains William Stanton and Joseph Gallup and others such as Amos Gallup, William Denison and George Denison.[133]

The British initiated the next action by trying to board a sloop and schooner that had earlier dashed into the harbor for safety as the British ships approached. The defenders temporarily warned them away but soon the four British vessels, now including the *Rose*, formed a battle line and returned with guns blazing. This time they were successful in bringing away the two ships. Not satisfied however, the ships continued their bombardment of the village where much damage was done.

At noon, Major Smith called a cease fire and sent a flag of truce out to Captain Wallace on the *Rose*. He hoped to reason with Wallace and end the affair. He explained that his men were fired upon without provocation and only returned fire in self defense. Wallace's response, in effect, called Smith a liar and expected him to step aside and accede to his demands. A second round of communications was even more emphatic. Wallace simply wrote his intention to resume firing and blamed it on the defenders.[134] One of his tenders then came close to Major Smith's wharf and explained Wallace's intention to fire the town because of continued resistance. His ships then lined up to shoot broadside and continued their bombardment from about 4 PM until dark.

The number of defenders grew steadily all day in spite of the miserable weather. Many came from New London alerted by an express rider earlier in the day. By dusk there were about 800 men, more than enough to repel any landing party. They still had no cannons but many of their muskets had sufficient velocity to reach the ships in the harbor.

After dark the British ships gave up the fight and sailed away. Wallace had achieved none of his goals. He failed to confiscate the cattle and one of the two ships taken from Stonington Harbor was forced into New London by the stormy weather and reclaimed by the colonials. While many houses were damaged, the village was not destroyed. The soaking rain and wet conditions prevented fires caused by incendiary munitions from starting or spreading. No villagers or defenders were killed and only one man was wounded. The British left with four dead and an undisclosed number of wounded.

There was a frantic rush to establish naval forces in an attempt to stop British marauding along the shores of New England and stop or reduce the amount of supplies reaching the now British occupied city of Boston. Rhode Island and Connecticut were the first to respond by initiating the establishment of state navies. General George Washington followed when he took initiative to establish his own navy in Massachusetts Bay. Finally, the Continental Congress acted in November, 1775 to authorize a Continental Navy.

In June 1775, Rhode Island became the first state to establish a navy when it commissioned two sloops to try and stop British raids that were being carried out within Narragansett Bay to obtain food and supplies. On July 1, Connecticut resolved to commission two vessels for naval service. On August 3, it took the first tentative steps towards establishing a state navy when it chartered the 108 ton brig, *Minerva*, belonging to William Griswold of Wethersfield. The ship was moved to Middletown for conversion to a warship and to assemble its seventy-two man crew.[135]

The *Minerva* was ordered to sea in early October but the fledgling Connecticut Navy would have an inauspicious beginning. At the time, American forces under Benedict Arnold and Richard

Montgomery had begun a two pronged campaign to invade Canada. England hastily loaded two unarmed but unescorted ships with powder and weapons and sent them off to Quebec at the end of August. Learning of this on October 5, Continental Congress President, John Hancock sent a letter by express rider to Connecticut and further along the line to General Washington outside Boston urging them to intercept the vessels.[136] Connecticut immediately issued orders to Captain Giles Hall, Commander of the *Minerva*, to proceed according to these directions and intercept the two British vessels. The crew however, balked at the orders and all but ten or twelve of the crew refused to serve on the mission.[137] Meanwhile, General Washington was trying to scrape together seven vessels for his own Navy. He received President Hancock's express dispatch on October 11 and two of his ships eventually sailed from Beverly, Massachusetts by the end of the month. By the time these vessels reached the Gulf of Saint Lawrence the British supply ships had already passed.

Connecticut commissioned an investigation to ascertain the reason that its orders to the *Minerva* were disobeyed but there is no known documentation of the result. In December, the *Minerva* was quietly taken out of service. Its guns were removed in New Haven and the ship was then sailed into the Connecticut River and returned to its owner.[138] Most of the crew was discharged in New Haven and the remainder in Rocky Hill.

The fact that none of the *Minerva's* crew was punished for this incident suggests that there were extenuating circumstances. Perhaps the ship was not ready, seriously deficient or not seaworthy. Another possibility is that the enlistment agreements specified operations that did not include a voyage into the North Atlantic. Although the result of this episode was inglorious, Connecticut officials must have learned from the experience because nothing similar happened again.

As soon as General Washington took command in early July of the Army that was positioned around Boston, he recognized the need for a Navy. His prime consideration was to interdict British supply ships coming down from Nova Scotia without convoy protection.[139] Not waiting for Congress to establish a Continental Navy, General

Washington hastily acquired, provisioned and manned the *Hannah* and five more ships from Beverly to the north of Boston and Plymouth to the south.

General Washington had a ready source of experienced mariners within his own army. Many regiments of New Hampshire, Massachusetts, Rhode Island and Connecticut troops came from seaport communities. Washington selected Yale graduate, William Coit from Norwich to command one of his six ships, the sixty-four ton *Triton* which was renamed *Harrison*. The *Harrison* mounted only four cannons and six swivel guns. At the time of his selection, Captain Coit was a company commander in the Sixth Connecticut Militia Regiment. Coit selected his crew, mostly from his own regiment, and pulled out of the siege lines on October 24. His orders were to capture British supply ships heading into Boston but avoid confrontation with armed vessels.[140]

As the men approached Plymouth Harbor on October 25, they were appalled by the sight of the ship they were about to take in harms way. The *Harrison*, built in 1761, was considered ancient. Captain Coit kept his sense of humor when he suggested that the ship be donated to the Royal Society of England as a museum piece as he doubted that they had "or will have, until the day of judgment, any curiosity equal to her."[141] The ship's armament of four, four pounders, six swivels and two mortars received additional derision from Captain Coit. He jokingly claimed that the mortars had been with Noah on his Ark, the swivels came with the pilgrims in 1620 and the cannons came into the country with Lord Saye and Sele with the founding of Saybrook, Connecticut in the 1630s.[142] Furthermore, one of the cannon had a hardened steel spike driven into the touch hole and was unusable.

Despite the *Harrison's* inferiority, Captain Coit set sail the very next day but the local pilot promptly ran her aground. A more experienced pilot was acquired on October 30 but this one also ran the ship aground on a sandbar. Plymouth Harbor was notoriously difficult to sail in and out of. Four days later, the ship grounded a third time but then finally got out to sea with a rising tide.

Despite the problems and delays, Captain Coit was the first of Washington's commanders to accomplish exactly what the General desired. Within a couple of days the *Harrison* captured two vessels in route from Halifax laden with supplies for the British Army. The cargo included cordwood, geese, chickens, sheep, cattle, hogs, hay, potatoes, turnips, butter, cheese and fish.[143] When Captain Coit returned to Plymouth he took great delight in making the prisoners trod upon the same rock as the pilgrims while his crew gave three cheers to the success of American arms.

Due to the approaching winter, many of the Connecticut crewmen did not want to venture out on another cruise. General Washington however, wished to keep all six ships in operation. He had a very low opinion of New England militiamen, considering them crude and undisciplined. He had an even lower opinion of his ship commanders and their crews. He complained to Congress that "The plague, trouble and vexation I have had with the crews of all the armed vessels are inexpressible. I do believe there is not on earth a more disorderly set. Every time they come into port, we hear of nothing but mutinous complaints."[144] Furthermore, he often referred to Captain Coit as a "blunderer."[145] In spite of General Washington's scathing sentiments, Coit weeded out the malcontents and had no difficulty replacing any of his discharged crewmen.

Captain Coit's next cruise would reflect great courage against overwhelming odds. On November 23, the *Harrison* departed from Plymouth in consort with the *Washington*. Soon, both ships were chased by the twenty-eight gun, British frigate *Tartar* that was on convoy duty. During the night, the *Harrison* escaped. Alone now, Captain Coit veered northward back towards the convoy and found two supply ships anchored near the Boston Harbor Lighthouse. Ignoring three British warships within plain sight, he sped straight in and boarded the nearest supply ship. Finding that the crew had cut all of the rigging lines, Coit was unable to raise any sails to get the ship away so he started fires to burn it instead.[146]

A hasty departure was then necessary at the approach of the forty-four gun *Phoenix*, fourteen gun *Raven* and the armed transport *Empress of Russia*. As they opened fire, Captain Coit could hear the grape shot whistle about his ears. The *Raven* pursued for three hours but, when the wind died down, the crew of the much smaller, *Harrison* manned their oars and were able to pull away. Sir William Howe witnessed the event and mentioned this engagement as an example of rebel audacity when he said that "a remarkable instance of daring spirit was shown . . . within a short distance of the light house, and within view of his Majesty's ships, by a schooner that had actually taken one, and would have taken two transports loaded with forage."[147]

Captain Coit escaped into Barnstable Harbor on Cape Cod, spent several days making repairs and then ventured out again. He captured two more ships and returned to Plymouth with them. The legitimacy of one prize was questionable but the other proved significant. It was only a small fishing vessel of fifteen tons but it carried four Tories serving as pilots that were waiting to board British transports and guide them into Boston Harbor. Coit wanted to make another cruise and the crew was willing to do so but General Washington decided to take the *Harrison* out of service for the winter. The Connecticut men ended their service to Washington's Navy and returned to their regiment.

Captain Coit went on to take command of the *Oliver Cromwell*, a new ship being built for the Connecticut State Navy in 1776 but left this post before the ship was ready for service. In 1778, he commanded the privateer sloop, *America* and captured a British brig in the West Indies.

With the exception of Delaware and New Jersey, all of the states established their own navies which existed separately from the Continental Navy. These state navies varied considerably in numbers of ships and in their use or effectiveness. Massachusetts, Connecticut, Pennsylvania and South Carolina established the most active and effective state navies.[148] In New York, all harbors were occupied by the British from September 1776 through the end of the war so its navy was only in operation for a short period of time. A similar problem existed for Rhode Island when Newport was occupied by the British in December, 1776. This made it difficult for ships to operate out of Narragansett Bay. New Hampshire commissioned just one ship and it was lost soon after.

The Connecticut Navy eventually consisted of eleven ships plus a dozen additional armed boats that served in the capacity of provision ship, troop carrier, coast guard, submarine warfare or other miscellaneous duty. These ships provided valuable service not only in and around Long Island Sound but as far away as the Azores, West Indies and France. Nine of the eleven Connecticut vessels were either lost in action or were destroyed but only five actually participated in general commerce raiding missions. Four of these five commerce raiders were lost in action but they captured forty-three enemy vessels for a capture rate of almost eleven for each ship lost.

Little information is available regarding the New York State Navy due to the fact that it only existed until August 1776 when the British occupied New York and Long Island and due to the fact that it is not entirely clear whether the ships operated under General Washington's control or under New York State authority. In early 1776, New York built or purchased and fitted out three ships, the *General Schuyler, Montgomery* and the row galley, *Lady Washington*.

The *General Schuyler* was most noted for recapturing six American ships that had been taken by British frigates *Cerebrus* and *Greyhound* in the months prior to the invasion of New York. The *Montgomery*, operating out of Huntington, Long Island under command of William Rogers, was ordered to cruise the Sound in the spring of 1776. By June 6, Rogers had captured six vessels.[149] He then sailed around to the South Shore and took up station off of Fire Island. Here, six of his crew deserted on June 21 and there is no further record of this ship's operations.

It was necessary for Connecticut and New York Navies to assume responsibility for early wartime maritime action if any was to be conducted in 1775 and 1776. The Continental Congress did not authorize privateering until March of 1776 and little activity occurred that year. It took time to fit a ship out for privateering, acquire and mount cannons and obtain other necessary items that were all in short supply. Also, by the middle of 1776, Long Island Sound, the waters of southern New England and the approaches to New York Harbor were swarming with British warships in conjunction with their invasion of Long Island, Manhattan and White Plains and subsequent occupation of Newport, Rhode Island. During the winter of 1777, two British frigates, the *Amazon* and *Niger* were stationed within the eastern entrance of Long Island Sound and several others in Gardiner's Bay.[150]

It was a dangerous time for vessels to operate in or around Long Island Sound. Still, there was opportunity everywhere and sea warfare was about to blossom. At this juncture it is helpful to review the types of vessels that would become involved in the widening conflict. There were many names for ship designs and properly identifying a ship can be confusing. British ships of war were classified by the number of guns. Privateers and Connecticut State naval sailing vessels were identified by the number of masts, mast placement, sail configuration and rigging. Long Island Sound row galleys and whaleboats were determined based on size.

British warships had three major classifications. A ship of the line, also called a man-of-war, carried from sixty to one hundred or more guns. These ships were slow and could usually be avoided by smaller, faster ships. The British had 131 of these ships at the beginning of the war and 174 by the end of the war.[151] Frigates and small two-deck vessels carried between twenty and fifty-six guns. The British had ninety-eight of these ships at the beginning of the war and 198 by the end of the war. The large increase in the number of frigates illustrates the importance of these ships to the British war effort. Sloops-of-war generally carried between eight and eighteen guns all on the main deck. The British had thirty eight of these ships at the beginning of the war and eighty-five by the end of the war.

The British Royal Navy also used a rating system for their warships. The classifications changed during the seventeenth and eighteenth centuries as ship sizes and number of guns increased so there is frequent confusion regarding ship ratings. At the time of the Revolutionary War a first rate ship carried a minimum of 100 guns; second rate, ninety guns; third rate, sixty-four guns; fourth rate, forty-four guns; fifth rate, thirty-two; and a sixth rate carried less than thirty-two.

Most Long Island Sound privateers and Connecticut Navy sailing vessels fell into three categories. A brig or brigantine had two or more masts at least one of which was square rigged. A schooner had two masts with all sails being fore and aft rigged. A sloop had one mast with fore and aft sail rigging. In most cases the brig was largest, schooner next and sloop smallest. The majority of privateers were sloops.

Brig

Schooner

Sloop

Row galleys and whaleboats had similarities. Both could be rowed or sailed although not all whaleboats carried sails. The row galley was much larger and carried a crew of about fifty people with four or five cannons. The four row galleys built for the Connecticut Navy all had the same specifications; a sixty foot keel, eighteen foot beam and five foot depth of hold.[152] The smaller whaleboats ran between twenty and thirty foot keel sizes and were mostly privately built and owned. They often mounted a small swivel gun and crew size varied from ten to twenty-five people. The number of oars varied but was usually between eight to twelve oars. Another major difference was that the whaleboat was relatively narrow and was pointed at bow and stern. This made them more maneuverable and they could reverse course quickly without turning.

In certain situations, row galleys and whaleboats had significant advantages over traditional sailing ships. In tight quarters they could maneuver better with oars. This made them good for rivers, narrow passages, coastal and harbor guard duty. These vessels could also overtake most sailing vessels under certain wind conditions. The most obvious of these was where the wind was light or negligible. Where upwind travel was required, they could often overtake a sailing vessel because they could be rowed in a straight line whereas a ship under sail had to tack in a zigzag fashion if forced to turn because of the proximity of land or shallow water.

The second ship acquired for Connecticut's Navy was a small schooner of just fifty tons, initially mounting only four cannon. It was a nimble and fast sailing vessel however, and made a significant contribution to the war effort, not only by capturing six enemy ships but in a variety of other roles as well. This ship was incongruously called the *Britania* and was purchased in August, 1775 from a consortium of Stonington merchants who included John Denison and Edward Hancox for an amount not exceeding £200.[153] The schooner was renamed the *Spy* and sent to Norwich under the command of Robert Niles where it was fitted out and made ready for duty by January 1776. Captain Niles had just gained notoriety for seizing what may have been the first enemy ship within Long Island Sound. This was the brig *Nancy* belonging to Joshua Winslow, a Tory from Boston. Niles led a small boarding party that took the ship while it was lying in Stonington Harbor with a cargo of molasses.[154]

The first assignment for the *Spy* came at the end of January, 1776 when Captain Niles was ordered to assist with preparations for the defense of New York City. Even though the British still occupied Boston, General Washington expected an attack on New York City and ordered Major General Charles Lee to make preparations. Two Connecticut Regiments were being raised for duty under General Lee and the *Spy* probably helped with troop deployment, transportation of war supplies and other services.

In April, the *Spy* was ordered to cruise with Commodore Hopkins and the newly formed Continental Navy if they needed his ship, otherwise to patrol the waters of southern New England on his own. The Continental Navy had just returned to New London after a successful raid in the Bahamas. By May, Captain Niles was on his own, cruising outside of the Sound. On May 30, the *Spy* was intercepted by the British frigate, *Cerebrus* and chased into the safety of New London Harbor. Under great stress, the *Spy* lost its topmast while struggling through strong wind and tidal currents negotiating "the Race" between Fishers Island and Plum Island but made it to safety. A year later the *Cerebrus*, loitering around New London, would be the target of David Bushnell's experimental floating mines in an ingenious attempt to destroy a ship.

The third ship acquired for Connecticut Navy service was the brig *Lily Ann*, purchased from John Griggs of Greenwich on December 23, 1775 for £1,000. It was renamed the *Defense* and was a new ship with only one previous voyage logged; a trip to the West Indies. The 230 ton, three mast ship was then taken into New Haven where it was fitted and supplied for war. It carried a crew of 140 men and was armed with sixteen, six pounders, twenty-four swivels, one hundred muskets, fifty-nine pistols, fifty-one cutlasses and eleven blunderbuss weapons.[155] A six pounder had an effective range of about 200 yards. Also onboard were at least two dozen stink-pots that could be lit and thrown down the hatchways of enemy ships.[156] These were designed to force crewmen up on deck and hasten surrender when a ship was boarded.

While these early events were taking place, serious shortages and inadequacies existed that had to be remedied. Coastal defenses around Long Island Sound were non-existent. Food supplies had to be conserved and embargos enacted to prevent exportation. After the outbreak of war in April, 1775, the northern colonies quickly realized they did not have sufficient military supplies to sustain the war. In particular, there was a critical shortage of cannon, shot, gunpowder, lead for musket balls, cartridge paper, flint, linen and sail-cloth. Shortages of these supplies threatened to bring the drive for independence to a halt. Domestic production had to be stimulated and the capacity to manufacture some items had to be developed almost from scratch. An all out effort was mounted to resolve these strategic issues with the fate of the revolution at stake.

Connecticut quickly addressed the issue of lead for production of musket balls. A rich supply had been found in Middletown prior to the Revolutionary War and the mine was in the process of being developed by a consortium of foreign investors apparently under the direction of a British military officer by the name of Colonel James.[157] Connecticut seized the mine, probably early in 1775, and appropriated money in May to take over the operation and build a smelting facility. When the new overseers evaluated the mine they found that Colonel James had stockpiled seven tons of lead ready to be exported to England.

Expertise on how to smelt the lead was solicited in New York and the furnace was ready for operation by the end of 1775. Over the next two years it appears that a significant amount of ore was mined and smelted into lead for musket balls and other military supplies. The ore vein was rich but shallow, running only ten to twenty inches thick, contained in a vein of quartz. Its location was on a hillside in Middletown running down to the Connecticut River just upstream of the narrows. By early 1778, the vein was worked to a point where it dipped steeply underground right at the river and could no longer be mined profitably. Nevertheless, the mine had served its purpose by providing a large stockpile of smelted lead for the war effort.

Another critical supply was gunpowder, the manufacture of which required charcoal, sulfur and saltpeter. Charcoal was readily available locally and sulfur could be obtained from mineral springs on a number of the windward islands of the West Indies. A rich supply of sulfur existed on the island of Dominica which became available in 1778 after the French reclaimed the island from the British. The main problem to solve was the manufacture of saltpeter, or niter, which would serve as an oxidizer in the mixture. In colonial times, niter-beds were prepared by mixing manure with either mortar or wood ashes, common earth and organic materials, to give porosity to a compost pile. The heap was leached with water and the liquid, which then contained various nitrates, was converted with wood ashes to potassium nitrate. This was then crystallized and refined.

The process of making niter, or saltpeter, was cumbersome and time consuming with composting taking a year or more. The issue was to drastically reduce the time and effort required. Bounties were offered for the production of saltpeter and numerous production experiments were undertaken in 1775. By the end of the year a process was discovered to reduce the processing time to four days.[158] The first critical component was to use earth dug from beneath the farmer's barn or crib where their animals were kept. The second critical component was the manner of leaching, drawing off the lye, boiling, straining and re-boiling to reduce the substance. A small sample was then drawn and cooled. If crystals formed it was sufficiently boiled. The full batch was then left to cool, the lye was removed and the result was again placed in boiling water to dissolve the saltpeter. After cooling once more the saltpeter became clarified and the process was complete.

Hundreds of Connecticut farmers undertook this new process. Each operation was inspected and saltpeter certificates were issued certifying that quality standards were met. The saltpeter could then be sold to gunpowder manufacturers, the largest of which was Elderkin and Wales in Windham, Connecticut.[159]

It was also imperative to create a cannon manufacturing capability as soon as possible. Cannons were just as important, perhaps even more critical, to waging war at sea as they were to land warfare. They were also essential weapons for defense of harbors.

Connecticut was fortunate to have an excellent source of iron with mines in Salisbury, located in the northwestern corner of the state. A good forge and blast furnace was also located in the village of Lakeville, close to the mines. Ironically, this forge was owned by a Loyalist, Richard Smith of Hartford, who had purchased it in 1768. Conveniently, Smith and his family fled to Boston after the British took control of that city. The family subsequently moved to England and then to New York City and were allowed to return to Connecticut near the end of the war.[160]

Connecticut acted swiftly by simply confiscating the property and Governor Trumbull moved to place the iron mines, forge and blast furnace under military control at full capacity.[161] In January 1776, Colonel Elderkin was appointed to analyze the ore, charcoal and ironworks and take any measure necessary to improve upon and obtain maximum production. In March, Colonel Joshua Porter was appointed Chief Provider and Overseer of the works and the facilities were placed under twenty-four hour military guard. The cannons produced were solid cast as opposed to being cast around a core. The barrel was then bored to the appropriate diameter and caliber desired.

Several thousand cannons were produced along with huge numbers of cannon balls, grape shot and hand grenades, etc.[162] A majority of this equipment went to Connecticut coastal defense fortifications, Connecticut privateers and the Connecticut Navy. Some equipment was supplied to the Connecticut Militia and to military forces in other states as well. Many cannons were also sent to General Philip Schuyler in his capacity as Quartermaster for the Northern Division of the Continental Army. They would play a role in the crucial American victory at Saratoga.

Salt, while not a military item, was a crucial strategic commodity necessary for food preservation. In order to supplement the diminished supplies that were reaching America from the West Indies, the Connecticut General Assembly established a reward for local salt production in May of 1776 for anyone who erected salt works and vats. The bounty was paid on a graduated basis with the highest amount paid on the first 500 bushels produced and then a lesser amount for each succeeding 500 bushels.[163] Farmers and communities all along the coast of Connecticut responded by constructing salt pans in the tidal marshes for the evaporation of salt water. In Greenwich, for example, twenty-six salt pans were constructed in the harbor area.[164] These were destroyed by the British Army during a raid on the town in February, 1779.

While long term supply solutions were being developed, immediate remedies were also undertaken. One of these was a private venture initiated by David Hawley of Stratford. Captain Hawley's adventures during the Revolutionary War ran the full gamut of just about every maritime experience. He started as a merchant, became a privateer and then joined the Connecticut State Navy. He commanded several ships, played an important part in the Battle of Valcour Island in Lake Champlain and participated in the Whaleboat War in Long Island Sound where he led raids and performed patrol duty. He was captured three times but escaped or was exchanged on each occasion.

In the fall of 1775, a shortage of gunpowder and muskets existed in Stratford and Fairfield. In spite of an embargo prohibiting the exports he carried, Hawley sailed for the Bahamas in his sloop *Sally* loaded with salted meat and grain. He intended to purchase gunpowder but could only acquire the meager amount of 112 pounds.[165] He was able to obtain a more substantial 1,305 bushels of critically needed salt and eighteen hogsheads of sugar (122 bushels). Initially charged with embargo violation, Hawley's explanation of military motivation was subsequently accepted by the Connecticut General Assembly.

During the winter of 1776 a decision was reached to transport to Boston the fifty-nine cannon and mortars that were taken at Fort Ticonderoga and Crown Point. After successfully attacking Dorchester Heights on March 4, 1776, General Washington was able to place these weapons on the heights where he was then capable of striking ships in the harbor. The British were forced to either attack and retake Dorchester Heights or abandon Boston. They chose to evacuate and departed for Halifax on March 17 where forces were congregating in preparation for an attack on New York.

Also, during the winter of 1776, the newly established Continental Navy went into action for the first time and made a strong contribution towards relieving the military supply shortages. Under Commodore Esek Hopkins of Rhode Island, a fleet of eight ships was acquired and fitted out at various locations. At least eighty crewmen were recruited from southeastern Connecticut. The captain of the fleet's flagship, *Alfred*, was Dudley Saltonstall of New London.[166] The ships rendezvoused near Philadelphia in January but were unable to get underway until February 17 due to ice clogging the Delaware River.

Commodore Hopkins decided not to follow his original operating orders and instead, attacked and captured supplies from Fort Nassau and Fort Montague on New Providence Island in the Bahamas. The raids were unopposed and the confiscated equipment included eighty-eight cannon, fifteen mortars, 5,958 shells, 11,071 shot and twenty-four barrels of powder.[167] Taken prisoner was the Governor of the Bahamas and several other British officials. On March 17, the fleet departed for Newport, Rhode Island to deliver these valuable supplies to General Washington. On the way they captured two British merchant ships and then on April 4, two small British warships off of Block Island. Learning that a large number of British ships were in Narragansett Bay, Commodore Hopkins changed his destination to New London Harbor. But first, he decided to patrol just outside Long Island Sound in order to pick off a few more stray British ships.

At about the same time, David Hawley pulled away from the dock in Stratford. This time he was fortified with a privateering commission. His sloop *Sally* was also loaded with flax, rye, Indian corn, flour, beef and pork which would give him the dual mission of trade and the approval to pray on enemy vessels or at least the ability to try and defend his ship. The Continental Congress had just authorized privateering and Hawley was one of the first to sail with an authorization and one of the few to do so from Long Island Sound that year.

Captain Hawley was probably not aware of the rapidly changing developments in the war or that he was heading into a maelstrom of British naval activity. Just one day after his departure from Stratford, the *Sally* was captured by the British sloop-of-war, *Bellona*. Subsequently, Hawley and his crew were transferred to the twenty gun *Glasgow*, another British sloop-of-war.

On April 6, the *Glasgow* came face to face with the Continental Navy fleet. Confined below deck, Hawley heard a grenade explode topside which had been thrown by a marine from the main topsail of the Continental Navy Brig, *Cabot*. Cannon fire erupted immediately thereafter and shells continuously smashed into the *Glasgow*. Greatly outnumbered, British Captain Tryingham Howe managed a skillful fighting withdrawal towards the safety of Newport Harbor. Unfamiliar with Narragansett Bay, Captain Howe offered Hawley a substantial reward to act as pilot and switch his allegiance to England.[168] Hawley refused the offer but the *Glasgow* would still survive to fight another day when Commodore Esek Hopkins decided to call off pursuit.

Despite being heavily damaged, the *Glasgow* had gotten the better of the fight. According to David Hawley, the *Glasgow* had significant hull damage, "ten shots through her mainmast, 110 holes in her mainsail, 88 in her foresail, 52 in her mizzen staysail, some spars carried away and her rigging cut to pieces."[169] The *Glasgow* suffered only one killed and three wounded, all by musket fire. The Americans had ten killed and fourteen wounded.

Captain Hawley and his crew were soon on their way to Halifax, Nova Scotia as prisoners of war. Once in the harbor, Hawley and eight others managed to make an escape in a small boat. They sailed it across more than 200 miles of open ocean and landed at Old York, Maine. David Hawley's next adventure would begin as soon as he got home to Stratford.

Meanwhile, after the fight with the *Glasgow*, the Continental Navy sailed into New London Harbor on April 8 with the large stock of naval and military supplies they had seized from the two British forts in the Bahamas. Preceding their arrival were the four captured enemy ships (called prizes) which were brought in by sailors transferred to them (called prize crews). The Continental Navy brigantine, *Andrew Doria*, was immediately ordered back to sea on reconnaissance duty. Off Montauk Point, this ship recaptured the schooner *John and Joseph* which had been owned by Nathaniel Shaw of New London.[170] It had just been captured by the British frigate *Scarborough* off the coast of Georgia and was being taken to Halifax by a British prize crew.

George Washington arrived in New London on April 9 on his way from Boston to New York. British forces had just evacuated Boston and General Washington correctly anticipated that their next move would be to attack New York City.

Washington went onboard the *Alfred* to confer with Commodore Hopkins. Part of this discussion involved where to use the captured military equipment. Many of the cannons were directed on to New York but it was also agreed that some of the guns should be retained for defense of New London Harbor.[171] This would indicate his recognition of the value and strategic importance of New London in the coming struggle for New York, New Jersey and southern New England. Afterwards, General Washington viewed the four military fortifications being prepared around the harbor and then departed by land to continue his journey to New York.

As 1776 wore on, the shortage of salt became a crisis. While long term solutions would rectify the problem, a major effort was needed in the interim to obtain salt. At the beginning of October, the Connecticut Council of Safety voted to charter vessels under strict secrecy for the sole purpose of acquiring salt. Over the next year, eighteen ships were chartered and sent for salt to the French, Dutch and Spanish West Indies. Although the ships were supposed to be guarded by an armed vessel, four were captured but the rest were successful.[172]

At the beginning of 1775, there was only one fortification in Long Island Sound established to defend a harbor. This was an earth work in the center of New London. It was originally built in 1691 to defend against French privateers but was in poor condition. The fort was under the care of Captain Titus Hurlburt but the guns and equipment were deteriorated due to many years outdoors, subject to the elements.[173] In August of 1774, a committee was established to determine what should be done to repair equipment at this fort and improve its defenses. Finally, in April, 1775, the Connecticut Assembly appointed a committee to study the best way to defend all of the coast and its shipping. Planning went slowly and it was October before the first troops were assigned and early 1776 before much construction began. By then, defenseless Stonington had already suffered bombardment by the British Navy.

In addition to defenses around New London Harbor, fortifications were eventually established in Stonington, Black Point in Niantic, Saybrook, New Haven, Milford Point, Bridgeport, Fairfield, Norwalk, Stamford and Greenwich. Initially, armament was difficult to come by and was allocated as it became available, either on loan from New York, by capture or manufacture at the Salisbury Iron Works.[174]

New London Harbor was the most strongly defended port in Connecticut with four separate fortifications. The most formidable was Fort Griswold on Groton Heights. This would be the scene of a bloody battle against British troops under command of General Benedict Arnold near the end of the war. Across the river was Fort Trumbull which was only partially completed. New guns were also placed in the old fort at the foot of State Street near the center of New London. Finally, some cannons were placed on Winthrop Neck just north of town. Many of the guns captured by Commodore Esek Hopkins in the Bahamas were utilized in these fortifications.[175]

Initially, costal defense in Milford was simply a call in May, 1775 to mount some cannons on carriages which could be taken to the shoreline. By February, 1776, the Fort Trumbull earthworks were constructed near Milford Harbor. However, it was August before proper artillery could be obtained for the fort. Six cannon were made available from New Haven and efforts were made to acquire four more from the furnace at Salisbury. Establishment of an earth works on Grover's Hill at the entrance to Black Rock Harbor in Bridgeport was directed by the state in February, 1776. In August, two cannon were ordered from the iron furnace in Salisbury.

Norwalk finally obtained six cannons from the Salisbury foundry in the spring of 1777. Instead of concentrating them, the guns were placed at strategic locations around the harbor. The arrival of these cannons forced British General Tryon to make a last minute change in his plans to attack Danbury. Instead of landing his troops at Norwalk, he moved the landing site to undefended Compo Beach at the mouth of the Saugatuck River.[176] A fortification at Stamford was not established until late in 1781 and was not constructed for harbor defense. Its purpose was to protect Connecticut from land attack by British troops in the New York City area. This was necessary to fill the void left in the area after General Washington moved the Continental Army southward to confront Cornwallis at Yorktown.

Because Long Island was less developed, New York made no effort to establish fortifications to protect its harbors in Long Island Sound. After British occupation in the fall of 1776 however, eight fortifications were established by the British and their Loyalist allies for varying periods of time. These included Sag Harbor Fort (1776), Southampton Fort (1777), Fort Setauket (1777), Fort Franklin on Lloyd Neck (1778), Oyster Bay Camp (1778), Fort Salonga (1778), Fort St. George in Mastic (1780) and Fort Golgotha in Huntington (1780). Half of these forts would be successfully attacked by Connecticut forces after commencement of the Whaleboat War.

In addition to fortifications near the shoreline, lookout posts were established on higher elevations further back from shore. Sometimes, as in the case of Lantern Hill in North Stonington, these were as far as eight miles inland. Using a telescope at high elevation provided views all the way across to Long Island and many miles up or down the Sound. In the days of sailing vessels, tall masts and sails were visible from a long distance. After the British occupation of Long Island, Connecticut had a distinct observation advantage due to the fact that Long Island had no high elevations. In addition to Lantern Hill, other observation posts near New London were established on Pequot and Pendleton Hills. Covering the New Haven area were posts on East Rock, West Rock and at Fort Wooster's Beacon Hill. In the Fairfield area, posts were located on Greenfield and Tashua Hills.

The most important of all these lookout posts was Tashua Hill, at an elevation of 608 feet, located seven miles from the coast.[177] This is actually the highest elevation on the eastern seaboard between Florida and Penobscot Bay, Maine. Observers with telescopes could see half of the entire sound and quickly send messages by post rider to surrounding communities. Possibly, signaling systems could also have been used. This site has been recognized as one of the most strategic observation posts on the Atlantic coast during the Revolutionary War.

The real value of these observation posts is uncertain. They probably provided continuous intelligence to seaport communities regarding ship activity to help captains determine whether it was safe to sail or better to stay in port. They may have identified targets for possible interception and they would have been on the lookout for whaleboat raiders. Both sides resorted to crossing the Sound with their whaleboats only at night in order to avoid observation. It is clear that the observation posts did not provide much advantage where large scale British naval operations were involved even when the shoreline communities received advance information of fleet movement. The problem was that no one knew the objective of these military operations and a general alarm to assemble sufficient numbers of militia at any particular location could not be given until British troops were already landed. These large scale events included the British raid on Danbury in 1777, the raids on New Haven, Fairfield and Greenwich in 1779 and the raid on New London in 1781.

People reacted in various ways to the growing conflict but there were a few generalities that influenced the position taken by individuals or groups. The percentage of people in the population who were strongly committed to the Patriot or Loyalist cause was probably between thirteen to thirty percent on each end. The large middle ground of the population was generally passive but eventually had to declare themselves. Many in this category who leaned towards the

Loyalist side were convinced that England would win the struggle and they didn't want to be on the losing side. England was a dominant power and had the strongest military in the world. For many Loyalists, it was impossible to see how the rebellion could succeed. They objected to the strong arm tactics of the patriots and their newly imposed colonial rule, soon to become state governments, overseen by committees of safety. They wouldn't actively support the revolution but as long as they didn't engage in subversive activities they were usually allowed to remain with only mild censorship.

Loyalists in both Connecticut and New York were predominantly members of the Anglican Church which was controlled largely by England and was supported by taxes.[178] England's control of Anglicans was maintained in two ways. First, Anglican leadership refused to allow the establishment of an American Bishop. They feared that local leadership might cause American interests to diverge from those of England. Second, they required all new ministers to be ordained in England where it was unlikely that heretical thinkers would be approved. Anglicans generally believed in loyalty to the king and government, right or wrong; considered dissenters to be an unruly, ungovernable mob; feared anarchy and were afraid that independence would bring them down to the same level of equality as everyone else.

Hard core Loyalists in the New York City area tended to be elitist, generally well to do and aristocratic. Anglican ministers were convinced they were superior to dissenters who they considered as lacking intelligence and incapable of governing themselves or others. This attitude was summed up nicely buy Andrew Elliot of New York City in a letter to his brother in England. Prior to the August, 1776 British invasion of New York, about 1,700 Connecticut soldiers were camped near his house in Manhattan. Elliot depicted them as a "Civil, quiet set, very ignorant, awkward, lazy well-looking young men, they trample down my ground but do no other mischief although under no sort of command."[179] He further portrayed them as very handsome but poorly educated and undisciplined which must make them bad soldiers. He hoped they would not stay in town long enough to improve their minds.

Manhattan as well as Kings, Queens and Richmond Counties were Tory strongholds that feared growing radicalism in New England. After the battles of Lexington and Concord, patriots began to take aggressive action against outspoken Loyalists in New York City causing a number of them to flee to England. Many would return after the British occupied New York and Long Island in the fall of 1776 and then flee again in 1783 at the end of the war. One of these was James Rivington who published a weekly paper called the *Gazetteer.* This paper had the widest circulation in New York and was pro British.

Articles and editorials in Rivington's paper frequently upset his enemies. In May, Rivington had to be rescued from an angry mob and taken aboard a ship in the harbor where he remained for a month.[180] Later, an article attacking the radical patriot, Isaac Sears, finally brought a temporary end to his activities. Sears was a powerful merchant and the most aggressive agitator for independence in New York City. He had been a fearless, successful privateer during the Seven Years' War. In November, Sears went to New Haven, Connecticut and recruited supporters to accompany him back to New York. Passing through Westchester County they kidnapped Samuel Seabury, an inflammatory Anglican Minister. At Kingsbridge, the Sears contingent was joined by more than one hundred New York supporters who then marched to Rivington's office and destroyed his printing establishment.

Rivington departed for England in January 1776 but returned a year later after the British took control of New York. He resumed publication of the *Gazetteer* but, as British prospects for winning the war waned, Rivington changed his position and furnished information on British fleet signals to American agents.[181] He probably did this as part of an agreement which would allow him to remain in America. After the war he took an oath of allegiance and renounced his old beliefs.

Residents of Westchester County, north of New York City, had divided loyalties. After British occupation of Manhattan, the county became neutral territory and served as a buffer between British forces located in the southern part of the county around King's Bridge and Continental Army and Connecticut militia forces to the north. Unfortunately, this created a terrible situation for residents who lived in no man's land. Anarchy would rule.

In Connecticut, Loyalist tendencies very closely mirrored the Anglican population. The entire eastern half of Connecticut had very few Anglicans with the numbers running from zero to nine percent in the various towns. The northwestern quarter of the state was somewhat higher but the largest numbers of Anglicans resided in the southwest quarter of the state. The towns in this section were over fifteen percent Anglican with some communities as high as twenty-five to fifty percent of the population.

Fairfield County in Southwestern Connecticut, although predominantly Patriot, had the highest percentage of Anglicans and therefore, the most Loyalists in the state. A recent analysis of records indicates that approximately 1,500 adult males, or twenty-five percent of Fairfield County's adult male population, were committed Loyalists.[182] In Stamford, fifty-seven percent of the Loyalists were Anglicans while Congregationalists made up only eight percent.[183] In Norwalk, Anglican Church membership increased in the middle 1700s and supported a full time minister by 1757. This was a harbinger of growing Loyalist sentiment.

The remainder of Connecticut and also Suffolk County, occupying the eastern two-thirds of Long Island, were overwhelmingly patriot in sympathy. In Middletown, for example, not one property was confiscated from an accused Loyalist. Because of its Patriot disposition and its interior location, Middletown was selected to house many Loyalist prisoners including ex New Jersey Governor, William Franklin, son of Benjamin Franklin, on good behavior. One tavern however, was cited and warned not to allow these Tories to congregate in their establishment.[184] Another indicator of Patriot sentiment was military service. According to the census of September 1776 there were 692 males of military age in Middletown, 588 of whom were in military service whether militia, Continental Army or other service.

There were always a few Loyalists even in the staunchest Patriot territory. When the British attacked Stonington on August 30, 1775, Stephen Peckham piloted Captain Wallace's ship, *H.M.S. Rose* into the Harbor. Sometime after the battle, Peckham was captured and made to apologize to the townspeople from a platform constructed under a large sycamore tree. In the apology which was read by Nathaniel Miner, Peckham attributed his actions to workings of the devil.[185] The event may have been staged to frighten Peckham into thinking he was going to be hanged but no further punishment was inflicted.

New London had a few prominent Loyalists who eventually went over to the British side. One was Robert Winthrop, a descendent of John Winthrop, Jr. who organized the settlement of southeastern Connecticut in 1646, then called Pequot Plantation. Robert served in the British Navy and eventually attained the rank of Vice Admiral. Another was senior customs official, Joseph Chew. While Chew had done much to help merchants circumvent British trade restrictions, he remained a Loyalist. He left New London in 1772 and moved to New York. When the British took control of Long Island he became a supply officer at the newly constructed British fort at Sag Harbor. Yet another was New London's Anglican Minister, Reverend Matthew Graves of St. James Episcopal Church. Contrary to the usual trend, his parishioners were mostly Patriot and they did not like it when Reverend Graves continued to read prayers for the monarchy during church service. Finally, in 1779, he was physically removed from the pulpit and banned from preaching. Soon afterwards, Reverend Graves moved to New York. His church was subsequently destroyed during the British attack on New London by the fires set under orders of General Benedict Arnold.

Chapter Six

Battle Lines Are Formed: 1775–1776

British forces withdrew to Halifax after their precipitous evacuation from Boston on March 17, 1776. They reorganized and awaited reinforcements in order to carry out a new strategy to crush the rebellion. The intention was to invade New York from both the north and south in order to split the colonies and isolate New England. The British Navy entered New York Harbor in June and began landing troops on Staten Island on July 2. The invasion of Long Island began on August 27. The result would be establishment of new battle lines that would last until the end of the war. Long Island Sound and Westchester County New York would become no man's land, caught between the front lines. A stalemate would develop but plenty of action would occur within this vortex of emotion.

General Washington took advantage of the time between March and the end of August to shift his forces from Boston to New York and prepare defenses. The troops in Boston were pulled out immediately and marched to Norwich, Connecticut where they boarded ships and sailed within Long Island Sound to New York.

The Connecticut Navy also stepped up its activities during the latter half of 1776. Captain Niles took the *Spy* out into the North Atlantic and positioned himself within the shipping lane between the West Indies and Halifax, Nova Scotia. There was plenty of activity here due to the need to supply British forces assembled in Halifax. In August, Niles captured two ships, the *Hannah and Elizabeth* and the *Hope*, both bound for Halifax from the West Indies with rum and sugar. Prize crews were put onboard both ships but the *Hope* never made it back to New London. It was retaken by the British and the prize crew consisting of Lieutenant Timothy Parker and five others were later incarcerated in a prison ship in New York.

One of the most hazardous assignments at sea was that of prize crew. The number of men placed on a captured ship was barely enough to sail it and nowhere near enough needed to keep all sails in top trim to avoid recapture if pursued. Also, no one could be spared to man the ship's cannons or other weapons. The standard operating procedure was for prize ships to avoid encounters with any ship, friend or foe. Still, many prize ships on both sides were recaptured before making it into port.

Conditions aboard most British prison ships were dreadful and survival was measured in months. In December, Lt. Parker sent an appeal to Connecticut Governor Trumbull for help and advised him that Lord Howe would only exchange men "taken under arms but by a like number taken in arms."[186] They would not accept commercial or privateer prisoners as exchange for military prisoners. Lt. Parker's appeal was successful and the appropriate prisoners were exchanged early the next year.

Captain Niles captured another ship off of Stonington in October 1776 which carried a cargo of 8,000 bushels of wheat bound for New York. As the year came to a close, the *Spy* was ordered to cruise the Sound in order to gain intelligence on British movements, harass the enemy and protect American shipping.

The Connecticut Navy brig, *Defense*, commanded by Seth Harding, captured six ships on its first cruise. The first capture was made within the Sound and the next two were taken in the Atlantic, east of the Sound. Captain Harding then sailed the *Defense* into Massachusetts Bay in mid June, just in time to participate in major action by assisting General Washington's small fleet which was still in operation.

Although the British evacuation of Boston in March had been hasty, it was carried off smoothly. In June however, an inbound convoy of at least thirty-one ships from England was unaware of Howe's evacuation. These ships carried soldiers from the Scottish Highlands plus war supplies, provisions and the families of some of the officers. A few of the approaching ships were warned before entering Massachusetts Bay and diverted to Halifax but many others in the scattered fleet continued in. They were chased and harassed by five ships of General Washington's fleet, initially without success.

On June 15, two more unsuspecting British ships carrying supplies and 206 soldiers entered Massachusetts Bay and headed for the maze of islands protecting Boston Harbor. These were the *Annabella* with little armament and the *George* with six, six pounders. They were intercepted and chased by four of General Washington's schooners. The *Annabella* grounded on Alderton Shoal while the *George* anchored off George's Island and prepared for action.

As daylight faded, General Washington's schooners discontinued the attack. Meanwhile, having heard the cannon fire, the Connecticut brig, *Defense* headed towards the action. The captain of one of General Washington's schooners came aboard the *Defense* and briefed Captain Seth Harding on their daylong efforts to capture the two British ships. This led to a testy exchange between the two captains. When hearing that the four schooners had suffered no casualties during the engagement, Captain Harding exclaimed that this was because they had not gotten close enough to do any good.[187] The irritated schooner commander then threw a challenge back to Harding daring him to do what he had just declared. Captain Harding responded by saying that he intended to do just that.[188]

At ten o'clock that evening the American flotilla, now including all five of Washington's Navy ships, approached the *George*. The *Defense*, true to Captain Harding's word, took up the most dangerous position directly starboard and 200 yards from the *George*. Four of the other vessels anchored off the bow and the last ship off the stern. Captain Harding then opened a dialog with Major Menzies aboard the *Hancock* to establish the ship's identity and demand its colors be struck to America. After several strident exchanges, Major Menzies derisively shouted, "Aye, I'll strike," while at the same time opening fire on the *Defense* with a broadside.[189]

The battle raged at close range for one and a half hours with most of the fire concentrated on the *Defense*. Major Menzies died almost immediately and seven other Highlanders were killed. Another twelve Highlanders plus the ship's quartermaster were wounded. In spite of their heavy casualties, the British struck their flag only when they ran out of ammunition and no hope of escape existed. There were nine wounded on the *Defense* and a total of four wounded on the other five American ships. The British dead were buried on one of the islands in the harbor while Major Menzies was taken to the State

House in Boston and then buried ceremoniously with full military honors.

On the very same day as Menzies burial, the *Defense*, along with General Washington's five ships, intercepted and captured the *Lord Howe*, another British troop transport. Altogether, these engagements took 437 prisoners which included fifty-five women and twenty-eight children who were family members of the soldiers.[190]

A few days later, this little group of ships sallied forth one last time to intercept eleven transports accompanied by two British men-of-war. Finding the ships too well guarded, they abandoned the hunt and returned to Boston. By this time, there was squabbling between all the ship commanders. The issue regarded the apportionment of each ship's share of the prizes. Captain Harding wanted the lion's share claiming his ship contributed the most but, of course, the others didn't see it that way.

The *Defense* discontinued its association with General Washington's fleet and returned to New London in September. It remained in port until the following March due to hazardous conditions. The British Navy was everywhere in support of their military operations in Newport, Rhode Island, Long Island and New York.

In January, 1776, the Connecticut Legislature authorized construction of the state's largest naval vessel, a three mast brig of 300 tons named the *Oliver Cromwell*. It was constructed at Uriah Hayden's shipyard in Essex, then part of Saybrook. Records indicate construction costs of about £1,750 pounds. Delays in construction, fitting, rigging and armament occurred due to the enormous, simultaneous demand for war material and supplies that were so urgently needed at this time. On August 1, the ship was struck by lightning which damaged the main and mizzen masts. On August 20, the *Oliver Cromwell* finally sailed over the Saybrook bar and out of the Connecticut River for the short trip to New London for further preparations.

Before the end of the year, many of the original officers and crew assigned to the *Oliver Cromwell* had to be replaced due to desertion (forty-eight), expiration of service commitments (twenty-seven) and other reasons (six).[191] The attrition was primarily due to lack of pay, idleness and better opportunities aboard privateering vessels. The first cruise of the *Oliver Cromwell* did not occur until May of 1777.

By then, there was a dramatic increase in privateer vessels offering more lucrative prospects for prize money. Sailors were anxious to participate in the action rather than remain idle.

Also, in the winter of 1776, Connecticut commissioned the building of four row galleys but only three were built right away. The *Whiting* was built in New Haven, the *Crane* in East Haddam and the *Shark* in Norwich. All were constructed with the same dimensions: sixty foot keel, eighteen foot beam, five foot hold and seven inch dead rising (space between hull timbers and floor of ship). Each ship had a crew of about fifty men, with four or five cannon and a number of swivel guns.

By July, all three row galleys were ready for action but their life span would be brief. The British were preparing to invade New York and their fleet already clogged the mouth of the harbor at Upper and Lower New York Bays. Soon 32,000 troops would be ashore on Staten Island. General Washington desperately needed ships and requested the loan of the three Connecticut row galleys along with their crews.[192]

On July 16, the Connecticut Council of Safety issued orders for the *Crane* and *Whiting* to proceed to the Hudson River and three days later the same orders were issued for the *Shark*. Under similar orders, two row galleys from Rhode Island were also making their way to New York through Long Island Sound.[193] These vessels were the *Washington* and the *Spitfire*. They had already seen action in Narragansett Bay when they recaptured two American ships recently taken by the HMS *Scarborough*. The success of this mission was due to the fact that the captured ships were anchored directly off the stern of the *Scarborough* where its cannon couldn't train on them. The two row galleys were able to dart in and cut the ships away without confronting serious cannon fire although musket and swivel gun fire would have been exchanged.

The *Crane and Whiting*, along with the two Rhode Island row galleys, reached the Hudson River by August 1. They may have avoided British ships in New York Harbor by traveling up the Harlem River and Spuyten Duyvil Creek around the north end of Manhattan Island. The four ships rendezvoused with the *Lady Washington*, a New York row galley and a whaleboat whose name and affiliation is unknown.

The six vessel fleet soon had a mission. They were ordered to attack two British frigates that were busy bombarding and raiding Hudson River communities for food and supplies. The two frigates were the forty-four gun *Phoenix* and the hated, twenty-four gun *Rose*. The combined American fleet was badly out-gunned by about four to one. They mounted a total of about fifteen to twenty guns, most of which were smaller than ten pounders.[194] New York's *Lady Washington* carried only one gun mounted on the bow, but it was the fleets largest, a thirty-two pounder.

It took twelve hours for the fleet to work their way up-river to Tarrytown where they found the *Phoenix* and *Rose* hard aground.[195] The Hudson River is two and a half miles wide at this location but, consequently, more shallow. The attack began at one o'clock on August 3 under command of Lt. Colonel Benjamin Tupper onboard the *Washington*. Despite the disparity in armament, the Americans had a good chance of defeating the British frigates if they could use the advantage of row galley maneuverability to attack the bow or stern of the enemy ships. Under the circumstances, their chances were excellent.

With the British ships stuck on a gravel bar, the chance for success was even better. Unfortunately, the tide was rising and the two frigates floated free just as the ships came into range. They immediately brought springs upon their cables which enabled them to pivot broadside to the oncoming Americans.[196] This is a procedure whereby a hawser line is attached to the anchor cable, then moved aft on the ship and hauled in to swing the boat while still anchored. This maneuver doomed the American attack yet the determined fleet continued to press forward.

The first shots were exchanged between the *Phoenix* and *Lady Washington* who was in the lead but Commander Tupper called her back into line in order to protect his largest cannon. A fierce engagement developed lasting more than two hours. Every ship was hit and the British mixed in some grape shot when the distance came closer. Commander Tupper finally called off the attack after losing several guns including the thirty-two pounder on the *Lady Washington* which was split open and its restraining tackle carried away. One of the mortally wounded sailors cried out "I am a dying man, revenge my blood my boys, and carry me alongside my gun that I may die there."[197] The

Americans retreated downriver to Dobbs Ferry. The *Phoenix* considered pursuit but decided that it was too risky considering the headwind they faced.

British losses are unknown. The *Lady Washington* claimed to have hulled the *Phoenix* six times but the British admitted only two hits. Total American losses were two killed and thirteen wounded.[198] Losses for Connecticut were one killed, three wounded on the *Whiting* and one wounded on the *Crane*. Rhode Island losses were four wounded on the *Washington* and one killed, three wounded on the *Spitfire*. The whaleboat had two wounded.

The bulk of General Washington's forces withdrew from Manhattan in October but General Lee decided to stay and fight at Fort Washington which was located on the Hudson River near today's George Washington Bridge. The British Army chose to temporarily bypass this stronghold and go on to defeat Washington's forces at the Battle of White Plains on October 29. The Rhode Island row galleys departed for home before this occurred but the British maneuver apparently sealed the fate of Connecticut row galleys, *Crane* and *Whiting*. The two ships found themselves trapped between two British naval forces, unable to escape upriver, back out to Long Island Sound through the Harlem River or downriver to the Atlantic Ocean. Both crews escaped ashore and the two ships were probably burned to prevent them from falling into enemy hands.

Shark, the third Connecticut row galley, must have been operating independently of the others, farther to the north, for it escaped the trap. Its commander, Theophilus Stanton, and at least some of the crew discontinued their service on October 29 and returned to Connecticut. Roger Fanning replaced Stanton as commander from October 29 to December 18 and then served as the ship's "keeper" until February 15, 1777.[199] Still in the Hudson River at this time, the *Shark* was probably sold or placed under some other American military authority until October 1777 and then burned to prevent falling into enemy hands.

It is known that two American row galleys and several other ships were abandoned and burned near Fort Montgomery in October 1777 when the British captured this American fortress defending access to the Hudson River Highlands.[200] Two of the other ships destroyed were Continental Navy frigates, *Congress* and *Montgomery*. These vessels had been built only the year before in Poughkeepsie and never made it out of the Hudson River.

One other Connecticut state naval vessel was put into operation in 1776. That was David Bushnell's submarine, the *Turtle*. David Bushnell was a young farmer from Saybrook who first attended Yale in 1771 at the age of 31. The students frequently held fervent discussions regarding resistance to British economic repression of the colonies. Bushnell was interested in developing a mine to explode gunpowder underwater. He felt that if he could develop a means for attaching these devices to the hulls of British ships the colonies would severely threaten England's ability to maintain control.[201] The symbol of England's great strength was its massive navy. If their ships became vulnerable in American harbors England would have difficulty asserting her authority.

Bushnell chose a secluded location on the Connecticut River to work on a submersible vehicle. He built a shed to conceal his work and told people he had taken up fishing. Secrecy was necessary to prevent any information from getting to Tory spies. Bushnell's submarine was ingenious but still quite cumbersome to operate. When it was completed, Bushnell's brother, Ezra, was placed on leave from the Seventh Connecticut Regiment in order to train on operating the craft. Ezra fell sick however, just before the first mission was scheduled and had to be replaced by Sergeant Lee.

On September 6, the *Turtle* was taken aboard a sloop and brought down to the South Ferry Landing on the southern tip of Manhattan. General Washington still occupied Manhattan but had retreated from Brooklyn and Long Island on August 29 after being defeated in two battles. The British fleet was anchored in the harbor and the Americans chose Admiral Howe's flagship *Eagle* as their target. After being towed part of the way by whaleboat, the *Turtle* was cast off. Sergeant Lee hand cranked the screw propeller and maneuvered under the ship but was unable to attach the explosive charge. The auger either struck the heavy iron rudder connection or else was unable to penetrate the copper sheathing of the hull.

After failing in a second attempt to maneuver under the hull, Lee decided to retreat before daylight. On the long trip back however, the British spotted him from a fort on Governor's Island and sent a boat out to investigate. As they drew near, Lee released the explosive keg which activated a one hour timer on the device. The British hastily turned and rowed away, uncertain about the danger they were approaching.[202] Lee made good on his escape. The gunpowder keg floated towards the anchorage and the subsequent explosion sent up an enormous column of water. No ship was damaged but the spectacle caused great consternation and a flurry of activity in the fleet as the ships prepared for action.

In the following months two more attacks were made by the *Turtle* on ships in the Hudson River but neither was successful. Although Bushnell's submarine worked perfectly well as designed, there were just too many difficulties and hazards delivering and attaching the explosives to enemy ships. Bushnell went home and turned his attention to the development of floating mines. He would have opportunities to test these interesting devices the following year.

Simultaneous with the invasion of New York from the south, British forces moved down from Canada to Lake Champlain. Spearheading the advance were thirty ships under command of Sir Guy Carleton. These were followed by 7,000 foot soldiers. A frantic effort was mounted to build ships in order to blunt the spearhead or turn the ships back if possible. Ship builders and workers from Norwich, Connecticut were rushed to Skenesborough at the southern end of Lake Champlain. There, the Connecticut workers hastily constructed four ships using green lumber out of necessity. Altogether, General Benedict Arnold's Navy consisted of seventeen vessels, most of which were new construction. However, one of the ships was a schooner confiscated from the Tory, Philip Skene and another was a schooner captured from the British. The latter ship was the *Royal Savage* which was the largest boat in the fleet mounting six—six pounders, four—four pounders and twelve swivel guns.

A recruiting effort was mounted in Connecticut to enlist sailors to man the ships. Two of the Connecticut vessels were row galleys. The *Gates* was commanded by Frederick Chapel and the *Trumbull* by Seth Warner of Saybrook. The other two were gondolas. The *New Haven* was commanded by Giles Mansfield and the *Connecticut* by Captain Grant. David Hawley of Stratford, Connecticut was chosen to command the schooner *Royal Savage*. He had only recently escaped imprisonment in Halifax. Upon his return home, Hawley accepted a commission in the Connecticut Navy as a second lieutenant on the *Oliver Cromwell*, the largest of Connecticut's naval warships which was under construction on the Connecticut River in Essex. These orders were almost immediately superseded by the pressing need for seamen on Lake Champlain. His new orders, written this time by the Continental Congress, were to recruit sailors and report to Benedict Arnold near Valcour Island located in the northern portion of Lake Champlain just below Plattsburgh. Captain Hawley arrived on September 28, 1776 with twenty-six men, one of whom was an Indian named Mel Wahlee.[203]

Sir Guy Carleton's fleet was seen approaching Valcour Island on October 11. Fifteen of General Arnold's seventeen ships were available and took positions across the channel on the west side of the island. Construction of the *Gates* was not quite finished and the *Liberty* was away obtaining provisions. After spotting the Americans, the British fleet reversed direction around the island and headed upwind to engage the badly outnumbered and out gunned American ships. The *Royal Savage* was damaged early in the battle and, with insufficient room to tack, Captain Hawley ran aground on Valcour Island. Twenty of his crewmen were captured but the other thirty were able to scramble aboard other vessels under protecting fire from Arnold's ships.[204]

Hawley transferred to the row galley *Washington*. Onboard this vessel was Brigadier General David Waterbury of Stamford, Connecticut who was General Arnold's second in command. The battle continued all afternoon and into the evening. The *Washington* was severely damaged and Hawley took charge of the vessel after its Captain, John Thatcher, was killed.[205]

The remnants of the battered fleet miraculously escaped during the night by rowing silently through the British ships that were anchored in a position to block such an attempt. Next morning, the British, mortified by the American's escape, started out in pursuit. Hawley's row galley was so shattered and contained so many dead and wounded it could not keep up with the rest of the fleeing ships and was captured at Split Rock on October 13. For the second time, David Hawley became a prisoner of war but, to his good fortune,

Carleton did not wish to hold any prisoners. He, General Waterbury and 108 other prisoners were released the next day at Fort Ticonderoga under a parole of honor.[206] This meant the men could return to their homes with a promise not to participate in the cause of the revolution until they were exchanged.

Most of General Arnold's fleet was sunk or destroyed to prevent capture and the Americans suffered eighty casualties. While the action was considered a defeat, it was immensely important because it caused the British to cancel their offensive and withdraw until the following year. It wasn't long before David Hawley was exchanged. He would re-join the Connecticut State Navy the following spring.

Meanwhile, General Howe was preparing to move his forces from Staten Island to Long Island. The New York Provisional Congress ordered that livestock be driven towards the interior of Long Island to keep the British from acquiring these supplies. If necessary, the livestock was to be destroyed rather than let it fall into the hands of the enemy. General Washington also recognized the vulnerability of Fishers Island which had been previously plundered by the British and ordered that all livestock be removed from the island for safekeeping on the mainland. The owners were reimbursed the £570 appraised value.[207] After it was learned that Kings County would not resist the British invasion, an effort was made to confiscate, remove or destroy the livestock and grain supplies of any Loyalist in that area who did not cooperate.[208] This effort was only partially successful. British forces landed in Brooklyn on August 22 and were victorious in the Battles that took place from August 27–29. They quickly took control of western Long Island and then began extending their authority eastward to Montauk Point.

The Congress of New York sent a letter to Connecticut shoreline towns on August 31, 1776 requesting aid to those on Long Island who wished to flee from British and Tory control. The Connecticut Council of Safety immediately ordered committees in New London and Groton to assemble protected convoys of transports, armed vessels and troops in order to evacuate Long Island residents. Communities all along the shoreline responded. The town of Guilford, for example, responded by sending the sloop Polly which made five trips to bring over people, horses and livestock.[209]

Records indicate that eighty-one Connecticut ship captains responded to the evacuation appeal. An additional forty-eight from Long Island also participated. This brought the total to 129 but there were probably more and multiple trips were often made.[210] Estimates are that about 5,000 people, or one out of every six, fled Long Island for Connecticut during September and October of 1776. Most of these were living in Suffolk County and represented about one third of the population of eastern Long Island.

In Sag Harbor, thirty-six families initially refused to sign the oath of loyalty to the king and most fled across the Sound to Connecticut.[211] The majority of the men joined New York, Massachusetts or Connecticut military units while others engaged in privateering from Connecticut ports. One of these was William Havens, a relative of James and Nicoll Havens on Shelter Island. William helped to obtain vessels to transport many refugees off Long Island, including himself. He served in the New York militia and then resigned to become a privateer in 1780 where he enjoyed amazing success operating out of New London. Two other Sag Harbor mariners joining him in New London were Joseph Conkling who commanded four different ships and Edward Conkling who commanded the *Eagle*. Edward was killed in 1779 when his ship was captured by the British.

Many large British warships wintered in the bay between Shelter Island and Long Island. At least eight ships of the line are recorded as anchoring there with the smallest being seventy-four guns and the largest carrying 120 guns.[212] For the most part, farmers were allowed to trade with the ships. Food supplies could be sold at a very high price and usually commanded payment in gold and silver so this trade was lucrative for the farmers.

Thomas Dering and James Haven, two Patriots living on Shelter Island, responded to British control in different ways. Both were chosen in 1775 and 1776 as delegates to the Provisional Continental Congress. After the Battle of Long Island, the Dering family decided to leave Shelter Island as refugees while the Haven family chose to remain.

Thomas Dering first came to Shelter Island in 1760 when his wife, Mary Sylvester and her sister, inherited their father's mansion along with about 1,200 acres of land. They fled to Middletown, Connecticut in September 1776 where they remained until the end of the war in 1783. The British occupied the Dering land in the interim and cut down most of the trees, using them for cordwood to supply their forces. James Haven chose to stay and did not experience mistreatment maybe because of his relatively isolated location on Shelter Island. That all changed in September, 1781. After attacking Groton and New London directly across the Sound, the British plundered Shelter Island. The homes of both Nicoll Havens and James Haven were ransacked.[213]

In Port Jefferson, the division of loyalty in the Strong and Smith families proved interesting. Selah Strong married Anna Smith in 1760. Selah was a patriot and was chosen as a delegate to the Provisional Continental Congress. Several of Anna Smith's brothers were Loyalists who fled the area prior to British occupation and Selah helped to protect their property.[214] After British occupation however, the shoe was on the other foot and Selah became the object of animosity. Selah was arrested in 1778 and Anna's Loyalist brothers returned the favor by helping to obtain his release. Selah was exiled to Connecticut for the remainder of the war while Anna remained on Long Island where she became a spy for the Patriots.

Many refugees from Long Island served the cause of the revolution from the Connecticut side of the Sound. Two men from Setauket, Suffolk County would have an enormous impact. These were Caleb Brewster and Benjamin Tallmadge. Both men, like David Hawley, served in the military for the entire duration of the war. Brewster was a childhood friend of Tallmadge. He was a descendent of Mayflower passenger William Brewster of Plymouth Plantation and of Roger Ludlow, a founder of Fairfield, Connecticut in 1639. Tallmadge's father was a Yale graduate who moved from Connecticut to Setauket, Long Island when he was ordained as a minister.

Brewster was a man who craved action and disliked the boredom of farm life.[215] He left home at age nineteen to sign on with a whaler out of Nantucket. He joined the Brookhaven Militia in 1775 and then the Continental Army as a Lieutenant when the British occupied Long Island. Unable to return home, Brewster became a refugee and joined the military side of the Whaleboat War where he operated primarily out of Black Rock Harbor. His initial action was to help patriot refugees escape Long Island with some of their belongings.

His most notable passenger was William Floyd, a signer of the Declaration of Independence.[216] Between October 28 and November 8, 1776 he was part of a group of whaleboats that crossed the Sound three times during which they captured two sloops in Setauket Harbor, killed sixteen Loyalist militiamen and captured another forty-six.

Benjamin Tallmadge went to Yale like his father and was a classmate and close friend of Nathan Hale. According to his memoirs, upon graduation in 1773 he was appointed superintendent of the high school in Wethersfield, Connecticut.[217] He accepted a Lieutenant's commission in the militia on June 20, 1776 and participated in the battles around New York. His oldest brother was captured during this campaign and died of starvation in a British prison.[218] In December, Tallmadge was commissioned a captain in the Continental Army. While Tallmadge and Brewster operated under different military authority, they would often work closely together on whaleboat operations. Both men would also have important roles in espionage activities—Tallmadge as organizer and intermediary with General Washington while Brewster functioned as courier of information back and forth across the Sound.

Prior to the establishment of any spy network, Nathan Hale volunteered to obtain intelligence on British plans following their invasion of Long Island. General Washington had successfully withdrawn his troops from Brooklyn, across the East River to Manhattan and wanted to know where the British might strike next. On or about September 12, Captain Hale was transported across the Sound from Norwalk on the sloop *Schuyler*.[219] This was probably a Connecticut Navy vessel in the process of being fitted out for commerce raiding missions that would commence the following spring.

Events moved so rapidly that any information Hale obtained was outdated before it could be delivered. General Washington began his withdrawal from New York City on September 12. British forces landed on September 15 at Kips Bay, Manhattan and the Battle of Harlem Heights took place on September 16. Instead of aborting his mission, Captain Hale decided to cross to Manhattan behind British lines and follow General Howe to the American lines. In Harlem on September 21, he searched for a boat that might take him around the lines but was intercepted by sailors who had come ashore from the man-of-war *Halifax* stationed in the Sound off Whitestone Point.

Incriminating evidence was found on Hale and he was executed the very next morning.

News of the execution saddened General Washington and Captain Tallmadge, Hale's friend and Yale classmate. Future espionage operations would be better planned and organized.

After a delay of several weeks, Howe embarked his troops at Kips Bay and ferried them to the north side of Long Island Sound. He landed some men at Throg's Neck and more at a better location just to the northeast at Pelham in Eastchester Bay. General Washington left a detachment of men at Fort Washington and then withdrew the rest of his troops across King's Bridge into Westchester County. After the Battle of White Plains on October 28 and the fall of Fort Washington on November 16, General Washington withdrew further to the northern portion of Westchester County, the Hudson River Highlands and northern New Jersey.

New battle lines were formed that would remain pretty much intact for the remainder of the war. Long Island Sound and Westchester County, situated between the lines, became neutral territory or no-man's land. The land portion was an area of about thirty miles on the east side of the Hudson River between British Army positions at Kingsbridge, just north of New York City, and the Hudson River Highlands around Peekskill. Roving gangs of Loyalists and Patriots, only quasi sanctioned as irregular militia, fought each other within this realm and terrorized the inhabitants. The Loyalists, known as "Cowboys," specialized in stealing cattle which they would sell to the British in New York City.[220] The British Army and Navy created a great demand for food sources over and above what could be furnished from within their occupied territory. The largest band of plunderers was a Loyalist corps commanded by James De Lancey.[221] The Patriot bands, known as "Skinners," sought to intercept the Cowboys and confiscate the cattle they had taken. They would then skin them and sell the hides and meat separately or sell the cattle to the Continental Army positioned in the Highlands.

Fear, suspicion and apathy ruled as supporters on each side raided, robbed, pillaged and destroyed at will. As if matters couldn't get any worse, the situation descended into anarchy with lawless bands torturing and robbing their victims. A favorite tactic was to hang a man until he almost expired and then cut him down. Once revived, the process was repeated over again.[222]

Coastal areas of Westchester County and the Bronx were also tenuous territory. On City Island at the mouth of Eastchester Bay there was a tacit agreement between the combatants that the island would be possessed by British or Loyalists during the day and by Patriots at night.[223] It was an important area for market boats to congregate before making the run through Hell Gate with provisions to sell in New York City. The deep water anchorage between City Island and Hart Island and the surrounding waters were marginally controlled by the British but were often a target for rebel raids. The entire length of Long Island Sound was fertile ground for privateer and naval ship action and land raids back and forth across the Sound became common.

After the British occupation of Long Island, many Connecticut committed Loyalists decided to move there. Passive Loyalists who chose to remain were usually allowed to do so but the most outspoken or potentially subversive were either arrested or expelled. A few people even changed sides during the war. Samuel Hawley of Redding (not to be confused with David Hawley) started out as a Loyalist but remained in Connecticut until April 1777. When British troops marched through Redding on their way to raid a supply depot in Danbury, Samuel feared he would later be arrested due to the anger this action would generate against Loyalists. He therefore joined them not to fight but to travel with them when they returned to their ships standing off Compo Beach in Westport. After sailing with the troops back to New York City he made his way out to Long Island but soon had a change of heart. He claimed to be a Loyalist only because of his belief the British would win. In January 1778 he returned home, requested a pardon and swore an oath of fidelity.[224] He was pardoned and discharged from any further prosecution.

The total number of Connecticut Loyalists who fled to New York or Long Island is unknown. Perhaps the largest number of refugees came from the Norwalk area where about 1,000 fled.[225] Many of the young men joined Loyalist military units or otherwise aided the British cause. There were numerous families in Norwalk and Stamford with the Hoyt name and their sentiments were divided. While the majority of Hoyts were Patriot, at least seventeen adult males were committed Loyalists.[226] Several eagerly aided the British even before the invasion of New York and occupation of Long Island. Jesse Hoyt joined the British fleet in New York prior to the Battle of Long Island and served as a pilot for Admiral Howe guiding his ships into the Harbor. Joseph Hoyt of Stamford went on the British warship, *Asia* in January 1776 and recruited forces for the British. Later, Stephen Hoyt raised an entire company for the Prince of Whales Regiment.[227]

Most of the Hoyt Loyalists fled to Lloyd Neck and the Huntington Bay area directly across Long Island Sound where they would become active participants in the Whaleboat War that was to develop. If their families didn't initially go with them they were harassed into leaving or were inevitably, run out of town. Such was the fate of Mary Hoyt, wife of Jesse, and their five children. Frequently abused, they were finally robbed by an angry mob and then banished from town in February, 1777.[228] They were forced to make their way through the British lines into New York City.

Another Loyalist refugee was Fyler Dibble of Stamford. His father was an Anglican minister who chose to maintain a low profile on the issue of independence. Fyler, however was an outspoken critic even though he was Captain of the local militia. He fled with his family to Long Island in August 1776 and soon joined a Loyalist military unit.[229] His troubles were only beginning however when local Patriots on Long Island ransacked his home in October while the British were still extending and strengthening their control. He then moved to Oyster Bay but was the target of a whaleboat raid in 1778 by people from Connecticut who used to be his friends and neighbors.[230] This time, Dibble was kidnapped and sent to jail in Hartford to be used as a bargaining chip in a future prisoner exchange.

On July 31, 1778, the Norwalk Town Selectmen sent a petition to Ezekial Williams, Deputy Commissary General of Prisoners of War within the State of Connecticut, requesting that Dibble be exchanged for William Smith Scudder, a prisoner being held by the British.[231] Dibble's father gave his bond assuring his son's cooperation in the prisoner exchange. He was eventually exchanged and returned to Long Island. He moved again but his home was ransacked two more times by whaleboat raiders in 1779 and 1780.

A number of Rhode Island Loyalists also fled to Long Island and settled in Mastic where they built a fort on the shore of Great South Bay. Benjamin Tallmadge, now a major, kept tabs on the construction of this fort through a spy network he helped establish. When completed, he would launch a successful attack on this stronghold utilizing both whaleboats and a march across the island to reach the fort.

Taking prisoners became a vital objective of naval and privateer actions as well as the Whaleboat War that was about to develop. The importance of prisoners was that they could be exchanged for release of prisoners held by the other side. For American prisoners held by the British under inhuman conditions, the possibility of exchange often meant the difference between life and death. The British kept prisoners in various New York public buildings, sugar houses, churches and on prison ships located in Wallabout Bay on the Brooklyn side of the East River. The most notorious of these was the *Jersey* where many thousands died from freezing temperatures, starvation or disease.

For the Americans, the matter of what to do with British prisoners of war became an issue by the end of 1775 as none of the colonies were well positioned to deal with the problem. Prisoners could be crews from captured vessels, land based military personnel or Tories deemed to be dangerous or subversive. On several occasions, Connecticut was asked to accept prisoners from other states as well.

Depending on circumstances, Connecticut had two methods of incarceration. First, was in an existing county or local jail. Second, was under a parole of honor whereby prisoners were allowed to live in a designated community as long as they agreed to certain restrictions on their behavior and movement and they agreed not to communicate with enemies of the United States. Occasionally, prisoners on both sides were released to their homes under an agreement that they would not participate any further in the war until exchanged.

Until 1778, communications with the enemy in New York and arrangements for prisoner exchanges were accomplished on any ships flying a flag of truce. The safety of a flag of truce ship was strictly observed and was considered very important by both sides. In most cases these ships were either carrying prisoners for exchange or were traveling to the enemy to negotiate an exchange or parole. Often cargo was carried on these ships as well and was usually, but not always, allowed to pass. Such dual missions were particularly common between Nova Scotia and New England.

While this method worked, the British felt it provided too many opportunities for Americans to abuse the system and use it for gathering intelligence or engage in illicit trade. In January 1778, the British gave notice that unofficial flag of truce ships would be treated as spies.[232] An alternative system was then worked out where special ships were designated by both sides as "cartel ships." For the rest of the war, prisoner exchanges were carried out on these cartel ships.

The growing number of American prisoners after the Battle of Long Island, capture of Fort Washington and Great Britain's expanding area of occupation overwhelmed British capabilities. By the end of 1776 they held at least 4,000 military, more than 1,000 civilian and growing numbers of privateer and merchant ship prisoners. Every type of public building was pressed into service in Manhattan but the ultimate solution for the British was the prison ship.

Initially, transport and supply ships were used, supplemented soon after by the hulks of many old vessels. The first such ship used for this purpose was the *Whitby* in October, 1776 while the most infamous was the *Jersey*. It is estimated that as many as 11,000 (8,000 on the Jersey) died on these ships.[233] The prisoners died from starvation, exposure and a multitude of diseases such as yellow fever, typhus, and dysentery. At some point, sufficient capacity was achieved and a kind of equilibrium existed. The addition of new prisoners was offset by high death rates, prisoner exchanges and by small numbers who accepted service in the British Navy.

At the end of 1776, smallpox swept through one of the overcrowded prisoner spaces. The infected prisoners were transferred to a British warship. In the waning daylight hours of January 1, 1777, this ship was spotted approaching Milford Harbor flying a flag of truce. The ship disappeared from view however as a dense fog settled around it, completely masking its objectives. Unseen from shore, the vessel anchored and about 200 men transferred to landing barges and headed towards the beach near Fort Trumbull.[234] In the dark and fog, visibility was barely a few feet but sound still traveled. Isaac Miles, who lived fairly close to the shore, heard the sound of many people moving towards him. As he stepped out his front door into the frigid winter evening he was shocked to see his yard filled with sick, barely clothed men. He was further dismayed to learn they were prisoners of war who all had smallpox.

Milford quickly rallied to meet the crisis. The villagers took the sick men into their homes and then converted the meeting house into a temporary hospital. Captain Stephen Stowe, Dr. Elias Carrington and a few others volunteered to take care of the sick. Stowe must have had a premonition that he would not survive the ordeal as he made out his will and said good-by to friends and family.[235] Stowe died before the end of January as did forty-six others.

Layers of corruption within British administration of New York were to blame for much of the prisoner starvation. The two individuals most responsible for this were Joshua Loring and William Cunningham. Loring's wife, Elizabeth, was General William Howe's mistress and Howe appointed Loring to the position of commissary of prisoners in order to maintain his acquiescence to the arrangement.[236] Loring not only sold off most of the prisoner's rations, he padded his accounts by including many of the dead. Cunningham, in his position as provost marshal, admitted starving 2,000 prisoners to death while they were confined in city churches by completely cutting off their rations and selling them.[237]

A few prisoners accepted enlistment in the British navy as a last, desperate chance to stay alive. The case of Nathan Gorham of Stratford, Connecticut is a good illustration. Gorham served with the Stratford militia in Washington's Army at the Battle of Long Island. During the evacuation of Long Island, Gorham and two other men found a small boat. Using makeshift oars, they barely managed to cross the river ahead of the British and avoid capture. Their boat was carried by currents back towards the British Army and sank just as they reached the shore of Manhattan at Corlear's Hook, across from Wallabout Bay where the British were preparing to cross.[238] Gorham was lucky this time but his next adventure would land him on the prison ship *Jersey*.

After completing his militia obligation, Gorham sailed as first mate aboard a privateer out of Boston that was commanded by his friend, John Barlow. This ended badly when Captain Barlow made an error in target selection. The ship they overtook turned out to be a British man-of-war instead of a merchant vessel. Surrender was their only option. Gorham was sent to the prison hulk, *Jersey*, anchored in Wallabout Bay. This overcrowded prison was a death trap with ten to fifteen inmates dying every day. The only way out was through death, prisoner exchange or joining the British Navy.

When illness began to claim Gorham, he opted for self preservation and joined the British Navy. His bad luck however, was about to change. The ship he was assigned to encountered a strongly armed American Privateer in southern waters. Armed with some long range thirty-two pounders, the American privateer heavily damaged Gorham's ship forcing it into the Spanish port of St. Augustine, Florida. From there, Gorham managed to escape and stole a canoe which he used to paddle northward to American territory.[239]

Several high level British and Loyalist dignitaries were held prisoner in Connecticut. Officials and other important people were especially desired for their prisoner exchange value. Occasionally, such as the case of Fyler Dibble, specific individuals were targeted for capture due to anger with their actions or to use as bargaining chips in obtaining release of a prisoner held by the enemy.

Among the prisoners taken by Commodore Hopkins of the Continental Navy in the Bahamas were Governor Brown and several other island officials. A special committee was appointed by Connecticut Governor Trumbull to look after these people and insure their good treatment. The other British prisoners taken by Commodore Hopkins were transferred to the Windham County jail.

Another important prisoner was the Royal Governor of New Jersey, William Franklin, illegitimate son of Benjamin Franklin. For forty-five years, William and Benjamin enjoyed a close and supportive relationship. William served in the French war of 1744–1748 (King George's War in America) and later accompanied his father to London. He was appointed Royal Governor of New Jersey in 1762 and became a committed Loyalist, increasingly at odds with his father's beliefs.

In 1776, William's activities became overtly heretical to the rebellion and he was arrested. In June, the Provisional Continental Congress, declaring him to be "a virulent enemy to this country and a person that may prove dangerous...," ordered him taken under guard to Connecticut.[240] Governor Trumbull was directed to either obtain Franklin's parole of honor or place him in prison. Franklin decided to sign a parole of honor and was initially sent to Wallingford but then transferred to Middletown at his request. Franklin ignored the conditions of his parole of honor when he distributed Loyalist propaganda around the community.[241] Angry Middletown leaders petitioned for his removal and he was sent to Litchfield in April 1777 and kept under close confinement until his exchange and release at the end of 1778.

Another official taken prisoner in June 1776 was New York Mayor David Matthews. He was accused and convicted of subversive activities in the months leading up to the British invasion of New York. In August, he and other New York Loyalist prisoners were moved to Litchfield Connecticut. Matthews was ordered to Hartford but within a week was returned to Litchfield where he lived in the house of the County Sheriff. Before the end of the year he either escaped or was released through an exchange and returned to New York. In 1779 the State of New York charged him with treason and he fled to Nova Scotia at the end of the war.

Chapter Seven

A Swarm of Privateers: 1777–1783

The Continental Congress delayed the authorization of privateering until March of 1776. They were reluctant to take this step earlier in the war because of their hope for reconciliation with England. It then took many months for merchants to modify their ships for privateering duty and obtain armaments which were in scarce supply. The war at sea finally erupted in all of its forms in 1777.

Privateers were issued a letter of marque which authorized or commissioned them to attack and capture enemy vessels. They were obligated to bring the captured vessel to a maritime court where the legality of the capture was determined and authorization given for condemnation and sale of the ship and cargo. Letters of marque were initially issued by the Continental Congress. Many states then followed by issuing their own commissions as well.

During the course of the war there were approximately 2,000 American privateers in action in addition to armed vessels of State and Continental Navies. Overall, British losses averaged two or three for every American ship lost. Some 16,000 British seamen were captured in the process.[242] This forced the British to remove warships from military operations to perform convoy duty. From a strategic standpoint the economic impact was significant although it did not come close to being decisive. Still, persistent, aggressive American action over many years contributed towards bringing England to the peace table.

The Continental Congress provided letters of marque to approximately 218 Connecticut ships. Connecticut also sanctioned approximately 142 privateers during the Revolutionary War for action primarily within Long Island Sound. Together, this brought the total to 360 Connecticut ships engaged in privateering for at least part of the Revolutionary War.[243] It is estimated that the total number of enemy ships taken by Connecticut privateers was about 500.[244]

The letter of marque issued by Connecticut contained a unique provision. It authorized the seizure of British goods and the property of British subjects on islands adjoining Connecticut waters as well as enemy vessels.[245] This gave some legitimacy to raids made on Long Island where Loyalist property was plundered. Many of the privateer vessels sanctioned by the state of Connecticut were small, armed vessels such as galleys and whaleboats. These boats saw considerable action in the western portion of Long Island Sound closer to New York City.

There was also considerable enemy privateering action in Long Island Sound, the waters around southern New England and New York. In addition to British privateers, approximately 200 privateer commissions were issued to Loyalist ships operating out of New York and Long Island. These enemy privateers made 165 captures between September 1776 and March 1779.[246]

Due to the proximity of substantial British Army and Naval Forces, a tremendous increase in sea warfare took place in the waters around southern New England between 1777 and 1779. From a tactical and strategic standpoint, Connecticut privateers, along with the Connecticut Navy, achieved stunning success interdicting supplies to the British Army and Navy stationed in New York, Long Island and Newport. These efforts definitely influenced the British to shift their offensive operations away from the area in late 1779 and turn their attention to the southern states.

Privateers operated under a written agreement provided by the ship owner that established financial remuneration for the owner, officers and crew. A typical arrangement would give the owner or owners, one half of the prize value with the other half divided amongst officers and crew in proportionate shares based on rank.[247] Additional compensation was usually provided to the sailor who first spotted the prize and the first to board the ship and for anyone suffering permanently disabling wounds.

Privateer owners had to obtain bonds for each vessel which ranged between $5,000 and $20,000. The bonders were usually three people, one of which had to be the ship's captain. All captures then had to be libeled in a maritime court which determined whether the prize was legitimate. If approved, the ship and its contents could then be auctioned off.

American privateers were well built ships with priority given to speed as opposed to size and carrying capacity. Their superior sailing characteristics allowed them to overtake English merchant ships and outrun most English warships. The majority of privateers were equipped for offensive operations. It wasn't necessarily the number of guns that determined this but, rather the size of the crew. Attacking another ship required a large crew. Cannons had to be manned and a substantial boarding party was required to overwhelm the defenders if necessary. These men also fired muskets at the opposing crew as the ships approached each other. Additional sailors were also needed to sail captured ships back to port. A ship with six to twelve guns and a crew of thirty to eighty men was probably equipped for offensive missions. The same ship with a crew size of only ten to twenty men was probably engaged primarily in trade and tended to avoid other ships.

Privateer engagements with British warships were usually avoided. When a vessel outside of its gun range was identified as a British warship, the privateer usually fled if sailing conditions permitted and tried to escape from the inevitable pursuit. When identification occurred at closer range, the privateer often struck its colors and surrendered without a fight.

The convergence of two privateers was always a stressful event and commanders had to make a decision to attack, surrender or flee. The first issue was to determine whether the ship was friend or foe. This could be difficult since privateers often flew the enemy's flag in order to approach the victim before revealing their true identity. The second issue was to determine which ship was more strongly armed. Telescopes were used for this purpose but at night or under poor visibility this could be difficult to determine. Occasionally, having or not having the upwind advantage would affect the decision to further approach the other ship. Generally, but not always, the weaker ship would try to escape if possible but would surrender quickly if not. Pursuit could last for several hours or days. Sometime the fleeing commander attempted to lighten his boat and increase speed by throwing cargo and guns overboard.

Often a ship being pursued would take a few hits before surrendering. Privateers usually avoided all out battle at close range with both ships facing broadside to each other. Such events, when they occurred, were terrifying. There was no place to hide from round shot which could shatter hulls and masts and sever a limb, head or torso. Grape shot and canister were lethal and sharpshooters picked off individuals with musket fire.

A ship being chased within friendly waters would try to dash into a nearby harbor for safety. If none were attainable the Captain might decide to go aground intentionally, thus allowing his crew to escape ashore and avoid capture. The ship could be sacrificed but was often saved as well if sufficient gunfire could be brought to bear on the enemy from the shoreline. Intentional grounding was usually not employed in enemy territory but was sometimes successfully accomplished in sparsely populated territory where good harbors abounded. Nova Scotia was such a place because there where good prospects for traveling onshore and later stealing a local vessel before sufficient opposing forces could be mounted to capture them.

A good example of successful, intentional grounding was accomplished by Captain Caleb Trowbridge of New Haven, Connecticut. Early in the war he had served in the Continental Army, was captured and spent two years in prison. Finally, his wife, Anna Sherman Trowbridge, was able to purchase his release.[248] In 1781, Trowbridge took command of the privateer brig, *Firebrand* of New Haven and made two successful voyages to Holland capturing two vessels in the process.

On July 14, 1782, inside Long Island Sound, Trowbridge encountered a British galley and a privateer sloop who gave chase. Unable to escape or dash into a friendly harbor, Trowbridge grounded his ship on a sandbar or beach in Guilford, Connecticut. As the crew scrambled ashore, the enemy boarded the *Firebrand* and set it on fire. Rescue efforts were rapidly mounted by vigilant Guilford residents near the shore who organized a counterattack.[249] The villagers, along with those crew members who had managed to take weapons ashore, drove the enemy off of the ship and extinguished the fire. The villagers then brought up a field piece and commenced firing on the two enemy ships. Cannon fire was exchanged for two hours before the enemy abandoned the effort and sailed away. The vigilance and quick response by Guilford residents was undoubtedly fostered by their previous experiences during the war. Guilford had already been the recipient of at least four prior Whaleboat War attacks by British troops and Loyalist forces.

An aggressive privateering tactic that was often successful involved the element of surprise by concealment of the boarding party and holding fire until the last moment. This was employed by Silas Talbot of Stonington in command of the sloop *Hawk* on October 29, 1778 when he captured the much larger, eight gun British schooner *Pigot* in Narragansett Bay. The *Pigot* was named after Major General Robert Pigot, commander of the 3,000 British troops who successfully defended Newport during the recent Battle of Rhode Island.

The *Hawk*, traveling at night from Providence, Rhode Island, approached its prey anchored in the bay at one thirty in the morning. Captain Talbot bore straight toward the *Pigot* giving it little time to react to the attack that was rapidly developing. They hoped to quickly board and overwhelm its forty-five man crew, many of whom were asleep below deck. British marines on watch opened fire but the *Hawk's* sailors did not return fire until after their ship's jib-boom tore into the *Pigot's* fore-shrouds. They then unleashed a volley of small arms fire with musket balls and buckshot and immediately dashed across the jib-boom onto the deck of the *Pigot*. Its surprised crew surrendered immediately in the face of this fierce and resolute action.[250] The Americans suffered no losses.

Connecticut privateers operated in a number of different sectors during the war. A study of privateer activity yields interesting information about the course of the war, what cruising areas were most rewarding and which were the most dangerous. This analysis is based on information contained in Volume II of Louis F. Middlebrook's book, *History of Maritime Connecticut during the American Revolution 1775–1783*. A complete resource of all privateer activity does not exist but Middlebrook is the most comprehensive.[251]

Naturally, the most prolific area of activity was within the confines of Long Island Sound. During the war, at least ninety-eight

Connecticut privateering cruises resulted in engagements where 137 ships were captured by one side or the other. Connecticut privateer action within eastern & western Long Island Sound usually involved engagements with British or Loyalist privateers or with Loyalist merchant supply ships. These supply ships carried provisions from Long Island, such as cord wood, to British forces or residents in the New York City area or to the British Naval Base in Newport, Rhode Island prior to its abandonment in October 1779.

In addition to sloops and schooners, Connecticut privateers operating in the Sound also included a few row galleys traveling independently and many smaller armed boats or whaleboats operating together in groups of about three boats. These smaller vessels were more common and particularly effective in the western end of Long Island Sound where it was narrower and many coves and harbors existed. By 1782, the majority of captures in Long Island Sound were ships carrying on illicit trade between Connecticut and Long Island.

The second highest activity was a large area extending well out into the North Atlantic Ocean southeastward from the tip of Montauk Point, Long Island and northward to Nova Scotia and Newfoundland. Important shipping lanes existed within this segment with routes from England and Nova Scotia to New York, and from Nova Scotia to the West Indies. Connecticut privateers operated consistently here throughout the war where at least fifty-seven cruises resulted in engagements where ninety-four ships were captured by one side or the other.

The third area was in the West Indies although most voyages to the West Indies were for trade purposes rather than commerce raiding even though the captain and vessel might have held a privateer commission and the ship was armed. Usually these ships had smaller crews that were insufficient for boarding parties against enemy privateers. They avoided contact with other ships if possible and their guns served mostly as a deterrent to approaching ships. Many ships listed as privateers had no record of their cruises or of any captures and probably were engaged in trade only cruises. In these cases a confrontation occurred when no other choice presented itself and the Connecticut vessel was lost as often as a capture made. Records reflect at least forty Connecticut privateers making West Indies cruises involving engagements where fifty-two ships were captured by one side or the other.

Fourth, the most dangerous area for a privateer, was off Sandy Hook and the Atlantic approaches to New York Harbor. This compact area consisted of a roughly, fifty mile wedge of ocean funneling into New York's Outer Harbor. It was the most significant and rewarding area, yet the most dangerous for a privateer to operate, due to the density of shipping. New York was the primary destination for many British warships and for most British and Loyalist privateer or merchant vessels. Unless they chose to go through Long Island Sound, enemy vessels arriving or departing from New York had to pass through this funnel. A Connecticut privateer could capture several ships within a few days or be captured itself. They didn't linger in this area and cruises were brief to avoid being specifically targeted for capture by the British Navy. While most avoided this area there were still at least thirty-two Connecticut privateering cruises involving engagements with at least sixty-nine captures by one side or the other within the approach to New York Harbor.

Fifth, were cruises along the south shore of Long Island and into the bays behind the barrier beaches. These commenced in 1778 and most of the captures occurred within Great South Bay or near the Fire Island Inlet to Great South Bay. The inlet was not defended because Loyalist evidently felt their maritime interests were secure within the huge bay in back of the barrier beach. The first raid occurred in 1778 when the schooner *Suffolk* out of New Haven, commanded by the Long Island patriot refugee, Ebenezer Dayton, slipped through the Fire Island Inlet and captured twelve vessels mostly at anchor. Overall, at least thirty-five vessels were captured here during the war by Connecticut privateers.

Sixth, was the Atlantic Ocean seaboard south of New Jersey This area became important in 1780 when the British shifted their primary military operations from New York to Virginia and the Carolinas. British shipping between New York and the southern states increased and the area also included some of the shipping lane from the West Indies to New York. At least eighteen Connecticut privateering cruises were made here involving engagements where at least twenty-six captures were made by one side or the other, most occurring during 1781 and 1782.

Finally, there were engagements where no location could be identified or inferred from the record. At least thirty-two Connecticut privateering voyages were made involving engagements where at least fifty-three vessels were captured by one side or the other under these circumstances.

Commissioned privateers came from every port around Long Island Sound. The greatest concentration of these raiders originated from the Thames River ports of Norwich and New London. Of these, the majority of privateering voyages were made in vessels entirely or partially owned by three men, Nathaniel Shaw, Jr., Thomas Mumford and John Deshon.[252] They were owners of twenty-eight different vessels making a combined total of thirty-three voyages capturing ninety-eight prizes. Nearby, Stonington supported ten privateers and at least one, the *Lucretia*, sailed from Westerly, the only Rhode Island community within Long Island Sound.[253]

The Connecticut River supported a great number of privateers with eighty-six sailing out of this river's numerous ports. Of these, sixteen came from the Middletown-Portland area and another seventeen from the Wethersfield-Rocky Hill area.[254] Famous Connecticut River names such as Riley, Sage and Olmsted engaged in privateering and maritime enterprises. At least ten Rileys were involved and a Riley could be found among the crews manning most of the privateers sailing from Wethersfield-Rocky Hill. Gideon Olmsted of Hartford commanded at least five privateer vessels during the war.

Enemy privateers operating in the area could be British, Nova Scotian or New York Loyalist. Nova Scotia did not generate much privateer activity until about 1780. The majority of New York Loyalist privateers had their home ports in New York Harbor or the Bays on the Atlantic south shore of Long Island. A lesser number sailed from ports within Long Island Sound such as Setauket and the Gardiners Bay area. The greatest concentration of Loyalist privateers within the Sound were located at ports on either side of Lloyd Neck in Huntington. These included Northport, Huntington, Lloyd Harbor, Cold Spring Harbor and Oyster Bay. Privateering and whaleboat action emanating from these harbors became particularly aggressive after the formation of an organization called the Board of Associated Loyalists in 1780.

Although the Continental Congress authorized privateering in March of 1776, little activity occurred that year and the British Navy was everywhere, making it exceedingly dangerous to venture out. One privateer however, was successful in spite of the dangers. This was the *Broome*, a sloop with ten guns and crew of seventy, commanded by William Nott of Milford. During the latter part of 1776, Captain Nott captured six ships in the West Indies, four of which were headed back to England with produce and the other two were inbound from Halifax.[255] The *Broome* was subsequently captured and the crew exchanged at a later date.

In 1777, at least forty-two captures were recorded with the most activity occurring in the West Indies and within Long Island Sound. There was no activity identified on the south shore of Long Island and most privateers continued to avoid the Sandy Hook area and approaches to New York Harbor because they were so dangerous.

Privateer activity doubled in 1778 with more than seventy-seven captures recorded. The first raids into Great South Bay on the south shore of Long Island resulted in numerous captures. The most prolific hunting ground that year, with at least twenty-five captures, proved to be the area east and north of Long Island Sound. Engagements involved enemy ships traveling between New York and England or Nova Scotia and ships traveling between Nova Scotia and the West Indies. This area would continue to be fertile hunting ground for the rest of the war.

During 1779, at least ninety-six captures were recorded and Connecticut privateers became increasingly bold. Of significance, at least sixteen captures were made within the Atlantic approaches to New York Harbor in spite of the dangers involved. Also, there were at least fifteen captures within the western portion of Long Island Sound and another twenty-one within the eastern reaches of the Sound.

Nova Scotia was particularly vulnerable to privateers in 1777 and 1778. Aside from Halifax, other harbors still were not well defended and protection offered by British warships was only sporadic. Also, Nova Scotians had not yet developed a significant privateering force to challenge American ships. In Liverpool, American privateers were spotted offshore almost every day with several entering the harbor to take ships from their mooring. Construction of a fort armed with one cannon was begun but this proved insufficient to deter privateers and only led to the town being shelled as a punitive measure. The town decided to dismantle its fort and only contest privateers by militia musket fire if a landing attempt was made.

Great Britain finally began to foster local defenses and other measures in 1779. First, the British Navy organized convoys to protect ships traveling between Halifax and other Nova Scotia ports. Second, cannons were provided for proper defense of harbors and for installation on privateers. Liverpool received four, twelve pound cannons on May 7 and the town reversed its previous decision by completing construction of a fortified battery on June 1. Elizabeth Headley Perkins, Simeon Perkins' wife, was given the honor of firing the four cannons in a ceremony held on June 2.[256] Finally, Liverpool had sufficient firepower to prevent the approach of American privateers.

On October 11, 1779, Simeon Perkins and others purchased a schooner and began the process of converting it to a privateer vessel called the *Lucy*. Guns were authorized from the King's supply yard in Halifax and shipped to Liverpool under convoy around the middle of November.[257]

The *Lucy* departed January 5, 1780 on its first cruise and returned February 5 with two captures. In a quirk of fate, one of these was the schooner *Little Joe* homeward bound from St. Martins to New London, Connecticut. Onboard were Captain Giles Latham of New London and Erastus Backus and Peabody Clement of Norwich. Backus was undoubtedly a relative of Simeon Perkins' first wife, Abigail Backus and his old business partner, Ebenezer Backus. During their brief stay in Liverpool, the three captives were entertained at a dance held by Mrs. Dexter. Paroles were then accepted for Backus and Clement who departed under a flag of truce on the *Lucy* February 12.[258] Captain Latham was sent to Halifax as a prisoner of war.

Back in Norwich Connecticut, several of Simeon Perkins' relatives engaged in privateering activities. During the war, Perkins family members provided one third bonding for at least thirteen privateer vessels and Jabez Perkins and Company (Simeon's old business partnership) owned several privateers. His brothers, Hezekiah and Jabez, continued trading voyages to the West Indies and Hezekiah commanded several privateers as well.[259] Hezekiah was captured at least three times and Jabez at least once during the war. More distant relatives of Simeon, Jabez Perkins, Jr. and Jabez Perkins, 3rd, also commanded privateer vessels.

Hezekiah's first privateering command was the sloop *Maria* which was commissioned on December 1, 1778, carrying eight guns and a crew of thirty. He made a successful voyage to Holland and France. His second command was the schooner *Hazard* with ten guns and a crew of twenty-five. This ship was commissioned June 12, 1779 but was captured in the West Indies. Hezekiah was exchanged on August 17 and sent to Boston on a flag of truce vessel.

Simeon received information on the welfare of his brothers in Connecticut in a variety of ways. In April 1778, an American privateer cruising Nova Scotia waters forcibly took onboard Samuel Hunt of Port Mouton to act as pilot. Captain Low advised Hunt that Simeon's brother Jabez was a prisoner in New York. He had been there for some time and was in poor health.[260] Hunt informed Simeon about this after he was released by Captain Low. Simeon immediately made arrangements to help his brother. He asked Liverpool merchant Gideon White who was about to sail for New York to provide Jabez with anything he might need on his account.

Simeon received an update on September 13 when Banajah Collins informed him that he had been to Connecticut and had seen Simeon's brothers, Jabez and Hezekiah.[261] Both had been confined on New York prison ships the previous winter. Hezekiah had survived eight months of incarceration although he had been very sick and had to have two toes amputated from a frozen foot. Jabez also survived and had done quite well financially in the West Indies trade despite his imprisonment. After being released, he bought two farms in the Norwich area.

The Riley family of Wethersfield and Rocky Hill on the Connecticut River was also a major participant in the business of privateering between 1777 and 1779. In addition to furnishing crew members for a number of vessels, two were also ship captains. Ackley

Riley commanded the sloop *Abigail* which was credited with two captures and later, the sloop *Snake* which was credited with three captures, the third of which was a boat loaded with British goods for illicit trade from Long Island to Connecticut.

Several patriot refugees from Long Island played active roles operating out of Connecticut harbors. William Havens of Sag Harbor took up residence in New London. From October 1778 to 1780 he commanded the sloop *Beaver* carrying twelve guns and a crew of sixty-five. He is credited with the capture of sixteen ships, eleven of which were solo conquests.[262] Three of his captures were taken in his old home port of Sag Harbor and two were captured off of Sandy Hook near the entrance to New York Harbor.

The brothers Joseph and Edward Conkling, also from Sag Harbor, took up residence in Groton. Edward had a short but brilliant career in the waters of eastern Long Island Sound and Gardiners Bay. He commanded the sloop *Eagle*, which he owned along with two other shareholders. His ship carried six guns and a crew of thirty. Between January and May 1779 he participated in the capture of eight ships, some alone and some in company with other privateers. One of his assists involved a successful plan to capture an enemy brig called *Ranger* in January while it was docked in Sag Harbor. The *Ranger* was a Loyalist refugee privateer of twelve guns which had gained a notorious reputation. It had taken many prizes and occasionally landed men on Connecticut shores in search of plunder. Three ships were assembled for the operation. Conkling was joined by his friend and fellow Sag Harbor refugee, William Havens, captain of the *Beaver*. The third ship was the brigantine *Middletown* out of Middletown on the Connecticut River.[263]

Edward Conkling's good fortune came to a sudden and tragic end when the *Eagle* was captured in May while cruising off Stonington. Edward and some of his crew were murdered and his ship was taken to New York by a prize crew. Nothing is known about the circumstances but the death of crewmen under these circumstances was extremely rare. It suggests that Loyalists harbored a grudge against Conkling. In a strange twist of fate, on its way to New York, the *Eagle* mysteriously exploded and blew apart while anchored off City Island in Eastchester Bay, New York. Several of the prize crew were killed.[264] Presumably, the explosion occurred when the ship's powder magazine ignited.

Edward's brother, Joseph Conkling, had a distinguished career and survived the war. His first command was the legendary eighty ton sloop *Revenge* owned by Nathaniel Shaw, Jr. of New London. This ship carried a compliment of sixty to eighty men, twelve swivel guns and initially, ten cannons, later increased to twelve cannons. Edward made three voyages in command of this ship and his Lieutenant of Marines on each trip was John Palmer who kept a log of the events.

Conkling departed January 22, 1777 on his initial voyage with the *Revenge* and their first enemy contact came on February 10 against a ship of fourteen guns. The *Revenge* overtook her quarry and, as she passed, both ships fired broadsides at each other.[265] Conkling's ship suffered a hole in its foresail, one in its jib, three in its topsail and several through the hull but no one was injured. During a squall, the ships separated. For the next four days the ships remained in sight of each other but neither wished to renew the battle.

The *Revenge's* next encounter occurred on March 1. For a second time, Captain Conkling overtook his prey but, as he closed the distance, again discovered that he confronted a superior force. Conkling frantically jibed the *Revenge* to reverse course. The enemy gave chase and scored several hits but Conkling managed to pull away.[266]

Finally, on March 16, they captured their first ship; a schooner bound from Halifax, Nova Scotia to Dominica laden with fish and lumber. Conkling brought this prize into the French Island of Guadeloupe where he sold the cargo. On May 14 another capture was made. This was the schooner *Venture* returning to Halifax from Dominica laden with 7,000 gallons of rum.[267]

Captain Conkling's second voyage on the *Revenge* commenced on August 30. Instead of setting course for the West Indies, he cruised the North Atlantic shipping lane used by vessels traveling between the Canadian Maritime territories and the West Indies. This fertile area resulted in three captures in quick succession during September. One of the captures was the brig *William* bound from Dominica to Newfoundland laden with rum. All three captures were sent into New London for condemnation by the Maritime Court.

Conkling's third voyage began the following March and was made in consort with another sloop owned by Nathaniel Shaw, Jr., the *American Revenue* commanded by Samuel Champlin. Both ships carried twelve guns. Their first capture was the British ship *Lovely Lass* bound from London, England to New York with provisions for British military forces valued at £25,000.[268] The two ships then set course for the West Indies where they captured a ship bound from Montserrat to London laden with sugar and cotton.

After Captain Conkling's third voyage, command of the *Revenge* passed to Nathan Post of Saybrook while John Palmer continued on as Lieutenant of Marines. Captain Post departed with seventy-four men on July 30, 1778, one day after the arrival of Admiral d'Estaing's French Fleet in the waters off of Newport. France had just declared war on Britain and plans were made for the French Fleet to assist in the recapture of Newport from the British. This was intended to be a coordinated attack with American ground troops under command of General John Sullivan.

The *Revenge* spent over a month cruising between Stonington, Newport and Block Island, occasionally in consort with two other privateers, the *Beaver* (Captain William Havens) and the *American Revenue* (now commanded by Captain William Leeds) and in communication with the French fleet. The British Navy was also in the area shadowing the French. The three American privateers played cat and mouse with the British ships and generally provided early warning of any action that might spill into Long Island Sound.[269]

On the evening of August 11, the wind began to pick up and squalls drifted through the area. By August 13, the storm intensified and sea swells became large. The *Revenge*, now far out to sea, gave chase to a vessel which turned out to be a French ship which had come up from Cape Francois, Saint Domingue (Haiti). The storm was ferocious on August 14 but you would hardly know this from the entries made by John Palmer in his log. He noted that "this 24 hours began with a fresh breeze of wind and a large sea having some of the people seasick but nothing remarkable to end the first part [of the day]."[270]

This storm had a disastrous effect on the French fleet. Many ships were damaged and the fleet, driven by the storm, became widely scattered. After reassembling his ships, Admiral d'Estaing cancelled the fleet's mission to support the attack on Newport and sailed to Boston to make repairs. Newport would remain in British hands.

The storm diminished the next day and on the day after that the *Revenge*, in consort with the *American Revenue* captured the brig *Thetis* headed for Cork, Ireland. After removing some rum from this ship, the two American privateers each put five men onboard to sail their prize into New London. They were then joined by the brig *Hazard* out of Massachusetts Bay on August 16 and the three ships cruised together in the North Atlantic shipping lanes for the next eight days. During this period they were hit by another storm which John Palmer characterized as "uncomfortable weather."[271]

On August 27, the two Connecticut privateers again crossed paths with the *Hazard* who was now sailing with the brig *Vengeance* out of Salem, Massachusetts. They learned from the *Vengeance* that Newport was still in the hands of the enemy at the time they left home eleven days previously. The next day they spotted at least fifty ships convoyed by British ships-of-war. Captain Post and Captain Leeds decided to give chase, hoping to pick off smaller vessels straggling from the fleet. They found one but were held off by a British frigate that came out from the fleet in defense.

On September 3, a British brig turned out of the fleet to attack the two pesky Americans. After exchanging broadsides, the two American ships hoisted all sail to make an escape. The chase continued all night and the next day under abominable weather conditions. Captain Post tried to stabilize his vessel by withdrawing all cannons from their stations and placing them at the bottom of the ship to act as ballast. The *Revenge* was obliged to carry as much sail as possible in order to outrun the British brig but this almost led to disaster in spite of the extra ballast. A sudden and severe squall almost turned the ship over and damaged some of the rigging, booms and sails before they could haul them down.[272] At five o'clock in the afternoon of September 4, the British brig finally gave up the chase.

After this narrow escape and the damage sustained, Captain Post decided to head home from his position located near the Grand Banks in the North Atlantic. On September 14, they were spotted by a British frigate who gave chase to the crippled *Revenge*. Captain Post ordered three cannons and some drinking water thrown overboard to lighten the ship. The next day, two more cannons and five more hogsheads of water (63–140 gallons each) were thrown over. Later that day, another ship came into view and the British frigate broke off its pursuit of the *Revenge*, deciding to chase the other vessel instead.[273] Nearing home, the *Revenge* encountered two more British ships but managed to avoid them as the weather deteriorated and became foggy. The ship eased into New London Harbor on September 17. While only one capture was made, the cruise had been dangerous and the crew was glad to be home and feel the ground beneath their feet.

The *Revenge* had an illustrious career in a three year period between 1777 and 1779. In addition to cruises made by Captains Conkling and Post, the ship made voyages under two other Captains. Altogether, the *Revenge* participated in the capture of nineteen vessels.[274] Her most impressive engagement involved an encounter in the West Indies in early January 1777. Under the command of Captain Joseph Sheffield of Stonington, the *Revenge*, carrying ten guns and eighty men, intercepted two British privateers traveling from Liverpool, England to Barbados. Despite being outgunned, Captain Sheffield decided to attack the *Sarah* and the *Thames* each carrying twelve guns. In the space of four hours, Captain Sheffield chased off the *Sarah* and captured the *Thames* which he sent into Boston with a prize crew.

Another Long Island refugee engaged in privateering was Ebenezer Dayton, a merchant who had lived in Coram. He was an outspoken patriot, member of the Committee of Safety and a militiaman. This left him little choice but to flee with his family to Connecticut in September, 1776. After settling in Bethany with his wife Phoebe Smith and two infant children, he became an active privateer as well as a notorious participant in the Whaleboat War with Long Island.[275] He was determined to make the best of his situation and made valuable contributions as a privateer. His whaleboat raids however, crossed over the line of acceptability when he engaged in plundering residents and possible illicit trade as well. His combined activities would come back to haunt him and he would be specifically targeted by the British for revenge as the Whaleboat War became increasingly vicious.

In 1778, Captain Dayton purchased a schooner which he named the *Suffolk* after his former county of residence on Long Island. He was the first privateer to venture into Great South Bay on the south shore of Long Island. This may have been considered too risky by other privateer commanders but Dayton knew better because of his intimate knowledge of the area. With only two guns and a small crew aboard the *Suffolk*, he operated contrary to the norms for aggressive action.

Captain Dayton was successful because he found a weakness along the south shore of Long Island and exploited it. A significant number of ships were harbored within the large bay formed in back of the barrier beach which faced the Atlantic Ocean. Many of these ships were unarmed merchant vessels and owners felt safe from attack within these bays. In June of 1778, Dayton surprised them when he entered the Bay through undefended Fire Island Inlet and found easy pickings. He captured four vessels near Blue Point and another eight vessels near the inlet.[276] In 1778, the inlet was opposite Blue Point, much further east than it is today. Dayton looted some of the vessels and took others back to New Haven where they were all successfully libeled and condemned in his favor.

Not all privateering vessels were successful. Many, such as the schooner *Swallow* and the sloop *Gamecock*, were captured on their first privateering voyages before claiming any victories. The *Gamecock* of Norwalk, with six guns and a crew of fifty, was captured in 1776 by the British frigate, *Cerberus*. The *Swallow* of New Haven, with ten guns and crew of sixty, was captured in 1780 by the Nova Scotia privateer *Annapolis Rover* and sent to Halifax.

The effect of the war on the British West Indies was devastating and discontinuation of commerce with America caused great distress. The plantation owners wanted some reconciliation and complained that the survival of their sugar plantations depended on free intercourse with North America.

By 1776, commodities used to support the slave population were scarce and prices rose to four times their customary amount.[277] The shortage of food and supplies reduced slave rations to near starvation levels and caused an insurrection in Jamaica. The rate of insurance for merchant ships making the return trip to England rose to twenty-three percent of cargo and ship value. A visitor to Tortola in 1778 reported that there was a shortage of everything and "the inhabitants [were] in a state of lawless ferment."[278]

The frenzy of military and privateer action on the high seas and the probability of being captured dampened but did not stop merchant ships from trading with French, Dutch and Spanish West Indies islands. Over time, American merchants found ways to reduce the risks and continue trade with non-British islands.

While no method was foolproof and many ships continued to be captured, there were two ways to optimize the chance for a successful voyage. The first, and probably best way, was to sail unarmed utilizing a small but very fast sailing sloop or schooner. Most Long Island Sound vessels were of this type of construction anyway so little accommodation was needed. Because they carried no cannons, ammunition, men to man the cannons, additional men for boarding parties and prize crews, plus extra provisions for more men, their weight was less. This reduced weight was offset by the cargo they carried but they were still faster than British warships and most British privateers.

British merchant vessels, converted to privateers, were generally much larger because they had to travel more than twice the distance from their home ports to reach the West Indies and needed to have more cargo carrying capacity to make the journey financially worthwhile. The smaller, speedier Long Island Sound vessels sacrificed cargo capacity but could make many more voyages than British merchants. The safest way to make the journey was to avoid all ships whether friend or foe. This meant changing course when any sail was spotted to avoid convergence. If chased, the Long Island Sound vessel could usually outrun the enemy.

The second way was to travel as an authorized privateer in a small, fast sailing sloop or schooner. While six to ten cannons would typically be carried, along with a few extra men, the primary mission was trade, not capturing ships. They would generally avoid other ships as well but, if an unarmed British merchant vessel was spotted, they would have the physical and legal capability of capturing it. If chased, they could throw their guns and cargo overboard if needed to gain extra speed.

Sudden encounters with other vessels required a rapid reversal of course and often this was accomplished by jibing the ship. Normally, a sailing vessel is turned into the wind and the sails gently and automatically shift to the opposite side as the tack is made. When jibing, the wind comes over the boat's stern and the sails must be manually hauled in while the turn is made and then let out manually as the wind moves to the other side. In light wind, this is not a difficult procedure but requires great skill in heavy wind conditions. If not done properly, the sail is violently whipped from one side to the other, often resulting in damaged sails, booms, masts and rigging.

The log books of John Palmer provide insight on how trade missions to the West Indies were accomplished during wartime. After a stint on the privateer *Revenge* in 1778, he made several voyages on merchant vessels in 1779. He sailed on the sloop *Fairplay* which departed Stonington on March 26, bound for Hispaniola.[279] On April 4, they spotted a sail to the southeast of their position, altered course to the southwest and maintained that heading all night in order to loose the other ship. On April 6 they spotted 3 ships and jibed their own vessel in order to quickly turn to an opposite course now heading north. The three ships began to chase the *Fairplay* and, although the wind was light, she steadily pulled away from her pursuers. By sunset, the ships were out of site and the *Fairplay* returned to a southerly course.

On April 9, another ship was spotted to their windward. It was a schooner which they believed was American since it was bound northward and held its course. At noon on Saturday, April 10, they spotted Hispaniola along with another ship headed in the same direction. The other ship did not threaten them so they guessed it was going into the same port they were (probably a French port on Saint Domingue, now Haiti). The next day they entered port after stopping at the fort for clearance. The captain went ashore in town and learned that because provisions were very scarce he could get a good price for his cargo.[280] He decided to stay there and negotiate his trade rather than shop for a better price at another port or island.

The *Fairplay* remained in port for over a month. This delay may have been due to British naval activity in the area at that time. They departed on May 15 in convoy with a French fleet and some other American vessels. In all, there were thirty-six vessels and the decision to wait and sail with them was probably made for reasons of safety. The fleet sailed northward past Great Inagua and West Caicos islands and then through the Caicos passage.[281] The *Fairplay* sailed north with the French Fleet for seven days and took its departure on May 21.

Ships were spotted on May 29 and 30 but did not give chase. As they approached New England, the weather turned foggy. Soundings were periodically taken to determine depth of water under them. The sounding device picked up grey sand at the floor of the ocean and measurements showed the depth in fathoms to be steadily decreasing at thirty-two, twenty-two, thirteen and then five.[282] Martha's Vineyard suddenly loomed up out of the fog and the *Fairplay* quickly turned away from the shore. The fog continued the next day and no land could be seen but the depth increased to between fifteen and twenty fathoms.

The weather finally cleared on June 3 and the *Fairplay* put in at New Bedford where they sold their cargo. John Palmer didn't get home to Stonington until June 27 and didn't remain for long. He immediately signed on with the forty-five ton merchant schooner, *Little Rebecca* which headed out to sea on July 1.

The *Little Rebecca* was commanded by Joseph Dodge and was bound for the Dutch island of St. Eustatius. A major transshipment center, this tiny island was a powerhouse of illegal trade prior to the American Revolution. The population soared to 20,000 during the early years of the war when the island became a critical supplier of strategic items that were in short supply in America. These included arms, ammunition, salt and duck cloth for sails. At times, there were as many as 200 ships in the harbor and the island became known as the Golden Rock. The British finally invaded and took possession of the island in 1781 but it was taken by the French the following year and then returned to the Dutch after the end of the war. St. Eustatius continued its importance as a transshipment center during the difficult years after the war until the end of the eighteenth century.

Initially, the *Little Rebecca* traveled with three other merchant ships. Two days out, they were chased by five vessels and, sailing close to the wind, quickly out ran them. A few days later the ships separated and traveled alone. The *Little Rebecca* was periodically in and out of sight of another New London sloop. On July 12, the *Little Rebecca* was chased by two ships. Captain Dodge bore away from them, raised all sails and soon disappeared from their sight. One of the ships continued to give chase however, and appeared the next day. Again,

Captain Dodge had no difficulty slipping away from this pesky enemy vessel. The determined pursuer still didn't give up and appeared on the horizon for the third day in a row and was given the slip for a third and final time.[283]

On July 17, seven sails were spotted but they were soon out of sight. The next day, they broke open their last barrel of fresh water and had to restrict the quantity consumed to two quarts per day per man.[284] On July 25, they approached the island of Barbuda and then headed southwest towards St. Eustatius. They were chased by a sloop with all sails raised but managed to bear away and escape by the time they reached Nevis and St. Kitts. They ran along the south side of St. Kitts and then turned north towards St. Eustatius where they arrived the next morning.

The delivered cargo was not identified but, for the return trip, they loaded 186 bushels of salt taken directly out of another sloop, a large quantity of ginseng tea and a number of bolts of duck (sail cloth).[285] They departed on August 4 bound for Boston where Captain Dodge would sell most of the cargo.

Over the next nine days they spotted eleven individual ships and a fleet of thirty vessels but none came after the *Little Rebecca*. On August 14, they encountered a sloop to the east and a schooner to the south. The winds were very light and they soon noticed that the sloop had taken out their oars and was rowing towards them.[286] Captain Dodge broke out his oars as well and they rowed first north and then to the west. The sloop gave up the chase by nightfall and, on the next day, neither ship was in sight. Soon however, they spotted a brig ahead of them so they came about to avoid closing the gap with that ship.

On August 16 they were chased by another brig but out ran them in the space of two hours. On August 18 they began to sound the bottom as they traveled and recorded readings of forty-five, thirty-two, twenty-one and then twenty fathoms with a bottom content of grey and white sand. On August 19, they encountered a fleet of twenty vessels which they identified as fishing schooners working an area around Crab Ledge. One of the schooners informed them they were near Chatham on Cape Cod. They soon spotted land and Captain Dodge ran north around the tip of the Cape and brought the *Little Rebecca* into Boston harbor on August 21. They unloaded the ginseng tea, duck cloth and 163 of his 186 bushels of salt and set sail for home.

Chapter Eight

Connecticut and Continental Navies: 1777–1779

Along with growing power and numbers of privateering vessels emanating from Long Island Sound ports, the Connecticut State Navy also reached its peak capability between 1777 and 1779. This was not a simple task. It was easier to find sailors to man privateers than military ships of State or Continental Navies. The primary reason was that privateering offered a greater probability of substantial prize money. Also, the privateer attempted to avoid encounters where they were weaker than their opponent so risk of injury or death was reduced. Their preference, if possible, was to coerce an enemy ship into surrendering without engaging in battle. Navy ships, on the other hand, had military objectives, so voyages were much more hazardous and offered less monetary reward.

Although military crew members received wages and privateer crews did not, their entitlement to prize money from captured ships was less. In November 1775 Congress issued regulations covering prize courts and prize share entitlement. Privateers were allowed the entire value of their prize which was then distributed to the ship owners, officers and crew. In the case of Continental or State Navies, the crew received only one third of the prize value when transport or supply ship captures were involved and one half when the ship was an armed vessel of war. The rest went into government coffers.

Congress improved Continental and State Navy crew shares in October 1776 in an attempt to encourage more aggressive action. The share was increased to one hundred percent for capture of war vessels and fifty percent for other vessels. This helped but did not overcome the disadvantages of serving on navy vessels as opposed to privateers.

The Connecticut naval ship, *Defense* sailed from New London in March of 1777 under the command of Samuel Smedley of Fairfield. It had been in port since the previous September after returning from action in Massachusetts Bay. Its previous commander, Captain Harding, stepped down due to health reasons but, subsequently accepted command of the Connecticut naval ship, *Oliver Cromwell*. He would later be appointed by the Continental Navy as commander of the frigate *Confederacy* which was under construction on the Thames River in Preston.

In a little over a month, Smedley captured four vessels within the Atlantic shipping lanes east of Long Island Sound. These ships were heavily laden with supplies bound for the British Army in New York.[287] After this cruise, the *Defense* went into Boston where extensive renovations were undertaken to lengthen and widen the ship.

The *Spy* was also ready for duty again in March 1777 and was ordered to sail to Maryland or Virginia to obtain a supply of flour. In June, two additional cannons were mounted onboard bringing the total to six. The *Spy* then spent most of the summer cruising in the western end of the Sound from New Haven towards New York as far as it could prudently go. Three enemy ships were captured, the largest being the eighty ton *Dolphin*.[288] The *Dolphin* was later purchased by the State of Connecticut and used to acquire critical supplies in the West Indies.

The twenty gun *Oliver Cromwell* was finally prepared for its first mission in the spring of 1777 under command of Seth Harding. It was the largest of Connecticut's naval vessels at 300 tons, eighty foot length of keel, twenty-seven foot beam width and twelve foot depth of hold.[289] Harding encountered difficulty recruiting a sufficient number of crewmen due to competing interests and better opportunities for men serving on privateer vessels. He managed to scrape together a minimum crew of 102 and set sail on May 21 to find additional crewmen elsewhere. In New Bedford, Massachusetts he recruited about eighty more crewmen.

Ready at last, Captain Harding eased the *Oliver Cromwell* out of New Bedford harbor on June 5 and set course for the busy North Atlantic shipping lanes. He captured three ships in July and sent them into Boston, however, only two arrived. The *Restoration* was recaptured by the British ship, *Ambuscade* along with its prize crew. Another setback occurred when most of the British prisoners taken by Captain Harding on the other two captured ships managed to escape. They were sent overland from Boston to New London. From there, the officers were sent to Governor Trumbull's war headquarters in Lebanon, Connecticut and the rest of the British crewmen were put onboard a ship for a prisoner exchange in New York. On the voyage down Long Island Sound, the prisoners managed to overpower the crew and escape with the ship by slipping into a Long Island port now under British control.[290]

Meanwhile Captain Harding's health again deteriorated. He took the *Oliver Cromwell* into Boston and relinquished command to the ship's senior Lieutenant, Timothy Parker. While the ship was being re-supplied and outfitted, a determination was made to cruise south together with the *Defense* which was also in Boston undergoing structural modifications. They would depart together in February, 1778.

Meanwhile, David Hawley was ready for a new assignment in the spring of 1777. He was given command of the Connecticut Navy sloop, *Schuyler* mounting six guns. His crew of forty was recruited from Stratford and Fairfield. By midsummer he had captured eight merchant ships within Long Island Sound, many with supplies destined for the British Army and garrisons in and around New York City.[291]

Although quite successful, Hawley was dissatisfied with his military rank of Lieutenant in the Connecticut State Navy. He had carried the rank of Captain during his participation with the Continental Army and Navy in the Lake Champlain campaign and may have also been concerned by the smaller share of prizes received by military personnel versus privateers. When his enlistment expired at the beginning of November, David Hawley brought the *Schuyler* into New Haven Harbor and declined to take her out again.[292] This rift appears to have been quickly resolved since he soon took the helm of the *Schuyler* for another mission.

In December, Connecticut militia General Israel Putnam devised a plan to disrupt British supplies that were supporting their New York military operations. He planned to attack the port of Setauket, Long Island in order to destroy these supplies, capture or destroy ships in the harbor and overwhelm the fort if that was feasible. A similar attempt had been made in August utilizing whaleboats that had only been partially successful.

At Norwalk on December 9, Putnam loaded troops aboard four transports and sent them across the Sound accompanied by three Connecticut naval ships, the *Schuyler, Spy* and *Mifflin*. Little is known about the mission and it appears they were again, only partially successful. The attack was discontinued when word was received that enemy ships were on their way from Huntington Harbor to the west.

The patriots feared having their line of retreat cut off and hastily re-boarded their ships to escape back across the Sound. All of them made it except for the *Schuyler* which tangled with the approaching British frigate, *Falcon*. Having no chance against this warship, Captain Hawley drove his vessel aground at Old Field Point, Long Island.[293] He hoped this would allow his crew and the troops he carried to escape ashore but they were all captured. For the third time, David Hawley was a prisoner of war and this time he was probably incarcerated at Newport, Rhode Island.

After David Bushnell's submarine, Turtle, proved unsuccessful in several attempts to sink a British ship he switched his focus to the development of floating mines. In 1777, the British frigate, *Cerberus*, lurking outside New London Harbor, provided an opportunity to test his new device. He rowed out to an anchored schooner that had just been captured by the *Cerberus* and fastened a line to the bow with mines attached to each end. When the *Cerberus* returned, it anchored off the stern of the now booby trapped schooner. Four sailors were sent over as guards.

About eleven o'clock in the evening, Commodore Simmons discovered the line caught around the bow of the schooner and trailing to the rear. The four guards were ordered to investigate. They hauled in the line, lifted the device onto the deck of the schooner and curiously began to examine it. Unknown to them a wheel was set in motion on the mine to trigger a timed explosion when an iron spike attached to it was bumped. In the process of hauling the mine aboard ship the spike was bumped and moved, thus releasing the wheel. The explosion "blew the ship in pieces and set her on fire."[294] Three of the sailors were killed immediately and the one survivor was blown into the water, seriously injured.

Although the *Cerberus* escaped damage, the device worked.[295] An added benefit was the immediate departure of the *Cerberus* for New York, ending its blockade of New London Harbor. Delighted by the possibilities, Bushnell enhanced his design so that the explosive charge was carried in a submerged configuration beneath the two floating casks. A spring-lock device connected the casks which detonated the mine when the casks rubbed against the ship hull.

Bushnell was soon presented with an opportunity to try his new devices. The British Army under General Howe occupied Philadelphia in September 1777 rather than going to the aid of General Burgoyne at Saratoga. Within three months they had cleared Delaware Bay of American ships and defenses. Hoping to prevent the British from continuing up the Delaware River north of Philadelphia, Colonel Joseph Borden and Francis Hopkinson sent for David Bushnell whose work with mines had now become well known.

In the middle of the night, several days after Christmas, about twenty sets of mines and kegs were taken aboard a whaleboat and rowed downstream towards Philadelphia. The objective was to have the mines float downstream and into the anchored British ships during darkness so they wouldn't be spotted. The plan went awry immediately due to the fact that neither Bushnell nor his rowing partner was familiar with the Delaware River. They put the mines overboard too far from the ships and miscalculated the speed of the current that would carry the mines. Drifting ice also interfered with the mines and significantly delayed their progress.

Matters took another turn for the worse when two boys spotted a keg and rowed out from shore to see what treasure they had found. The mine exploded as they hauled it into their tiny boat killing both of the boys.[296] A few days later another set of kegs was spotted from a barge close to the British fleet. Again, the mine exploded as it was being pulled onboard, killing four of the crew and wounding the rest.

The British quickly sounded the call to battle stations. The Battle of the Kegs had begun. For the rest of the day ship cannons roared in an intense bombardment aimed at every piece of debris floating in the water. Nervous British captains took no chances. While the rebels failed in their primary objective, Bushnell's efforts achieved an unexpected notoriety lifting the morale of patriots during the dark days of Valley Forge. The Battle of the Kegs was widely reported in rebel papers and the British were ridiculed.[297] With gleeful derision patriots memorialized the "battle" in song, story and poem.

After the Battle of the Kegs, Bushnell returned to Yale where he earned a Masters Degree in 1778. In 1779, incensed by the British raid on New Haven, Bushnell immediately volunteered for service in the newly formed Corps of Sappers and Miners.[298] This was an ideal place for him where he could utilize his knowledge of explosives. He was appointed Captain by Governor Trumbull and saw service at Yorktown and other locations.

The *Oliver Cromwell* and the *Defense*, both in Boston for renovations or re-fitting, were ready to sail again in late February, 1778. Captains Parker and Smedley confirmed the agreement that both ships would cruise together on a voyage through the West Indies. Sometime after weighing anchor, a smallpox epidemic broke out on the *Defense* with about fifty sailors becoming infected, two of whom subsequently died. Captain Smedley did not abort the mission and continued in tandem with the other ship.

Near St. Kitts, a passing French ship warned them of two large, heavily armed British vessels nearby that were bound from Bristol, England to Jamaica. The Connecticut ships immediately altered course and intercepted the twenty gun *Admiral Keppel* and the eighteen gun *Cyrus*, both British privateers. The ships were equally matched in cannon firepower but the Connecticut ships carried three times the number of crewmen as did the British ships.[299] Technically, this gave them an advantage in musket fire and boarding strength but fifty men aboard the *Defense* were disabled with smallpox at the time of the encounter.

A stiff engagement of three glasses (one and a half hours) ensued before the British ships surrendered. The *Defense* sustained significant damage but only two wounded. Losses on the *Oliver Cromwell* and *Admiral Keppel* were equal with two dead and six wounded on each vessel. One of the dead on the *Oliver Cromwell* was James Day, Captain of Marines. The *Admiral Keppel* and the *Cyrus* were sent back to New London and arrived there safely.[300]

The two Connecticut ships then separated but both soon made their way into Charleston, South Carolina for repairs. In June the *Defense* engaged three British ships off of Charleston and captured two of them before heading back to Boston where it arrived on August 3. With enlistments up, many of the crewmen were released from duty in Boston and most of the remaining sailors were subsequently dismissed back in New London where they were free to return to their homes in Stratford and Fairfield.[301]

Meanwhile, the *Oliver Cromwell* attempted to fulfill a previous order to pick up a cargo which included indigo for delivery in France. After leaving Charleston with this cargo on August 24, the *Oliver Cromwell* suffered through a hurricane which knocked down all her masts. Captain Parker was forced to cancel his voyage to France and limp back to New London for repairs. Before the end of the year the *Oliver Cromwell* made one more capture, the brig *Medway* off of Cape Cod.

The *Spy* received a fateful new assignment in 1778. Initially, it was ordered to convoy the eighty ton *Dolphin* to the West Indies. This ship had been captured by the *Spy* in western Long Island Sound the previous September and was purchased by Connecticut to use as a supply ship. Staves, hoops and lard were loaded to trade specifically for rum.[302] Rum was considered an essential commodity necessary to sustain the morale of soldiers and sailors. The *Dolphin* sailed alone however, as an important new mission was given to the *Spy* which superseded the West Indies voyage.

The final voyage of the swift sailing *Spy* was made in June in the role of a dispatch courier to American Commissioners in France. Six copies were made of the newly ratified Treaty with France for friendship, commerce and alliance. This document was so important that the Marine Committee of the Continental Congress requested that six copies be carried secretly on six different ships in order to insure that at least one document arrived safely.[303] Connecticut was called upon to provide one of the six vessels. The *Spy* left from Stonington with this historic document and arrived in Brest after a speedy voyage which took only twenty-one days. Supposedly, this is the only treaty document that reached its destination.

Captain Niles' return voyage would not be as quick and he would not see home again for more than a year. The *Spy* was captured and the crew taken to England. Captain Niles managed to escape and made his way to France. His second attempt to reach America ended the same way and he was sent to Fortun prison where he was eventually exchanged. He finally reached home on July 23, 1779.

Also during 1778, several ships operated in the western portion of Long Island Sound under the military direction of General Gold Silliman. While little is known about these ships, the schooner *Mifflin* was particularly effective as a commerce raider under command of Captain John Kerr. During the first half of 1778, the *Mifflin* captured seven vessels in Long Island Sound.[304] It was then taken out of service and sold. Its commander, John Kerr, accepted a commission in the Continental Navy where he served as a lieutenant.

The Connecticut State Navy reached its culmination in 1779 but it would be the last year for major ship operations under Connecticut military authority. Authorities were anxious to send the *Oliver Cromwell* back to sea and in January, ordered Nathaniel Shaw to obtain supplies and make other preparations to get the ship ready for sailing as soon as possible. However, the usual problem of obtaining a crew for a navy vessel kept the ship in port for a considerable period of time.

Captain Smedley of the *Defense* was also unable to recruit a new crew due to the extreme shortage of men and their preference to serve on privateer ships with a potential for more lucrative cruises. When he received orders to sail on a mission into Long Island Sound, Smedley pressed into service a militia detachment stationed in New London even though many of them were not sailors.[305] He also obtained a pilot supposedly knowledgeable of local waters but on March 10, 1779 the ship foundered on Goshen Reef offshore from New London

Harbor. A successful effort was mounted to save the guns and most of the supplies before the *Defense* sank. The price for this valiant effort was high as four or five lives were lost when the ship unexpectedly rolled over and went down during salvage operations.[306]

The *Oliver Cromwell* was finally ordered to sea by Governor Trumbull on May 3 with instructions to Captain Timothy Parker to recruit additional men at Stonington, Martha's Vineyard and Nantucket if necessary to obtain a full compliment of men. Captain Parker found sufficient, additional crewmen in Stonington and then headed into the Atlantic without further delay. There were several black and Indian sailors onboard, including at least two Mohegans, Abimilech and Benjamin Uncas. Also onboard was twenty-three-year-old Jabez Perkins, 3rd of Norwich, Captain of the Marine contingent and a relative of Simeon Perkins of Nova Scotia.[307]

There were five quartermasters; a sixth had deserted prior to the ship's departure from New London. The quartermaster was an important position with responsibility for the helm usually located on the quarterdeck (hence the position title). The Quartermaster had considerable interaction with the navigator and ship captain. Often two quartermasters were on duty with each watch because it often took two men on the wheel of larger ships to hold the rudder and move it for course corrections, tacking and other maneuvers.

Almost immediately after their departure from Stonington, four enemy ships fell prey to the *Oliver Cromwell*. One of these, the *Hazard,* had changed hands three times. It was originally a British merchant ship captured by an American privateer, subsequently captured by a British privateer and finally recaptured by the *Oliver Cromwell*.[308] Captain Parker convoyed the four ships with their supplies and more than sixty prisoners back into Long Island Sound by the end of May. Not wishing to incur further delays or loose crewmen, he sent the prize ships into New London Harbor alone for libeling in Maritime Court. In order to fill in for the prize crews that were placed on the captured ships, he conscripted a few of the British prisoners. His crew at this time totaled approximately 140 men.

Captain Parker then set course to round Montauk Point and head for the dangerous waters south of Sandy Hook, New Jersey where British maritime commerce, privateers and naval ships began to funnel into New York Harbor. The approaches to New York Harbor were especially dangerous at this time. British General Clinton was in the process of increasing and supporting his military forces for a major offensive up the Hudson River with hopes of reaching Albany. There was considerable British shipping and naval activity in and out of New York Harbor.

At twenty-seven leagues south of Sandy Hook (about eighty-five miles) the *Oliver Cromwell* was spotted by three British warships, the *Daphne, Delaware* and *Union* who all gave chase. A day later, at eleven o'clock in the morning of June 6, the *Daphne* caught up to the *Oliver Cromwell*. During the initial phase of battle, the *Daphne's* main top mast was shot away. It temporarily fell behind while clearing the damaged mast and rigging but caught up again three and a half hours later.[309] The battle resumed and fighting was fierce for another hour and a half.

At close range, standard tactics called for British sharpshooters to concentrate their fire on the helmsmen in order to kill or seriously wound every man who attempted to grab the helm. The objective was to disrupt steering and gain positional advantage. They succeeded in killing three of the five quartermasters—Charles Cheeseboro, Thomas Stanton and Michael Ewan. Cheeseboro was a descendent of William and Anna Stevenson Chesebrough, the first family to settle in Stonington in 1649. Stanton was a descendent of Thomas and Ann Lord Stanton who established the first trading post on the Pawcatuck River, Stonington in 1650.

With losses mounting and the other British warships approaching, the *Oliver Cromwell* was forced to strike its colors. Seven were killed on the *Oliver Cromwell* but there is no information on the number of American wounded or any of the British casualties. The prisoners were disbursed onto the three British warships. Some were then impressed into British service and some incarcerated on the prison ship, *Jersey*. Nine of those held on the *Daphne* managed to escape. For the second time, Captain Timothy Parker was a prisoner of war.

When word of the *Oliver Cromwell's* capture reached Governor Trumbull, immediate arrangements were made to assemble appropriate numbers and ranks of British prisoners to accomplish an exchange which was carried out in August. Jabez Perkins, III was among those released only to be lost at sea in October 1780 during a severe hurricane in the West Indies. At the time of this hurricane,

Perkins was probably in command of the Sloop *York,* an armed trading vessel owned by Jabez Perkins & Co carrying six guns but only ten crewmen.[310] Simeon Perkins of Nova Scotia did not learn of this devastating hurricane until December 31, 1780 when he received some newspapers from New York.[311]

The British lost no time repairing and refitting the captured *Oliver Cromwell* for privateering service based out of Huntington Harbor, Long Island. The following advertisement appeared on the front page of Rivington's *Royal Gazette* on July 21, 1779.

The Frigate RESTORATION

(formerly the OLIVER CROMWELL)

Is now fitting for sea, and will be ready in six Days to join the Associated REFUGEE FLEET, lying at Huntington Harbour, And intending soon to pay a visit to the Rebel Coast.

All gentlemen who are desirous to enter on board said Ship as Officers, shall be provided for agreeable to their merit; and all good seaman who wish to join this determined Band of LOYALISTS, are desired to repair on board said ship, lying at the Navy-yard, where they shall receive FIVE GUINEAS advance, THREE POUNDS Sterling per month, and One Share of all Property taken from his Majesty's revolted Subjects by Sea and Land.

Mr. LEONARD flatters himself, that this encouragement will be sufficient to induce every well wisher to his Majesty and the British Constitution, to engage in an undertaking, where profit and honour are inseparably blended.

N. B. [Note carefully] as MR. LEONARD is determined, at all events, to adhere punctiliously to the orders of the Commanders in Chief both by Sea and Land, he warns all persons who are engaged in either service not to apply, unless with permission [from their military unit], for he must and will reject them.

The story of the Connecticut Navy ship, *Guilford* is fascinating, not for its brief period of naval service, but rather for the circumstances of its acquisition. It was purchased by the state in April of 1779 and was burned at its wharf a few months later during the

British invasion of New Haven.[312] It never saw action as part of the Connecticut Navy.

Previous to its capture, the sixty ton sloop, known as the *Mars*, was a British privateer carrying eight guns. While cruising in Long Island Sound on February 6, 1779, the *Mars* captured the American merchant sloop, *Lucy* and its crew commanded by Giles Sage of Middletown. The six Americans were transferred to the *Mars* as prisoners while the *Lucy* was sailed down the Sound to New York by a prize crew. On February 21 however, the *Mars* was driven onto the rocky shore of Guilford, Connecticut by severe weather. Desperate to lighten his ship and float it off the rocks before American military forces or residents arrived, Captain Samuel Rogers began to throw heavy equipment overboard. The crew managed to jettison two cannon, the anchors and anchor cables before time ran out.

Two separate forces acted almost simultaneously to subdue the British crew and take control of the *Mars*. On land, a nine man military contingent led by Captain Darius Collins arrived. They were part of a garrison charged with protecting the Guilford shoreline. About the same time, five of the six prisoners on the *Mars* managed to break free and come up on deck. Captain Giles Sage was not with them as he was probably held in a separate compartment and was not able to free himself. The British privateers surrendered to this combined force.

The *Mars* was subsequently floated off the rocks by Captain David Landon and several associates. This group also retrieved the anchors and cable and sailed the ship into Guilford Harbor. Finally, the two cannon were salvaged from the ocean by Solomon Leete and Associates.

Action then moved to the courtroom in New Haven for libel and condemnation proceedings in this complex case. There were numerous competing claims to all or a portion of the prize. Three separate groups made claim to the entire ship and all of its supplies and equipment. There was even an allegation of jury misconduct adding excitement to the proceedings. This involved a juror who was seen conversing with Captain Giles Sage. The juror's wife was a cousin to the wife of Captain Sage.

After three considerations, the jury finally returned a verdict on April 4. Solomon Leete and his associates were awarded the two cannon they salvaged from the ocean. Captain Giles Sage was awarded the supplies he personally owned that were transferred from the *Lucy* when it was captured by the *Mars*. These were a barrel of sugar, a barrel of coffee and a certain amount of rum. The five *Lucy* crewmen who broke free of their confinement were awarded one half of the ship and equipment. Three quarters of the remaining half was awarded to the military unit consisting of Captain Darius Collins and his eight men. Finally, one quarter of the remaining half plus the anchor and cable was awarded to Captain David Landon and his crew for getting the ship off the rocks and bringing it into Guilford Harbor.

Captain William Nott was appointed to command the *Guilford* but he resigned his commission and brought the ship into New Haven. He was replaced by David Hawley who took command on July 2 just as the British were moving to attack the town. Hawley had been out of action since his capture one and a half years earlier while participating in the raid on Setauket Long Island. The *Guilford* was not prepared for action and there was little Hawley could do against the more than forty British naval ships assembled for the invasion of New Haven. However, he was able to remove the anchor, cables, sails, ammunition and supplies before British forces burned the *Guilford* and other ships in the harbor.

Construction of the *New Defense*, Connecticut's last major naval vessel, began in early 1779. This was one of four large row galleys that were originally authorized in 1775 but only the *Crane*, *Whiting* and *Shark* were previously built. The town of Branford initially applied to build one of the four row galleys in 1776 but the request languished.[313] Branford renewed its effort in 1779 when the town sponsored and pushed construction forward and then petitioned the Connecticut legislature to accept the vessel as its fourth row galley. The General Assembly voted approval on April 7, 1779.[314]

Some of the equipment utilized by the *New Defense* was salvaged from other vessels. One anchor and cable was furnished from the *Defense* which sank off New London in March. Another anchor and cable plus the mainsail were taken from the *Guilford* before it was burned by the British in July.[315] Authorization was given for about eight cannon and it is known that two, twelve pound cannons came from New London and two more twelve pounders came from New Haven.

The mission assigned to the *New Defense* was to guard the coast and harbors of central Long Island Sound and interdict illicit trade. It probably didn't commence these duties until late in the year and its operational life was short lived. The *New Defense* was captured around February 1, 1780. Its crew was placed on prison ships in New York where twenty of them died.

By now, Connecticut's eleven major naval vessels were all captured, destroyed or taken out of service and no more would be commissioned during the war. Naval activities however, continued at the whaleboat level. The larger ships had done their jobs well but the nature of sea warfare in and around Long Island Sound was about to change.

Long Island Sound mariners also made a strong contribution to the newly formed Continental Navy in a variety of positions. For example, the crew of the brig *Alliance* included ten men from the Fairfield and Southport areas alone.

Dudley Saltonstall of New London was in command of the Continental Navy flagship, *Alfred* during the fleet's cruise to the Bahamas in 1776. He was later given command of the *Warren*, another Continental frigate.

Elisha Hinman of New London was commissioned as a Captain in the Continental Navy on August 13, 1776. He took command of the fourteen gun brig, *Cabot* after its return from the Bahamas expedition and made a cruise to the West Indies where, in late October, he captured a sixteen gun British privateer loaded with sugar, rum and cotton.[316] He captured six more ships in November before returning to New London for the winter.

On March 23, near Cape Ann Massachusetts, Hinman encountered the much larger, thirty-two gun British ship-of-war, *Milford* and desperately tried to slip away on a northeastward course, probably determined by wind direction. The chase continued for two days and ended when the coast of Nova Scotia loomed up out of the horizon. With no more room to maneuver, Captain Hinman drove the *Cabot* aground on Cheboque Point near Yarmouth Nova Scotia.[317] The crew managed to take all of the small arms and escape ashore.

They evaded capture and commandeered another vessel which took them safely back to New England.

Not long after this, Captain Hinman was appointed to command the Continental Navy ship, *Alfred*. Command of this ship had passed from Dudley Saltonstall to John Paul Jones and then to Hinman. In consort with the new Continental frigate *Raleigh*, two captures were made. On March 9, 1778, however, they were intercepted by British warships *Ariadne* and *Ceres*. The faster sailing *Raleigh* escaped but the poor sailing *Alfred*, now alone, was forced to surrender.

Captain Hinman and the officers were taken to Fortun prison near Portsmouth England. Within a week Hinman and four of his officers escaped. They bribed the jailors to look the other way while they dug their way out and escaped to France.[318]

The Continental Congress authorized construction in Connecticut of Navy frigates *Trumbull* and *Confederacy*. The thirty-six gun, 700 ton frigate, *Trumbull* was built in Portland on the Connecticut River. The ship was launched in September 1776 and work continued on its construction. It wasn't until then that its builders became concerned that the deep draft on this ship would make it difficult to negotiate the sandbars at the mouth of the Connecticut River. In February 1778, it was floated down the river for further fitting. Despite new depth charts and channel mapping of the river mouth, the *Trumbull* was unable to negotiate the shallow waters and underwater sandbars.

The ship remained in the river until August 1779 when Elisha Hinman thought of a way to get it out. He devised a plan to raise the ship a bit by placing water casks on either side of the vessel, attached to ropes strung under the hull.[319] The casks were filled with water to the point they barely floated and were then pumped out to lift the ship. The plan worked and the *Trumbull* was then taken to New London for final fitting out. Its first voyage would be made the following year.

Meanwhile, the thirty-two gun Continental Navy frigate, *Confederacy* was under construction in Preston as previously mentioned. Much of the timber used for construction was harvested on property confiscated from two Loyalists.[320] It was launched November 8, 1778 and towed downriver to New London where it was rigged and fitted out. Seth Harding of Norwich, who previously commanded the

Connecticut Navy ship *Defense*, was given command and many of the crewmen were recruited from Norwich and New London. Its first mission was to cruise the Atlantic coast and perform convoy duty. On June 6, 1779, the *Confederacy* and the *Deane* captured three ships, drove off two British frigates and brought the convoy safely into Philadelphia.

Its next mission was a voyage in November, 1779 to transport the French Ambassador, Count de Gerard and his family back to France. Also taking passage was the first U.S. Ambassador to Spain, John Jay, and his family. A violent storm off Newfoundland shattered the ship's three masts and filled the hold with six feet of water. With remnants of the masts lashed together, the *Confederacy* was pushed southward and limped into the French West Indies island of Martinico. The dignitaries transferred to the French frigate, *L'Aurore* and continued on to Europe.

Silas Deane of Wethersfield, Connecticut played a significant role in America's struggle for independence, not as a sailor but as a diplomat. He was instrumental in obtaining military supplies and other assistance from France and he was a signer of two all important treaties with the French in February 1778. One was the Treaty of Alliance and the other was the Treaty of Amity and Commerce. A Yale graduate and member of the first Continental Congress, it was Silas who financed the expedition to capture Fort Ticonderoga largely from his own funds. It was Silas who wrote the first rules governing the Continental Navy and it was Silas who selected and purchased the *Alfred*, flagship for the first fleet action of the Continental Navy.[321]

In 1776, Silas went to France as a secret representative of Congress to enlist French support and obtain supplies. He recruited many French officers and men, including Lafayette, and negotiated for cannon, small arms and clothing to equip 25,000 men. After the treaty was signed in 1778 but before ratification by the Continental Congress, Silas made arrangements for at least eight ships to make the journey to America loaded with supplies. Most, but not all, made it safely.

One French ship that failed to reach its destination was the *Duke de Choisel*. It was packed with military supplies and about one hundred men including two French officers. They carried a letter of introduction to Philadelphia financier, Robert Morris that was written by Silas Deane.[322] The *Duke de Choisel* was intercepted off Nova Scotia by the British warship, *Blonde* and chased into Liverpool Harbor where it went aground on April 24. British salvage efforts were made difficult when the vessel rolled over on April 26, killing three of the *Blonde's* crewmen who were onboard at the time. A hole was cut in the hull and salvage resumed. The *Blonde* departed on May 12 and its Captain gave Simeon Perkins authority to remove the remainder of the small arms and clothing.

Word of the wreck of the *Duke de Choisel* quickly reached American officials. On May 19, two American privateers entered Liverpool Harbor. The townspeople decided not to engage or molest the privateers as long has they did no harm. Simeon was summoned aboard the *Washington*, one of the two privateers. Captain Preston advised Simeon that his mission was just to recover the arms and clothing so an agreement was reached and Simeon was awarded a salvage percentage.[323] After loading the supplies on their vessels the Americans broke their agreement. That evening, men came ashore and ransacked several houses and stores including Simeon's. The privateers left the next day but returned a day later and cut loose a sloop that had just arrive from Bermuda and towed it out of the harbor.

Chapter Nine

Between and Behind the Lines: 1777–1779

Hostilities within Long Island Sound and on both shores increased dramatically to keep pace with the war at sea. There were major British military operations to obtain provisions, destroy Continental Army supplies, punish the inhabitants or attempt to lure General Washington's Army out of its Hudson River Highland defenses. The Highlands was a twenty mile stretch of the Hudson River with mountains on each side stretching from today's Bear Mountain State Park to Newburgh. At its heart were Fort Montgomery and West Point. Also, significant whaleboat actions took a wide variety of forms. There were retaliatory whaleboat raids and other raids with military objectives that captured forts, encampments or ships in harbors. The sole objective of other whaleboat raids was plunder.

Angry and vindictive refugees from both sides of the Sound entered the fray. Usually they targeted communities where they used to live and often, previous friends and neighbors were their victims. An important objective was to obtain prisoners for exchange and increasingly, civilians were kidnapped for this purpose.

In the Fairfield area, William Wheeler's Diary reflected great concern over the number of Tories from all the shoreline towns who could, and often did, pilot enemy vessels "into every place they pleased to come."[324] He also commented on the liberty pole placed by Whigs (Patriots) on Greenfield Hill. Erected during the day, it would be cut down at night by Tories. Even a sheathing of iron around the bottom didn't stop the Tories from returning at night with a ladder and cutting it above the plates.

Long Island Sound was no man's land and the shoreline was, although sparsely defended, the front line. Actions were sometimes contested near the shore but often penetrated a considerable distance inland. Raiding party movement across the Sound was mostly at night to avoid detection during the crossing. Both sides also developed espionage operations primarily to keep tabs on significant, strategic intentions. Passage of information to General Washington traveled from New York City to Setauket, Long Island, then across the Sound by whaleboat to Connecticut and finally to the Continental Army headquarters in the Hudson River Highlands.

The British military conducted occasional foraging raids on the coast of Connecticut. Throughout the war, there was a chronic shortage of provisions in New York. There were a number of reasons for this shortage which often reached crisis proportion. First, there were many more mouths to feed. British Army forces totaled about 25,000 men and there were thousands more navy personnel. There was also, a large influx of Tory refugees who flooded into New York from many of the American states and there were a large number of American prisoners incarcerated in New York. Second, American privateers captured many supply ships coming from Great Britain and Nova Scotia. Third, market boats from Connecticut, a major pre-war supplier to New York, were discontinued although a lively illicit trade would develop late in the war. Fourth, Long Island and Westchester County market boats bound to New York with supplies were interdicted by Connecticut whaleboat men and privateers.

The first foraging raid occurred at Milford in March 1777 when the British ship, *Swan*, accompanied by three tenders, sent a forty person foraging party ashore at Gulf Beach near Pond Point. Their objective was to steal livestock and other food supplies. The landing site selected for this raid was probably chosen because it was on the opposite side of the Milford Harbor inlet from where Fort Trumbull stood. Defending militia at Fort Trumbull could not risk crossing the inlet under the watchful eyes of gunners on the *Swan* and would have to march all the way around the harbor to confront the raiding party.

Vigilant farmers near Pond Point however, were already taking action to preserve their livestock. The wife of Miles Merwin acted quickly to spread the alarm. She hitched a horse to her carriage, grabbed her baby and a copper kettle and raced into the village, banging the kettle all the way.[325] Animals were rounded up and driven inland before they could fall into the grasp of the swiftly moving raiders. The rapidly growing resistance convinced the raiding party to abandon their quest and retreat. The frustrated raiders had just enough time to wreck the interior of the Merwin home. The British had hoped to fill their three ship tenders with livestock and food. Instead, they came away virtually empty handed with just two hogs and a little cheese.

The British ship, *Schuldham* was also employed to obtain provisions in 1777. It was stationed at the deep water anchorage off of City Island, Pelham, New York. Its primary duty was to function as a guard ship near the narrows and the Hell Gate passage leading into New York City but it also scoured the coast to obtain provisions by raid or coercion. Its crew also intimidated and mistreated local Pelham residents. Determined to put an end to this, twelve whaleboat men from Darien, Connecticut obtained intelligence on *Schuldham's* anchorage and information about a small market sloop that often sold provisions to this vessel. A plan was developed to seize the market sloop and then approach the *Schuldham* posing as its regular crew.[326]

The Darien men sailed or rowed their whaleboat along the shore and portaged it over Rodman's Neck to keep out of sight and insure surprise. After boarding the merchant sloop they headed for the *Schuldham* in the early morning hours. As they approached they proclaimed to the night watch that they were fleeing from enemy whaleboats on the Sound and wanted to get around to the lee side of the British ship for protection.[327] Several men then boarded the *Schuldham* unchallenged and put a gun to the captain's head as he came up from below deck. The crew quickly surrendered and the ship was sailed back to Stamford. On the way, they captured six more small market vessels.[328]

Lack of provisions also plagued the Continental Army. Shortages would be a chronic problem throughout the war but they were particularly acute in early 1777 due to the harrowing retreat of Washington's forces from lower New York over the previous several months. Connecticut responded to General Washington's appeal and provided a large amount of food, shoes, clothing and rum. During the war, Connecticut supplied more food and cannons than any other state and was officially recognized by George Washington as "The Provision State."[329]

The Continental Army provisions were initially stored at Peekskill on the Hudson River near the General's fortifications in the Highlands. They were moved to Danbury, Connecticut because it was thought to be a much safer location and didn't need to be closely guarded. Danbury was twenty miles inland from Long Island Sound and twenty-eight miles east of the Hudson River.

Loyalist informants advised General Howe of the supply depot relocation and the General ordered a raid to destroy these supplies. General Washington also had informants and had received advance intelligence about British preparations, knew the numbers of the regiments involved and had a good idea that they might try to destroy the provisions stockpiled in Danbury that supported his Continental troops assembled in the Hudson Highlands.[330] Nevertheless, he was unwilling to split his forces and commit to defending multiple locations.

Under the overall command of General William Tryon, a fleet of twenty-six ships set sail carrying 1,550 regular British troops and 300 Loyalists, many of whom were Connecticut refugees familiar with the target area and its roads. Simultaneously, a diversionary force of ships was sent up the Hudson River to confuse the Americans. As the British fleet approached, Connecticut forces tracked its progress from coastal watch sites and from the strategic observation post high on Tashua Hill.[331] They did not however, know where the intended landing sight would be and militia troops were already in disarray. Under orders from General Gold Silliman, some troops were shifted eastward to Fairfield and others were in route westward to the Hudson River in response to the diversionary tactic.

In the late afternoon of April 25, 1777 the British fleet anchored off Compo Beach near the mouth of the Saugatuck River in Westport, Connecticut. General Tryon had originally selected Norwalk for his landing site but shifted it to Compo Beach at the last minute due to the recent arrival and positioning of six cannon at strategic locations around Norwalk harbor. Compo Beach was undefended and the landing was unopposed but riders were soon on their way to give warning and call people to arms. When the British returned to their ships three days later, the high hill overlooking the beach would by hotly contested as its loss would pose a severe threat to re-embarkation.

Led by Loyalists, the British forces marched eight miles inland before camping for the night in northern Fairfield. The only resistance that could be mounted the first day was a small ambush involving eighteen men hidden behind a stone wall. They fired one or two volleys killing a major and wounding three other troops and then retreated into the woods.

On the next day, General Tryon reached Danbury at four o'clock where his troops destroyed large quantities of military supplies, food, tents, shoes and several houses in the village. Overnight, drunken soldiers rampaged through the streets and burned many more homes and buildings. Their activities were virtually unopposed but that would soon change. Militia forces were being gathered south of Danbury to contest the return of General Tryon's forces to their ships on April 27.

Word of the attack reached Colonel Henry Ludington in Kent, New York at nine o'clock in the evening. That night, while Danbury burned, Ludington's sixteen-year-old daughter, Sybil, galloped forty miles through Putnam and Dutchess Counties, alerting men to assemble. These troops arrived in time to skirmish with British troops retreating to their ships. With New York militia forces pressing the enemy from the north and Connecticut militia positioning themselves along the escape route to the south, the British were in a desperate situation. Their superior military discipline and skill however, would see them through the crisis.

Heavy but unsuccessful resistance was mounted in Ridgefield where Connecticut's General Wooster was killed and General Benedict Arnold's horse was shot from under him. On April 28, the patriots established an ambush at Old Hill in Westport but the British were warned of this by Loyalist, Deliverance Bennett and managed to circumvent the hazard.[332] Another attempt to head off the British failed when the militia refused to follow General Arnold's audacious orders to attack across the exposed Kings Highway Bridge.

The final battle took place at Compo Hill overlooking the beach where the British had to re-embark on their ships. This was a fierce engagement which could have led to disastrous consequences if the British were not able to hold the heights. Despite being re-supplied from one of their ships, the British forces ran out of ammunition. Close to being overwhelmed, the four defending Regiments, led by

Major Stewart, mounted a charge with fixed bayonets.[333] The experienced British soldiers were masters of this terrifying form of attack and successfully drove the Americans off.

The British suffered approximately 160–200 killed, wounded and captured and the Americans about sixty. British losses and the risks involved were severe enough to cause them to change their strategy for future raids on Connecticut soil. Three nights and 4 days on land allowed enough time for significant numbers of militia troops to assemble and deploy. Never again would British forces remain on Connecticut soil for more than one night and two days.

A plan was almost immediately devised to retaliate for General Tryon's successful raid on the supplies at Danbury. After the British occupied Sag Harbor, Long Island, they established a supply depot and built an earthworks fort on a hill overlooking the harbor. The site they selected was Sag Harbor's burying ground and disruption of the graves caused outrage in the community and with those Sag Harbor Patriot refugees who had fled to Connecticut.

Colonel Return J. Meigs of Middletown, Connecticut was selected to lead a strong whaleboat raid against the fort, supply depot and ships in the harbor. He collected thirteen whaleboats in New Haven and proceeded to Sachem Head in Guilford where reinforcements were added and the raid was further organized and planned. Their sanctuary was a small, isolated, but very beautiful and well protected cove at the tip of Sachem Head. When the expedition was ready to depart, Colonel Meigs had a compliment of 170 men, thirteen whaleboats of about twenty feet in length, two small, armed sloops for protection and one unarmed sloop to carry prisoners and booty.[334] At least two of the men were Patriot refugees from Sag Harbor who guided the raiding party.

The convoy headed out into the Sound on May 23 and landed on Hashamomuck Beach on the North Fork of Long Island. A short portage took the thirteen whaleboats across the peninsula into Southold Bay undetected while the three sloops remained back at the beach. The portage also allowed them to avoid the strong tidal currents running through Plum Gut. They then traveled through the Bay and

Shelter Island Sound at night, arriving at Sag Harbor at two o'clock in the morning. The attack was a complete surprise. The fort and nearby barracks were quickly overrun by the men who swarmed through with fixed bayonets. Twelve ships in the harbor were burned and destroyed, the largest being a brig carrying twelve guns. The supplies were also destroyed including 120 tons of hay and a large quantity of grain, merchandise and rum. Six defending soldiers were killed and a total of ninety were taken prisoner from the fort, barracks and wharf area.

The raiding party suffered no casualties and returned to Sachem Head Harbor in Guilford a little more than twenty-four hours after they had departed. With them were the ninety prisoners and fifty captured muskets. One of the prisoners was Joseph Chew, erstwhile Customs Inspector at New London but now a Loyalist supply officer.[335] The prisoners were subsequently exchanged. Surprisingly, Chew would surface once again in New Haven where he would have a crucial role in the events that occurred there in July of 1779.

The spectacular success of this raid had significant impact beyond the mission itself. It served as a model for future operations. Both sides took notice of how effective small whaleboats could be and employed similar tactics in the Whaleboat War that would soon develop. Guilford, because it served as the launching site for this raid, was singled out by Loyalists for future punitive action and revenge raids.

Only a few weeks later, the British struck back at Guilford with an attack at the Sachem Head Cove where Colonel Meigs had mounted his raid. This action had no military objective and its sole purpose was to punish Solomon Leete for having allowed the use of his property around the cove as a staging area for the raid. Few people even lived in this isolated location. On June 17, several tenders with troops from a British ship landed in the harbor. They proceeded to burn Solomon Leete's house before being chased away by militia.[336] Another minor raid was made in December of 1777 with small damage done to the home of Timothy Shelley.

Two other whaleboat actions in 1777 illustrate the wide spectrum of motivating factors. They ranged from purely personal or emotional issues to ones motivated by more objective rationale aimed at crippling the other side's capacity for carrying on the war. The majority of whaleboat raids were never recorded however, so a definitive analysis is not possible.

As the Whaleboat War between Long Island and Connecticut began to heat up there was opportunity for refugees to seek revenge against people they were angry with in the communities they had fled from. In June 1777, one such raid targeted the home of William Palmer of Southport, Connecticut. The objective was to kidnap William's daughter, Mary and the raid was organized by a spurned suitor for her hand in marriage.[337] The Tories entered the Palmer home and found only Mary present when they entered. After stealing as much as they could take, the house was set on fire and Mary was carried off to Long Island. A sizeable rescue party was quickly raised and soon got underway on Captain Amos Perry's sloop, *Racer*. It was a fast ship and, with good wind, managed to overtake the Tory whaleboat before it reached Long Island. Mary was rescued and, in the process, she kindled a relationship with Joel Hawkins, one of the rescue party members. She and Joel were later married.

The other side of the spectrum involved an attack on Fort Setauket, Long Island which was made in August 1777 as part of a coordinated effort whose primary goal was to take back Staten Island from the British. This opportunity arose after General Howe embarked the majority of his troops and moved south to capture Philadelphia. He left only 4,000 regular troops and 3,000 Loyalists behind to defend New York and Long Island. General Washington also moved most of his troops southward to defend Philadelphia but still approved a plan with a main objective of capturing Staten Island. The plan was to make a feint at Kingsbridge and a diversionary attack across the Sound against Fort Setauket in order to draw British defenders away from the city.[338] General Sullivan would then lead a detachment of Continental troops onto Staten Island.

Fort Setauket was an improvised fortification constructed by Lieutenant Colonel Richard Hewlett, a Long Island Loyalist. Hewlett had contemptuously confiscated the Presbyterian Church, whose minister was Benjamin Tallmadge's father, to use as a fort.[339] The church was desecrated and many of the gravestones were overturned. Four swivel guns were mounted in gallery windows and the first floor was used as a horse stable. Finally, an earthwork topped with a palisade surrounded the church. Hewlett had a force of 150 Loyalists to defend this fort and the harbors it protected.

The attacking force, also numbering about 150, was led by Colonel Parsons. They departed from Norwalk Harbor on August 14 in a sloop and six whaleboats, one of which was commanded by Caleb Brewster. Major Tallmadge was not involved in this operation as he had been recalled by General Washington to rejoin the main army for the campaign around Philadelphia.[340] The troops brought a six-pound brass cannon which they mounted on a huge, ten foot high boulder. They spent five hours cannonading and probing the fort's defenses but did not press the attack because it was only a diversion. The rebels then withdrew back across the Sound before they could be cut off. The primary objective of seizing Staten Island also failed when General Sullivan's forces were repulsed on the island a few days later.

In early 1777, General Washington took action to establish an espionage network within the occupied territory of New York City and Long Island. He selected Major Benjamin Tallmadge (code name John Bolton) to organize the operation because he had grown up in Setauket, Long Island. Tallmadge graduated from Yale in 1773, was a classmate of Nathan Hale and taught school in Connecticut before joining the Continental Army. His goal was to obtain intelligence on British military activities from their headquarters in New York City and transmit that information to General Washington by transporting the messages across Long Island Sound.

Numerous spies were recruited with different functions. Typically, the elaborate process would begin with intelligence collected in New York City by someone like Robert Townsend (code name Samuel Culper, Jr.).[341] Townsend was an influential man who lived in Oyster Bay but had business interests in New York City and was a Loyalist newspaper reporter as well. This combination provided an excellent opportunity to obtain information and cover to deflect suspicion. Always a Patriot, he had signed the Loyalist oath of allegiance out of necessity since the population of Oyster Bay was overwhelmingly Loyalist in sentiment.

The information Townsend obtained was then given to Austin Roe during his frequent visits to either Oyster Bay or Manhattan. He owned a tavern in East Setauket, farther out on Long Island. This provided his cover by justifying his trips as necessary to purchase supplies. Roe then turned the messages over to Abraham Woodhull (code name Samuel Culper, Sr.), a prominent Setauket descendant from Richard Woodhull, an original settler. Abraham was in charge of the day to day operation of the spy organization, known as the Culper Ring.[342] He was also responsible for evaluating the intelligence messages and forwarding appropriate ones to General Washington.

The next step of the journey involved the critical phase of transferring the information without detection to Lieutenant Caleb Brewster coming from Connecticut in a whaleboat. Caleb was a childhood friend of Major Tallmadge and had intimate knowledge of the Long Island seashore. He had joined the New York militia at the beginning of the war and then transferred to the Continental Army after the Battle of Long Island.

The message transfer process was facilitated by Anna Smith Strong (code name Nancy). When her husband, Selah Strong, was imprisoned in the prison hulk, *Jersey* and then banished to Connecticut, Anna became a spy for the patriots. Six different boat landing and hiding places were established to keep the British and Tories off their track and minimize suspicion. Anna devised a signal system using her laundry and clothes drying line to alert Woodhull and tell him where he could safely meet Lieutenant Brewster.[343] A black petticoat meant Brewster was onshore and the number of handkerchiefs hung amongst the garments determined which of the six landing places he could be found.

Finally, back across the Sound, Lieutenant Brewster gave the messages to Major Tallmadge who passed them on to General Washington wherever his headquarters happened to be. The complex system worked quite well and the identities of the Long Island participants remained unknown until the twentieth century.

Whaleboat forays were also launched strictly for plunder and Ebenezer Dayton became proficient in this shady form of profiteering. While he had done good service as a privateer on his schooner

Suffolk out of New Haven, he exercised poor judgment in his selection of targets during whaleboat raids. Even Patriots in the Culper Spy Ring made an effort to stop Dayton's activities because they often harmed people sympathetic to the American cause and threatened to undermine that support.[344]

An example of Dayton's opportunism involved an incursion in February, 1778 when he led a band of twelve patriots onto Long Island where they roamed for several days. His itinerary included a stop in his home town of Coram where the band of marauders took two wagon loads of dry goods owned by Obadiah Wright of Southampton who was a friend of the American cause. Later, Obadiah brought action against Dayton in the New Haven Superior Court which ruled in his favor.[345] In other cases, goods in Dayton's possession were attached by the court and returned to the victims or its equivalent value forfeited.

Militia members on both sides were often targeted. Stephen Hoyt, a Loyalist refugee from Norwalk, led a raiding party of twenty-four men from Huntington, Long Island to Norwalk where they targeted Samuel Richards and an encampment of militia near his home. Richards and about 17 militiamen were captured and spirited away to Long Island.

In November 1778, a sizeable retaliatory raid was carried out. Twenty Patriot whaleboats glided into Huntington Bay with the primary goal of capturing Tory refugees from Connecticut. It was known that many of these frequented a public inn called The Cedars. The landing force managed to capture sixteen people and kill several others who resisted.[346]

The year 1779 was destined to become a pivotal one in the American Revolution. Great Britain had become frustrated by the general stalemate and William Howe's inability to engage and crush the Continental Army in all out battle. General Howe resigned in 1778 and peace overtures had not born fruit. Sir Henry Clinton replaced Howe and his actions followed a new strategy that was mandated by King George, III. If peace efforts failed, the King ordered General Clinton to directly confront Washington's army if possible and engage it in a general military action. If unable to accomplish that, Clinton was ordered to make a series of destructive raids against the coast of New England, supported by the navy, and also to maintain a blockade in the north.[347]

The King's orders placed Long Island Sound and its shore communities at the epicenter of the war. Although considerable mayhem and destruction was carried out, the British strategy failed. By the end of 1779, Great Britain abandoned its naval station at Newport, Rhode Island and revised its strategy to re-focus future military action against the southern states.

Supply shortages continued to plague the British military and civilian population in New York. The British Navy made their third foraging raid on Fishers Island. This time they offered no compensation and burned most of the buildings and anything they couldn't take with them. After this, the island was virtually uninhabited and was taken over by people engaged in illicit trade.[348] Small warehouses or shacks were hastily built. Illicit goods were off loaded and stored. At an opportune moment the goods were smuggled into Connecticut ports in small craft.

The British Army also mounted a large foraging raid in February with 1,500 troops under command of General Tryon. His troops departed from Kingsbridge at eleven o'clock in the evening of February 27 and arrived at Horse Neck (southwest Greenwich, Connecticut) at ten o'clock the next morning. The area was plundered, houses damaged and military supplies were destroyed. A detachment also destroyed a schooner and two small vessels in the harbor plus twenty-six salt pans and a large quantity of stored salt. General Tryon began withdrawing his forces in the late afternoon when he learned that the rebels would be able to collect 1,000 troops to confront him the following morning.

Also in February, General Washington received intelligence from both Caleb Brewster and Abraham Woodhull that the enemy was repairing and building a number of flat bottom boats and other transport.[349] This indicated the British intended to land a substantial number of troops and Connecticut was the most likely target for such an attack. In March, Woodhull further advised that General Clinton was at the eastern end of Long Island recruiting Loyalist troops to build up his attack force. General Washington advised the Connecticut militia to go on alert and man all of the seaside forts but then cancelled this order when Sir Henry Clinton returned to New York.[350]

It was apparent from the above that during the winter and spring General Washington was aware of the warning signs of an impending raid or invasion of Connecticut. He refused to split his forces however, and was committed to remain in the Highlands and defend the Hudson River.[351] Connecticut would be a sacrificial lamb if necessary. Solid evidence of immanent attack was sent by the Culper spy ring on July 1 but the letter did not reach Washington until July 7, too late to do any good.

Another incident occurred that should have been taken as a warning or prelude but was not. On May 2, Connecticut Militia, Brigadier General Gold Silliman was kidnapped from his Fairfield home by a small group of Loyalist whaleboat raiders. Historians have viewed this kidnapping as simply part of the game to obtain high ranking prisoners for their exchange value. In reality, the timing was probably orchestrated to remove the single most important man who was in a position to thwart the British attacks that were about to be made. General Silliman, a 1752 Yale graduate, was commander of the militia in southwestern Connecticut including all of the military outposts and fortifications in Fairfield County. He was also the one that would have rallied the troops to defend against invasion. He had previously served in this capacity during the attack on Danbury in 1777 and before that in the Battle of Long Island.

The kidnappers departed at night on a whaleboat from Lloyd Neck on Long Island. Only nine men were involved but at least two of them were previous residents of Fairfield so they had intimate knowledge of the countryside. They landed about midnight and marched approximately two miles inland to the Silliman home on what is now Jennings Road. As the raiders attempted to break down the door, General Silliman grabbed his loaded gun and fired through the window but it misfired and only flashed. The raiders then burst through a window and grabbed Silliman and his son, William. Silliman's wife, Mary recognized two of the attackers as Glover, a carpenter who had built their cider mill, and Bunnell who had made shoes for the family.[352] The attackers stole valuables, knocked out windows and then departed with Gold and William Silliman.

William was later released under a parole of honor agreement but Gold would not see home again for a year. It would take a concerted effort to find a high ranking Loyalist official to use for the exchange and it would take another kidnapping to obtain that person.

General Sir Henry Clinton finally initiated his new campaign on May 30. For the first phase of the operation he assembled newly arrived troops from England with troops recalled from the Chesapeake Bay area of Virginia. His primary goal was to confront General Washington but the British still had hopes of cutting New England off from the rest of the colonies, something they had failed to accomplish in 1777. The previous effort was a spectacular failure which ended with the defeat of General Burgoyne at Saratoga.

As Clinton's forces pushed north through Westchester County they burned and pillaged as they went. Much of this was the work of revengeful Loyalists and Hessian soldiers.[353] The town of Bedford, except for two Loyalist houses, was burned on July 2. Clinton met resistance along the Hudson River but General Washington avoided a major battle and withdrew most of his troops further northward into the Highlands. Clinton also began to encounter supply difficulties which threatened his campaign.

Thus thwarted, General Clinton then initiated the second phase of his plan which he thought would remedy both of his problems. He planned a series of raids along the Connecticut coast which would have two objectives. His first objective was to force General Washington to transfer at least some of his troops away from defenses in the Hudson River Highlands in order to protect Connecticut. The Royal Army then hoped to defeat these troops on flat ground which was to their advantage. General Clinton could then continue the march north and secure the entire Hudson River Valley. This reason is well known and has been widely reported.[354] His second reason for attacking Connecticut coastal communities is not well known. Connecticut vessels of all types were having a devastating effect on the British supply line through the Sound to New York. This was reported in the British Annual Register for 1779 as follows:

> "The numbers of small cruisers, whaleboats and other craft
> of that nature, from the Connecticut coasts, which infested the
> Sound, lying between that colony and Long Island, were so

watchful and constant in their depredations, and their situation afforded them such opportunities, that they nearly destroyed the trade to and from New York on that side, to the very great discommodity and distress of that city, as well of the fleet and army. Upon this account, General Sir Henry Clinton, and Sir George Collier, determined on a course of desultory invasions along that coast, with a view of curing the evil by cutting off the means of depredation in the destruction of their piratical craft, and so far as it could be done, of their other vessels and materials for building."[355]

This view is further corroborated by New York Loyalists who that year bemoaned the fact that the town was destitute of fuel because the rebels were capturing all of the wood boats in Long Island Sound. The populace was "disgusted and dispirited" by the military government's management of the city which caused the loss of allegiance of many Loyalist supporters.[356]

The British assembled a fleet of forty-eight ships In Long Island Sound carrying 3,000 troops and headed for New Haven, their first target. The ground forces were under the command of General William Tryon of Surrey England who had no sympathy for the colonists. He had moved from a British military career path into civil service, first as the chief executive of North Carolina and then Governor of New York. He was forced out of this position when George Washington's forces took control of Long Island and New York City in 1776. Tryon looked for an opportunity to re-establish his military career and sought the opportunity to raid Connecticut's costal communities. He gathered a mixed force of Loyalists, Hessians and regular British troops.

Onboard the fleet's flagship, Commodore George Collier and Major General William Tryon drew up a proclamation to the people of Connecticut urging them to renounce the rebellion and declare subservience to Great Britain in return for safety and preservation of their property. Rather than being conciliatory, the tone of the document was insulting and inflammatory. It called the people deluded, selfish and ungrateful and portrayed Great Britain's response to the rebellion as lenient, mild and noble when it had the power to destroy every dwelling on the coast.[357] Ironically (or perhaps by design), the proclamation was dated July 4, 1779, the third anniversary of the American Declaration of Independence.

Because July 4 was a Sunday, religious restrictions mandated that Independence Day festivities be held on Monday. Instead of an elaborate celebration, the people of New Haven were jarred awake at one-thirty in the morning of July 5 to the sound of cannon blasts warning of the approaching British fleet. At sunrise a mixed group of Hessian, Loyalist and British regular troops landed on both sides of the Harbor and began advancing towards New Haven. Militia drummers beat the call to arms and non-combatants began to stream northwards, away from the coastline.

Organized resistance however, took time to assemble and was only able to slow the British advance in a few locations. On the east side of the harbor, patriots skirmished with Hessian and Tory troops around Beacon Hill and Black Rock Fort before withdrawing. On the west side, a mixed group of patriots, including Yale students, defended the bridge crossing on the West River and forced the British to march northward and bypass this direct route into New Haven.

The heaviest fighting took place at Ditch Corner to the northwest of town (now the corner of Goffe and Orchard streets) where a small detachment of militia made a stand. After eleven defenders where killed and many others wounded, a British captain issued a demand for surrender. Militia Captain John Gilbert, himself wounded and his brother Michael, dead, asked if he and his men would be treated as prisoners of war. The British captain's reply was "no, you damned rebel" at which point he ordered a nearby soldier to shoot Gilbert.[358] Captain Gilbert immediately shouted back that "we'll never surrender" and shot the British captain. Gilbert was then killed in the return gunfire.

Although pillaging parties were organized that evening and the British destroyed some patriot supplies, ordinance and ships; damage to New Haven was slight. There is considerable evidence to indicate this was due to the influence of local Loyalists and a North Carolina Tory Colonel by the name of Edmund Fanning who had graduated from Yale in 1757.[359] The most important person was probably Joseph Chew who implored the British forces not to burn the town. He had been actively involved in Loyalist causes in New York and was well known in British circles. At the same time, he was exploring reconciliation with Connecticut officials and reuniting with his family in New London. Another reason for the clemency may have been the relentless buildup of Patriot military forces taking place around the city. Large scale destruction of property might have invited fierce retaliation so the British withdrew to their ships and sailed down the coast to initiate another hit and run raid. The next two communities would not be spared.

Patriot losses at New Haven were twenty-seven killed and nineteen wounded. General Tryon reported his losses to be approximately nine killed, forty wounded and twenty-five missing.

After departing New Haven, General Tryon sailed westward along the shore. In the foggy early morning hours of July 7, his ships were barely spotted as they sailed past the defenders ensconced in the fort overlooking Black Rock Harbor. The inhabitants joyously assumed the enemy was headed back to New York and would conduct no further raids along the coast. The thickening fog closed in but then suddenly lifted about 10 o'clock in the morning revealing the awful specter of British ships setting anchor off Kensie's Point in Southport.

Fairfield would not be saved and would fare much worse than New Haven. General Tryon had decided not to directly challenge the fortification at Black Rock Harbor and chose to circumvent it by landing at another location. Around eleven o'clock, 1600 troops went ashore at the town beach near Kensie's Point (Sasco Hill Beach). The American battery on Grover's Hill began firing their twelve pounders from long range, loaded with ball and grape shot against the marching British columns. Residents of Black Rock, including several women, soon took refuge with the troops on Grover's Hill.

By early evening the British occupied Fairfield Village and its Green. Much of southwestern Fairfield and the Greens Farm portion of Westport were already in flames but this didn't stop General Tryon from issuing his infamous proclamation requesting allegiance to the Crown in exchange for leniency and protection. The village men grabbed their weapons and rendezvoused at Round Hill to the northeast of town under the command of Colonel Whiting. In response to Tryon's demands, Colonel Whiting fired back a challenge of his own when he said "Connecticut has nobly dared to take up arms against the cruel despotism of Britain, and as the flames have now preceded your flag [of truce], they will persist to oppose the utmost that power exerted against injured innocence."[360]

Many of the villagers fled northward and either hid in various un-inhabited woodlands or went to houses of acquaintances. All tried to hide whatever valuables they could manage or take some items with them. Many of the Southport residents fled into the Pequot Swamp near the coast, the same swamp used unsuccessfully as a refuge by Pequot Indian remnants at the end of The Pequot War in 1637.[361] General Gold Silliman's wife, Mary sought refuge northward in Trumbull until the danger passed.

On the next day the pillaging and burning resumed. A few burn-ing houses were saved after the British troops moved on. The fire that was started in the Hobart House was extinguished by a little boy, a black slave who had hidden in the attic during the attack.

Some women bravely stayed at their homes to try and save their property but all entreaties fell on deaf ears. General Tryon was in a foul mood and would issue no orders to reign in the destruction. Patriot and Loyalist homes alike were put to the torch and anyone trying to save them was badly abused.[362] Several of the women were beaten, cut and bruised in their attempt to dissuade the enemy.

A Loyalist woman by the name of Spaulding overconfidently thought she could reason with the British forces and single hand-edly save the town from destruction. She convinced Mrs. Rowland, an elderly woman, to stay with her when others fled. The invaders however, tore off most of Rowland's clothing, dragged her about by the hair and threatened to kill her.[363] The most abusive and shame-less destruction was carried out by Hessian troops followed closely by embittered Tory refugees that fled from Connecticut earlier in the war.

At least four men were murdered by the British forces. Two of those murdered were servants. One was an Irish servant of the Penfield family and the other was an elderly, bedridden black slave belonging to the Lewis family. The black slave's execution was a case of mistaken identity when it was thought he had shot and killed a British officer who was approaching the house where he lived.[364] What really happened was a man by the name of Parsons fired out the window at British troops advancing down the road killing the officer in charge of the detachment. Parsons immediately fled out the back door and escaped. The British accused the bedridden slave of committing this act and bayoneted him in spite of his claim of innocence. The next day the slave's charred body was found amid the burned ruins of the house.

The local militia could not match the 1600 British troops landed plus their reserves and therefore, could not establish a battle line against the advancing invaders. They contested the British troops through skirmishes and constant fire from covered positions. The British leveled many stone walls knowing that these were preferred locations for rebel militia. They also sent a row galley with troops and an eighteen pounder brass cannon to assault the Black Rock Harbor Fort. Several attempts to take the fort were beaten off by the twenty-three defenders.

Around eight o'clock in the evening of July 8, the British sounded retreat and withdrew to their ships. The rear guard of Hessian troops however, continued the destruction, even burning several more homes plus the Meeting House and the Loyalist Church of England in spite of the fact that these few buildings were granted a written protection order by General Tryon. Angry residents pursued the retreating British forces as far as they could but were unable to inflict losses at the embarkation point. All of the stone walls near the beach had been leveled and covering fire from the ships was too strong.[365]

When it was over, eighty homes and many other buildings were burned. Eight or ten Fairfield residents had been killed and several taken prisoner. Residents of Fairfield reported finding the bodies of as many as forty enemy troops that had been left behind. Sixteen prisoners were also taken, fifteen of them Loyalists plus one British soldier. These figures differ significantly from those reported by General Tryon who stated ten killed, twenty-nine wounded and seven missing.[366]

Information about Fairfield's fate quickly reached Norwalk and the community expected they would be next in line for attack. Fearful residents spent all of July 9 removing what they could from their homes to transport northward, away from the coast. Meanwhile the British forces sailed across Long Island Sound to Huntington Bay in order to collect additional artillery supplies and await favorable winds. They did not land troops at Norwalk until after sunset on July 10. The next morning British troops marched up both sides of the Norwalk River burning most buildings and both churches.

During the interlude after the Fairfield attack, General Samuel Parsons and a small military contingent was detached from Continental forces in the Hudson River Highlands in order to coordinate the defense of Norwalk. Parsons managed to assemble 1,000 troops but most were positioned too far inland to effectively contest the British advance into the village. Sporadic fighting occurred and a counterattack was mounted but the British forces were still able to link up at the strategic Norwalk Bridge and then head back to their ships.

The primary objective of the Norwalk raid was to burn the village and destroy ships in the harbor. They succeeded in destroying 130 dwellings, 87 barns, 22 stores, 17 ships, 4 mills and both churches.[367] In the process, the British lost 3 killed, 26 wounded and 4 missing.

The British strategy of attacking Connecticut's coastline was a complete failure. Despite the intimidation and destruction, British forces achieved neither of their objectives. General Washington did not transfer any forces from the Hudson River Highlands to confront General Clinton nor any to shore up Connecticut defenses. As a result, Clinton's offense sputtered out and was forced over to the defense. On July 15, American General Anthony Wayne recaptured the fort at Stony Point on the Hudson. In the process he took 700 prisoners and suffered only fifteen casualties. Another 150 prisoners were taken at Paulus Hook, New Jersey on August 19.

Likewise, privateering and the Whaleboat War on Long Island Sound continued undiminished. An article in the *British Annual Register for 1779* reported that the raids on Connecticut "did not seem to produce any great effect with respect to its immediate object, of checking the depredations of the American cruisers; for so bold and numerous were they, that in a very few days after, two of the royal sloops of war were taken by them."[368] The article went on to complain that the expedition had only served to justify long standing complaints by Americans relative to British conduct of the war. Finally the article was critical of the entire endeavor.

"General Sir Henry Clinton's object was, to draw him down, if possible, from these facilities into the flat country, and thereby to bring on a general engagement in that sort of ground, which would have been adapted to the exertion of those peculiar advantages, and that decided superiority, which the royal army possessed. This was among the motives which led to the Connecticut expedition; and others of less note, were undertaken upon the same principle. It was, however a matter of no small difficulty to lead Washington into such an error; nor could any art in the laying or covering of the design, afford more than a very doubtful prospect of success."

After three years in New York the British had little to show for their efforts. Their attempts to move north along the Hudson River, lure General Washington into battle on favorable terms and subdue the incessant maritime threat from Connecticut ports had all failed. These failures led the British to shift their emphasis to the southern colonies in hopes of regaining control of the war (the British still referred to the states as colonies). They hoped to recruit large Loyalist forces in the South and better utilize their naval resources. Their ships would be in a better position to both defend their West Indies possessions and support operations in the southern colonies. On October 11, the Royal Navy abandoned its base at Newport, Rhode Island and on December 26, General Clinton sailed from New York City with most of his regular troops to invade Charleston, South Carolina.

The anger in Fairfield over the destruction of their town took a long time to dissipate. At a town meeting on July 20, the people voted to offer a reward for anyone who would capture General Tryon.[369] A committee was selected to raise the reward money. On August 31 however, the people voted to prohibit the importation and sale of goods plundered from inhabitants of Long Island. In spite of their great need, the people of Fairfield knew what it was like to be victims and didn't wish to replicate this on Long Island even if they were Loyalists. The people also voted to advise the Governor of the names of people known to be trying to sell contraband goods to Fairfield residents. A Mr. Bishop of Hartford was singled out in the record as a major offender.[370]

Individuals reacted to the devastation in different ways. Captain Samuel Smedley's house and all of his outbuildings located at the corner of Oldfield Street and the Old Post Road had been burned. His outrage motivated him to take command of a Fairfield based privateer vessel named appropriately, the *"Recovery."* This vessel was a captured British privateer of 200 tons and carried sixteen guns and a crew of ninety-five. It was owned by Joseph Williams & Co. of Norwich and was refitted in Rhode Island. The *Recovery* was commissioned February 18, 1780. Captain Smedley captured one ship and then was himself captured by the British warship *Galatea* in March. He was exchanged in May.[371]

Smedley next took command of the *Hibernia* carrying ten guns and fifty men and was again captured, this time by the British warship *Hussar* on October 25, 1780.[372] Smedley and his crew were sent to Old Mill prison at Plymouth, England. He remained there for some time but eventually managed to escape and reach Holland. He then took command of the Dutch vessel *Heer Adams*, a chartered ship loaded with military and naval supplies in support of the American Revolution. He arrived in Philadelphia with these supplies on September 12, 1782.

In the fall of 1789, ten years after the British raid on Fairfield, George Washington, the newly elected first President of the United States, made a tour through New England. He spent the night of October 16 at the Rising Sun Tavern near the Fairfield Village Green. In his diary, President Washington commented on the beauty of the area and the industrious people harvesting abundant crops and making cider. He also wrote that "The destruction evidences of British cruelty are yet visible both in Norwalk and Fairfield; as there are chimneys of many burnt houses standing in them yet."[373] He also commented that the principal exports of Fairfield and Norwalk were items supplied in the West Indies trade—horses, cattle, salted pork and beef, Indian corn and a small amount of wheat and flour.

Although overshadowed by British military actions just described, The Whaleboat War continued unabated during 1779. In Fairfield, Simon Couch recorded a raid in a letter to his father.[374] He was awakened by the enemy who fired through his door and smashed windows. They took some items from his house, cattle from his barn and livestock from several other houses before withdrawing. This occurred in June, just prior to the British destructive raid that burned the town.

In Norwalk, Reverend Moses Mather became the focus of repetitive raids by Tory refugees because of his venomous sermons railing against their treasonous behavior. The first of these occurred on July 29, 1779 when eight men, five of whom were former parishioners, ransacked his home.[375] Mather and four of his sons were kidnapped and placed in a New York prison but were released a month later.

Patriot raiders were also busy. Fyler Dibble, the Loyalist refugee who fled from Stamford to Long Island, continued to be a target in spite of moving several times in an attempt to throw the antagonists off his track. Jesse Brush, a Patriot refugee from Cold Spring Harbor, Long Island became infuriated when two Loyalist families occupied his house. He continually pressed them to leave. When they declined, he tacked a note on the barn door during one of his forays via whaleboat. The message said that "I have repeatedly ordered you to leave my farm. This is the last invitation. If you do not, your next landfall will be in a warmer climate than any you ever have lived in yet. 20 days you have to make your escape."[376]

In November, three Connecticut whaleboats landed to plunder houses of specific Loyalists in the Brookhaven area. Two of the raiders were patriot refugees from that location so they blackened their faces to prevent recognition. Their first targets were the homes of Colonel Benjamin Floyd and Andrew Seton. The next evening they approached the home of Solomon Davis but the element of surprise was gone. The raiders decided to cut short their adventure and make a hasty retreat back to Connecticut instead.

The kidnapping of General Gold Silliman back in May also needed to be addressed. General Washington did not show much interest in assisting with Silliman's release. He was not keen on using a high level prisoner under his control as a bargaining chip for a militia general. The matter was left for Connecticut to resolve. Connecticut however, had no one of sufficient rank or importance to interest the British in exchange for Silliman. Deliberations within Connecticut to resolve this problem included discussions with Governor Trumbull. It was decided to target the well known Loyalist

Judge, Thomas Jones who lived in the Fort Neck area of what is now Massapequa, Long Island.

The kidnapping operation had to wait until fall when longer hours of darkness would improve the chances for a successful whaleboat raid. Captain David Hawley of the Connecticut Navy was called upon to organize the affair. Although the operation was sanctioned under military authority, his two dozen raiders were civilian volunteers, not under militia or Continental control.

The group set off in one or two whaleboats in early November and landed at Stony Brook. They still had a considerable distance to travel but probably couldn't risk landing further westward where higher concentrations of Loyalists resided. At this point the men threatened to abort the mission if they weren't allowed to take some booty in compensation for the danger involved and the risk they were taking.[377] Captain Hawley was forced to concede since he was not able to use military law and the threat of insubordination or court martial.

The raiding party traveled at night to avoid detection and arrived at Judge Jones' house at nine o'clock on Saturday evening, November 6. The raiders heard music playing and people dancing and, surprised by how large the house was, described it as a "castle."[378] No one inside heard them knock at the door so they resorted to smashing a side panel to get inside. The intruders immediately grabbed Judge Jones and one of the guests by the name of Hulet. The men then proceeded to plunder the home before leaving in accordance with the agreement grudgingly extracted from Captain Hawley.

Two nights later the raiding party reached their whaleboats and sailed home without incident. The prisoner, Hulet, was subsequently exchanged for General Silliman's son, William. Judge Jones was hosted for several days by Mary Silliman and then taken inland to Middletown as it was felt too risky to hold him anywhere near the shore due to the potential for whaleboat counterattacks or raids by British naval and land forces.

Negotiations for the prisoner exchange and release of General Silliman dragged on. The British requested an additional prisoner, a Tory by the name of Washburn, who had been captured on July 8 during their invasion of Fairfield.[379] This was agreed and the prisoners were exchanged in February, 1780. By chance, each side released their prisoners at the same time and the two whaleboats met under flags of truce in the middle of Long Island Sound. Mary Silliman had sent along a large, cooked turkey to give her husband and the prisoners decided to have a fine meal out on the water.[380] Both Silliman and Jones had been Yale classmates so the dinner conversation must have been fascinating. After a pleasant interlude, the boats separated and the men returned to their respective homes at last.

The Patriots launched one major whaleboat raid under military authority in 1779. This was an attack on Fort Franklin and it was a spectacular success. William Franklin, Ben Franklin's son, supported the establishment of Fort Franklin on Lloyd's Neck, a central, strategic location which could defend and control activities in all of several bays and harbors. Loyalist operations in this area between Oyster Bay and Huntington Bay made it a strategic section of western Long Island Sound and a lair for Loyalist military, whaleboat and privateer action. This encompassed Oyster Bay, Cold Spring Harbor, Lloyd's Neck, Lloyd Harbor, Huntington Bay and Northport Harbor.

The attempt to disrupt this Loyalist stronghold at Lloyd Neck was mounted from Shippan Point in Stamford and was led by Major Benjamin Tallmadge and Captain Caleb Brewster. A force of 120 men departed in the evening of September 5, 1779 on a mixture of sloops and whaleboats. The surprise of the attack in the middle of the night was so sudden and unexpected that the entire garrison of about 500 men quickly surrendered. Although the fort was left intact, the raid was a spectacular success and produced many prisoners useful for future exchanges.

At the end of 1779, Patriots around Long Island Sound had cause to give a sigh of relief. The focus of the war had moved southward. Still, hostilities would continue for more than three years. The war in and around Long Island Sound was far from over. The Whaleboat War would actually increase in intensity and privateer activity would peak in 1781. The British Army and Navy would make one more devastating raid—this time against New London and Groton in 1781.

Chapter Ten

The Tide Turns: 1780–1783

After the British abandoned their naval base at Newport, Rhode Island in October of 1779 and transferred 8,500 regular troops from New York to Charleston, South Carolina in December, they still had 16,000 troops remaining in New York. British naval presence was temporarily reduced and, for a time, only one naval frigate was left behind for defense.

Due to diminished British naval activity in Long Island Sound and nearby waters, Connecticut had less need for larger naval sailing vessels and no more would be commissioned during the war. While there were still many enemy merchant vessels and privateers in the Sound, they could be managed by Connecticut privateers and did not pose a significant military threat in support of ground troop actions.

Naval activities, however, continued at the whaleboat level and the Navy supported both defensive and offensive whaleboat operations. Patrol boats were organized to cruise the Connecticut coast in order to detect enemy raiders and try to stop illicit trade. During 1780 these forces were organized into three sectors. One group patrolled from Stonington to Guilford, another from Guilford to the Housatonic River and the third group from the Housatonic River to the New York line.

With reduced British military presence in Long Island Sound, Connecticut stepped up activities directed against Loyalist supplies, ships, ports and fortresses. The whaleboat, it will be remembered, varied considerably in size and equipment but was generally a small boat, approximately twenty to thirty feet in length and often carried a swivel gun or small cannon. It was usually rowed with fixtures for eight to twelve oars and often carried a sail as well. The whaleboat was pointed at both the bow and stern and could carry ten to twenty-four men.

David Hawley's naval assignments were shifted to armed whaleboat patrol operations where he was in charge of as many as three boats. He captured two sloops and two schooners within Long Island Sound during 1780. On April 20 of that year, emboldened by the reduced presence of British forces, he mounted a three boat operation which sailed out of Long Island Sound and around Montauk Point to the south shore. Entering Great South Bay, Captain Hawley captured eleven ships. Seven of these were either destroyed or ransomed back to their owners and the remaining four were taken back to Fairfield as prizes.[381]

Surprisingly, the enemy had still not established any significant defenses within Great South Bay in spite of previous losses suffered there. That was about to change. Loyalist refugees from Rhode Island began construction of Fort St. George on Smith Point in Mastic. Major Benjamin Tallmadge kept tabs on its construction through his Long Island spy network. When it was completed, he would plan, organize and lead an attack to capture and destroy this fort.

Loyalists also vowed to step up the pace of the Whaleboat War and become more aggressive in its prosecution. In order to accomplish this goal, a "Board of Associated Loyalists" was established in 1780 to foster, coordinate and strengthen offensive and defensive activities against Patriot interests around Long Island Sound and northern New Jersey. William Franklin, recently released through a prisoner exchange, was a prime instigator and organizer of this effort.

The manifesto of The Board of Associated Loyalists fostered aggressive action. It encouraged Loyalists to prove their worth by "annoying the seacoasts of the revolted colonies, distressing their trade, spying behind the lines and serving as guides for the British when they were maneuvering in unfamiliar territory."[382] It claimed its moral position was "just vengeance against the patriots who were persecuting them."

Other profound changes were taking place within the British system as the war dragged on. British treatment of people on Long Island and New York, Loyalist or not, was arrogant and often brutally cruel. Food supplies and forage were often confiscated without any compensation. When payment was made, the farmer rarely received a fair amount. Corruption within the British military supply system was rampant. This included fraud, swindles, skimming, kickbacks and occasionally, murder.[383] Compensation was needed for a vast bureaucracy. To make matters worse, there were no civil liberties, civil government or civil courts. The territory was ruled by martial law and provided no way to adequately address even obvious problems.

The people who suffered the most were the very people who were most supportive of British occupation and who had viewed the British military as liberators. Disillusionment set in and respect for British rule plummeted.[384] The military hierarchy turned a blind eye to the corruption and the crimes of British authorities. Many Loyalists switched sides although they could not let this be known publicly. The British resented having to be there and didn't care if the people suffered as a consequence even if they were Loyalists. They even treated Loyalist militiamen as second class citizens of the empire.

Even staunch Loyalist supporters such as James Rivington became disillusioned. His newspaper, *The Royal New York Gazette*, remained overtly propagandist because of British censorship and threats to keep Rivington in line. Rivington managed to take advantage of his reputation as a committed Loyalist to obtain information from unsuspecting patrons in the coffeehouse he also operated. His crowning achievement was to steal a copy of the British fleet's signal book in 1781. This was delivered to French Admiral Comte de Grasse in time for his famous battle with the British fleet off the Virginia Capes which paved the way for victory at Yorktown.

By mid 1778, General Washington had considerable need to have someone manage the espionage activities around New York on a full time basis and he assigned the task to Major Tallmadge. In his memoirs, Tallmadge stated that "I kept one or more boats continually employed in crossing the Sound on this business."[385] He recruited Abraham Woodhull, a Long Island farmer, and others to gather intelligence. For the rest of the war, Tallmadge and his small Continental Army contingent would represent General Washington on the western end of Long Island Sound.

After Tallmadge's successful attack on Fort Franklin, he was promoted to Colonel. He then had a long conversation with General Washington about how they should conduct the war in the Long Island Sound theatre of operations. Based on intelligence he had gathered and his own knowledge, Tallmadge laid out his ideas for disrupting Loyalist operations on Long Island, combating illicit trade and dealing with the Cowboys in Westchester County. General Washington listened intently but made no commitment. The following summer however, Washington gave Colonel Tallmadge an independent command with significant, but not total authority to do as he wished.[386] His small detachment consisted of two companies of light infantry and a compliment of mounted dragoons. He took up station on the border of Connecticut and Westchester County, New York.

Controlling illicit trade was a difficult matter. Essentially, this trade involved the exchange of farm produce for British manufactured goods, cloth, linen and any other items previously supplied by the British that could no longer be legitimately obtained. Illicit goods brought into Connecticut were usually carried on ships owned by Connecticut merchants and sailed by Connecticut seamen. It was impossible to tell what ships were engaged in illicit trade without stopping inbound ships, searching them and finding British made products onboard.

More complex schemes probably involved pre-set agreements between a merchant on Long Island and another in Connecticut in order to avoid charges of smuggling. For example, an arrangement could be made to "capture" the ship coming from Long Island loaded with British goods. The Connecticut merchant (probably authorized by letter of marque) would then bring his "prize" into port for libel and condemnation procedures by the maritime court. After wining a favorable judgment, the merchant was free to sell the goods and the ship legitimately. Ultimately, profits would be shared with the Long Island merchant.

Nova Scotia's privateering capabilities continued to develop after 1780. Except for one episode where Liverpool's harbor fort was captured by American privateers and then relinquished, Liverpool

Harbor remained free from American incursions for the last three years of the war. The privateering conflict still raged however, and many captured American crews were brought into Nova Scotia ports. Generally the crews were exchanged or paroled and carried back to New England under a flag of truce. One of these missions had a sad ending for Simeon Perkins' son, Roger, of Norwich Connecticut.

Roger, it will be remembered, was born December 8, 1760 in Norwich. His mother, Abigail Backus Perkins, died two weeks later. Roger was raised by relatives in Norwich when Simeon left to take on the challenge of representing the Perkins and Backus family business interests in Nova Scotia. In 1777, at the age of sixteen, Roger sailed for Nova Scotia to be with his father. On November 1, 1781, he sailed as a crew member on Thomas Harrington's vessel to Boston under a flag of truce. They carried three paroled prisoners and some trade goods. After a successful exchange they began the return trip but were driven into Portsmouth, New Hampshire seeking shelter from a storm. After leaving Portsmouth, the ship was never seen again.[387] The fate of Roger Perkins, like thousands of others before and after, would be the slow, awful realization that he was lost at sea.

With the return of Harrington's ship long overdue, Simeon Perkins began to register concern in his diary. On December 14, he made an entry that indicated they were seen in Boston. An entry on January 14, 1782 indicated great relief to hear "that Harrington was seen at Portsmouth, which if true is much better news than I expected to hear."[388] Two additional reports mentioned that ship captains had spotted wreckage that had washed ashore but did not necessarily identify the wreckage as the Harrington vessel. Simeon made no further entries in his diary about the matter after January 19.

Long Island Sound privateers continued their activity in all operational areas during 1780 but the total number of engagements was down by about thirty percent from the previous year. This was probably due to the reduced volume of enemy shipping in northern waters which produced fewer targets. The shift of Great Britain's military strategy, now focusing on the southern states, reduced the threat of British military operations against Connecticut or within

Long Island Sound. This was a relief and may have generated a pause in the action or a temporary slowdown to reflect, regroup and determine new hunting grounds.

The peak year for Long Island Sound privateers was 1781 with at least sixty-seven cruises involving at least ninety eight engagements where captures were made. Heavy action took place in all cruising areas but the greatest number of captures (at least twenty-five) occurred within the Atlantic approaches to New York Harbor. As the war shifted to the southern states, the reduced British naval presence around New York Harbor emboldened more American privateers to frequent the area. British merchant vessels and privateers would have been more vulnerable and Connecticut privateers less vulnerable. A small but growing number of captures involved Atlantic coastal areas south of New Jersey. This reflected higher maritime traffic by the British between New York and their southern bases such as Charlestown, South Carolina.

Overall, activity by Long Island Sound privateers declined during 1782 although engagements within the Sound and along the Atlantic coast, south of New Jersey remained high. There were at least thirty-three captures within the Sound but the majority of these were vessels engaged in illicit trade between residents of Long Island and Connecticut. Many of the vessels captured here were unarmed and Connecticut ships as well as those from Long Island were fair game for privateers if they could prove that illegal trade activity was involved. An all time high of least fourteen captures were made in the Atlantic coastal area south of New Jersey. This showed the continued importance of British commerce between New York or Great Britain and the southern ports controlled by the British.

Captain Ebenezer Jones of Stamford was particularly active in the western end of Long Island Sound from 1780–1783. He is known to have made nineteen captures but his actual total may have been many more.[389] His most successful method of operation involved simultaneous attack by several small, armed boats which he owned. These were probably whaleboats or something slightly larger that could be sailed or rowed. His initial fleet involved the *Greenwich*

and *Spitfire*. By the end of 1781, he was in command of the *Rattlesnake, Viper* and *Saratoga*. As previously discussed, western Long Island Sound was ideal for this type of small vessel that could be rowed or sailed. It held numerous tactical advantages in confined spaces over pure sailing ships and its pointed bow at each end meant it could reverse course instantaneously without turning.

Several Perkins family members continued to be active in privateering from New London during the latter part of the war. Hezekiah, despite having been captured several times and nearly losing his life on the prison ship *Jersey*, went to sea again. In June of 1782, Simeon learned that Hezekiah was captured and taken into Bermuda but was soon exchanged and returned to Norwich.[390] He then took command of the Brig *Hancock* which was commissioned as a privateer on September 16, 1782. With eight guns but a crew of only sixteen, its mission would have been trade rather than commerce raiding.

The sloop *Mercury*, owned by Perkins, Fanning & Co., was commissioned July 12, 1781 and was captured August 10 and taken into New York. Captain Lathrop was subsequently exchanged and returned to New London under flag of truce. The Brig *Fair American*, owned by Jabez Perkins & Co., had fourteen guns and carried a compliment of ninety men. This vessel was commissioned July 18, 1781 and captured one ship while under command of Samuel Champlin and seven ships while under command of Peleg Eldred.[391] These latter seven were all brought into New London together on November 27, 1781.

Ackley, Ashbel, Richard and Justice Riley from the Rocky Hill, Wethersfield and Middletown areas of the Connecticut River were also active late in the war. Richard was a crew member on the brig *General Green* which carried 100 crewmen and sixteen guns. This ship was captured on its first voyage in 1782 by the British ship of war, *Virginia* and the crew was placed on prison ships in New York where many of them died. Records reflect that the dead included nine from Rocky Hill but not Richard Riley.[392]

Joseph Conkling and William Havens, both refugees from the Sag Harbor area of Long Island, continued their privateering careers. Conkling, in command of the brig *Whim* with twelve guns and a crew of forty was chased ashore in France. The cargo was saved and the ship was later floated off. He returned to New England in May 1781. In April of 1783 he captured the British brig, *Lyon* while in command of the brig *Hancock*. Meanwhile, Havens made two captures while in command of the brig *Jay* carrying twelve guns and seventy men. When the British attacked Groton and New London in 1781, both Conkling and Havens were hurriedly issued letters of marque and pressed into service in an attempt to save ships in the harbor by sailing them upstream to Norwich. At first, a north wind made it difficult for both the British fleet and American ships to make any progress. Conkling took command of the brig *Venus* but it was too late. This ship had to be abandoned and was burned in the harbor by Benedict Arnold's forces. Havens boarded the brig *Jay* but there is no further information as to whether this vessel succeeded to escape upstream.[393]

Prison ships continued their grim functions during the latter part of the war. Escape attempts were rare but they did occur. The severe winter of 1780 caused untold hardship to Americans held onboard the *Jersey*. In one way however, it aided the escape of a few prisoners including Ebenezer Bartram from Fairfield, Connecticut.[394] In January, Wallabout Bay froze solid and forty-seven men planned to break out of the hold, scramble onto the ice and walk away. Only Bartram and six others made it to the ice before a shower of bullets splattered around them. They managed to evade capture and reach the shore of Long Island but the bitter cold forced them to seek shelter. Fortunately, they chose the home of elderly, sympathetic residents who hid and fed them for several days until the search parties were called off. The old couple's son then guided them to Whitestone where they obtained a small boat and crossed Long Island Sound to safety.

Connecticut established a prison ship in New London in 1778 but it was used for only a year. Another prison ship, the *Retaliation*, was placed into service in May 1782 to house maritime prisoners. It was moored on the Thames River about two miles north of New London and remained there until the end of the war. The first compliment of 116 prisoners was hardly aboard this ship before an escape attempt was made. On June 2, 1782, twenty prisoners, who had been allowed on deck for fresh air, overwhelmed the guard. A total of eighty men then went ashore but the remainder decided not to leave.[395] Nine of the fugitives stole a boat and made good on their escape as did seventeen others. The rest were recaptured.

Sailors in the British Navy often tried to escape the ships they served on. These vessels were little better than floating jails. The living conditions were unhealthy and many did not want to be there. British crews often contained a considerable number of forcibly impressed sailors and captured Americans who had little other choice. In August of 1780, several British naval vessels were positioned in Gardiners Bay, Long Island. The French Navy had just occupied Newport Harbor the previous month and British General Clinton wanted to keep tabs on their activities. Six British sailors managed to escape from one of these ships while anchored in the Bay. They commandeered a small vessel and traversed the Sound into the safety of New London.[396]

The Whaleboat War increased in intensity during 1780 and 1781. On the Loyalist side, this can be attributed to William Franklin and the Board of Associated Loyalists whose purpose was to foster aggressive action against the Patriots around Long Island Sound and also in New Jersey. On the Patriot side, whaleboat raiders may have been emboldened by the reduced presence of the British Navy in Long Island Sound.

While some of the raids were launched for legitimate military reasons, more and more raids from both sides were motivated by pure thievery. On Connecticut's part, many of these raids were rationalized by Connecticut Letter of Marque provisions that allowed seizure of British goods and property of British subjects. These powers were not limited to vessels but included islands adjoining Connecticut waters as well. Many who continued to reside on Long Island were not Loyalist yet many of these people were victims of raids. As shown in Albert Overton's book *Plunderers from across the Sound* a number of property confiscations originally approved by Connecticut Prize Courts were later overturned by a Congressional Court of Appeals after the war.[397]

In Fairfield, Loyalist whaleboat raids were continuously annoying in 1780. In particular, ships and small boats anchored or located in harbors were the target of theft attempts, some successful and others unsuccessful. William Wheeler's journal reflected six raids on the coast of Fairfield in 1781 during which several houses were burned, livestock stolen and a few prisoners taken.[398] While there is no way to accurately determine the actual number of raids, one measure of volume was the number of tax abatement requests made due to damages and losses suffered from the thievery and plundering. In the Stamford area alone, the numbers peaked between 1780 and 1782 when 172 claims for tax abatement were filed.[399]

The Board of Associated Loyalists on Long Island decided to take punitive action against Ebenezer Dayton, a Patriot refugee who fled from Coram, Long Island. He was one of the early and more notorious of the whaleboat raiders fighting from Connecticut. The Board enlisted Alexander Graham, a Long Islander, to lead a raid into Connecticut for the purpose of stealing or destroying Dayton's property and retrieving property he had stolen from Long Islanders. Graham was a deserter from Washington's Continental Army who then accepted a commission from the British to help recruit Loyalists.

Ebenezer Dayton had taken precautions to discourage such an attack against him by moving his family to Bethany, about twelve miles inland from the Sound. He thought the distance inland would be a sufficient deterrent. That did not turn out to be true thanks to assistance provided by local Connecticut Loyalists. In March of 1780, Graham and another Long Island Loyalist crossed the Sound and traveled to Seymour, a town bordering Bethany. At Seymour they managed to recruit five more Loyalists from the surrounding area.[400] Their objective was to steal Dayton's money, jewelry and other valuable affects and destroy as much else as they could. Their plan was to store the valuables with a local Tory sympathizer and hide until the heat was off. They may have also planed to kidnap Ebenezer but at the time of the raid, Captain Dayton was away in Boston.[401]

The seven attackers entered the Dayton home at night. Dayton's wife, Phebe, screamed for help and was tied up while the marauders ransacked the house and then ate dinner. They departed with many sacks of valuable items and at least £450 pounds in coins.[402] The conspirators' plans soon went awry when they encountered a sixteen-year-old boy named Chauncey Judd who recognized many of them. They had to choose between either killing Chauncey or taking him with them to Long Island rather than hiding out for a period of time. In a close vote, the seven conspirators decided not to kill Chauncey.

Meanwhile, Phebe managed to free herself and get help. It wasn't long before an investigation determined who the perpetrators were and a pursuit initiated. The conspirators were tracked to the home of another Loyalist and were almost captured but managed to flee. Realizing their only hope now was to escape back to Long Island, they marched six miles to Derby where they stole a whaleboat.[403] Derby, which sat at the confluence of the Housatonic and Naugatuck Rivers, had shipyards and the river was navigable for the eleven miles down to Long Island Sound. The raiders, with their kidnap victim, Chauncey Judd, made it safely back to Long Island but their freedom was short lived.

The number of pursuers grew to over 100 by the time they reached the shore but only thirty were selected to cross the Sound in two whaleboats. They were led by William Clarke, another Long Island Patriot refugee who had been a neighbor of Dayton in Coram and knew the likely location where the conspirators would seek shelter.[404] The pursuit was eminently successful. Chauncey was freed and all but one of the conspirators was captured on Long Island and returned to Connecticut. Alexander Graham was sent to General Washington's headquarters in Morristown where he was hanged for being a deserter from the Continental Army. The others were sent to Connecticut's Newgate Prison in East Granby from which some of them later escaped.

Due to its propensity for overzealous action, the Board of Associated Loyalists was abolished in May 1782 by Sir Guy Carleton, successor to Sir Henry Clinton. The seminal event leading to its eradication occurred in April 1782 when a group of people within this association captured and then lynched Joshua Huddy, a New Jersey Patriot.

The town of Derby was significantly involved in the maritime greatness of the era, not only for its seaport and ship building activities, but for two of its native sons. These were Joseph and Isaac Hull. Joseph was the father of the more famous, Isaac Hull, future captain of the USS Constitution which achieved fame during the War of 1812.

Joseph, while serving with the Continental Army in 1776, was captured when Fort Washington surrendered and spent two years as a prisoner before being exchanged. He was then commissioned to command a fleet of whaleboats to harass and "annoy the enemy."[405] He commenced operations in 1779 and continued to the end of the war. His force is credited with the capture of several British supply boats and the recapture of an American ship which had been lost to the British. This last ship was being sailed into New York by a small prize crew hence it was probably undermanned and unable to defend itself from a swarm of whaleboats.

In one celebrated attack, Hull learned that British ships often loaded wood at an inlet near Throg's Neck. He decided to use tactics similar to those used in the successful capture of the British ship *Schuldham* several years earlier. If he could capture one of their supply boats he could use it to approach the larger schooner without rousing suspicion. Several whaleboats with fifty men made the journey and had no difficulty acquiring a firewood supply boat around midnight. With twenty men hidden in this boat, Hull approached the British schooner. The sentry onboard merely warned Hull to stay clear and avoid collision to which Hull proclaimed he shouldn't worry, there was sufficient room to pass.[406] Instead, he tied up under the bow and his men leaped aboard. A fight with casualties ensued but soon ended after the British Commander was shot dead as he came on deck from below. Hull then hoisted his whaleboat onboard the schooner and secured the wood boat to its side. All haste was then made to raise sails for the dash up the Sound to Black Rock Harbor in Connecticut. Along the way,

Hull managed to slip past three British vessels without arousing suspicion.

Colonel Benjamin Tallmadge's espionage organization was well organized by 1780. One of his concerns was to keep track of the construction of Fort St. George located at Smith Point on Great South Bay in Mastic near the south shore of Long Island. His agents on Long Island soon delivered excellent intelligence and drawings of the fortification whereby Tallmadge developed a plan to attack the Fort. General Washington however, thought the risks were too great. Not to be denied, Tallmadge personally crossed the Sound to obtain and verify information about the fort.[407] He also learned about a great quantity of hay and forage that had been collected at Coram. General Washington relented to Tallmadge's appeal and authorized the mission.

Colonel Tallmadge teamed up again with Captain Caleb Brewster and this time the assembly point was Black Rock Harbor in Fairfield. The combined force of Tallmadge's light infantry and additional volunteers from Fairfield, totaling about eighty men, departed from Black Rock Harbor at four o'clock in the late afternoon of November 21, 1780, just as the sun was setting. They arrived at Old Man's Beach near Mt. Sinai at ten o'clock but a storm forced them to delay their march across the island for another day.

The next evening, sixty of the men formed a strike force and set out for the fort, arriving there at four in the morning. The attack commenced almost immediately and was met with some resistance but was quickly overcome. The defenders suffered seven wounded and killed. Most of the killed were defenders thrown out of a second story window by the invading force that was angry at being fired on after the fort had struck its colors in surrender.[408] The attackers suffered only one casualty. Major Tallmadge's men then destroyed as much of the fort and its supplies as possible and burned one, fully loaded ship in the harbor. The troops departed with prisoners at eight in the morning.

The return march was made in broad daylight as the element of surprise was no longer an issue. At Coram, approximately mid-island, twelve men separated from the column to burn 300 tons of hay and forage which had been set aside for use of the British Army. By four o'clock, all were back and the whaleboats shoved off for the return trip across the Sound.

The Whaleboat War recessed for the winter of 1780–1781 and resumed in March. Reverend Moses Mather continued to elicit anger from Loyalist refugees who had fled from Norwalk. His home was plundered for a second time in March. This served to further increase his rhetoric and he railed against treasonous Tories in his sermons. Determined to further punish Reverend Mather, a large force of forty Loyalists led by William Frost, an ex-neighbor, and Joseph Hoyt, slipped across the Sound on Saturday night, July 21, 1781.[409] They surrounded the meeting house during Sunday service when it was filled with worshipers and took fifty adult male prisoners back to New York. About half of the prisoners were paroled soon after but the rest were not exchanged until December 27. By then, seven were dead from the appalling prison ship conditions but Reverend Mather survived.

Loyalists launched another raid in March but this one actually fulfilled a military objective. The previous summer, the French had landed a large force of 5,800 men in Newport, Rhode Island under command of General Rochambeau. Food supplies from Connecticut helped to sustain these troops while a plan for future military action was evolving. British intelligence learned that flour was being collected in Fairfield to supply these forces. The collection point was located at two mills owned by the Perry family on Mill River, two miles upstream from Southport Harbor in Fairfield. Four whaleboats with about forty Loyalists landed on March 4, proceeded to the mills and burned them.[410] They also destroyed about 200 barrels of flour and then departed with several sheep.

Guilford was once again the target of a Loyalist raid on June 18 at Leete's Island a location separated from the mainland by marshes and a small stream. This was a major raid which included some refugees previously living in the area. Apparently, it was motivated by revenge over a previously unsuccessful whaleboat raid where one of the raiders was shot and killed on the beach.[411] This time they came in greater numbers carried on two Loyalist ships along with convoy protection provided by the British Navy brig, *Keppel.*

A 150 man raiding force assembled at Lloyd Neck on Long Island and departed the evening of June 17. One of their leaders was the infamous refugee, Jesse Hoyt from Norwalk. Light winds slowed the journey so that the landing force was unable to go ashore until seven o'clock the next morning. They proceeded to burn several homes and barns. The thumb of Ambrose Leete was cut of by a Loyalist or British officer as he stood in the doorway of his home.

In the village of Guilford, a militia force with superior numbers was assembled. They marched onto Leete's Island and attacked straight away. Their first salvo wounded eight of the enemy who then began a retreat to their ships. In the ensuing fight, two patriot militiamen were killed.

The Loyalist forces re-boarded their ships under protecting cannon fire and looked for another plunder opportunity. They anchored off the neighboring town of Branford for the night but decided against any further landing because the residents were alerted to the marauders presence and were prepared to resist. Next morning the Loyalists returned to Long Island with little to show for their effort.

In 1780 and 1781, the Loyalists strengthened all of their fortifications around Lloyd Neck. These fortifications included an encampment on Oyster Bay, Fort Franklin on Lloyd Neck and Fort Slongo about eight miles to the eastward. They also stationed three naval warships and one galley in Huntington Bay to protect the whaleboat fleet. In April, 1781, Colonel Tallmadge developed a complicated, large scale invasion plan to destroy all of these installations.[412] General Washington tentatively approved the plan dependant upon complete secrecy, comprehensive knowledge of the enemy and absence of the British fleet.

The project had to be postponed when the British fleet returned to New York. General Washington then suggested that the plan might go forward if appropriate French warships could be employed to support the action. With an introduction provided by Washington, Colonel Tallmadge immediately went to Newport, Rhode Island and met with General Rochambeau and the French Fleet Commander.[413] Finding that the appropriate smaller warships were not available, the plan was again put on hold.

In May, Generals Washington and Rochambeau met in Wethsersfield, Connecticut and agreed upon a joint plan to attack New York. Unknown to Colonel Tallmadge, this plan included an assault on Fort Franklin. Unfortunately, Tallmadge was not consulted and the operation would prove to be a fiasco. The French Army was put in motion marching from Newport, Rhode Island through Connecticut to link up with General Washington's forces in Westchester County, New York. A contingent of 450 troops split off from the main body and loaded onto French ships near Stamford on the morning of July 13.

The French flotilla, consisting of at least eight major vessels, crossed the sound and entered Huntington Harbor to discharge the troops at the back of Lloyd's Neck. By eleven o'clock the troops were lined up 400 yards from the fort. Two of the defender's twelve pounders then opened up with grape shot causing casualties in the French lines. The attackers resolve almost immediately crumbled and no real attempt was made to charge the fort. Instead, a disorderly retreat occurred and the entire force returned to Connecticut. That same month, Loyalists made a smaller but far more successful raid against a Connecticut militia garrison. A force of sixty men embarked from Lloyd's Neck on a schooner and landed near Compo Hill in Westport. They easily overwhelmed the small garrison of militia that was on shore guard duty. Six were captured and imprisoned in New York. They were exchanged six months later.

The French failure at Fort Franklin on July 13, may have given Tallmadge reason to be concerned over the increased capabilities and state of readiness exhibited by the defenses. Nevertheless, he continued to promote and organize military operations directed towards Long Island. On October 9, 1781, he departed with 150 men to attack Fort Slongo in the township now known as Fort Salonga. This time the assembly point was the Saugatuck River in Westport. Following the same formula of his previously successful raids, Tallmadge's attack started at four o'clock in the morning and the

100 Loyalist defenders were easily overcome.[414] Twenty-one were taken prisoner but the remainder escaped.

Although the British focused their military strategy on the southern states, they kept a nervous eye on events occurring around New York and Long Island Sound during the spring and summer of 1781. General Clinton still had over 14,000 troops in New York while only 3,500 American troops remained in the area. In late June however, the French Army under Rochambeau began its march from Newport, through Connecticut to link up with General Washington in White Plains. Clinton was reluctant to send any more troops to General Cornwallis in the Chesapeake Bay region. Indeed, he even asked for the return of 3,500 troops if Cornwallis could spare them.[415] This prompted an irate response from Cornwallis although he did detach and send General Benedict Arnold back to New York.

General Arnold, whose first wife died in 1775, turned traitor in May 1779, shortly after marrying Peggy Shippan, a Philadelphia Loyalist. Embittered, he had been secretly passing intelligence to the other side through British Major André but was forced to openly switch sides in September 1780 when Captain André was captured and later executed. Sent to Virginia under Cornwallis, Arnold commanded 1,600 troops and captured Richmond.

General Clinton planned to initiate diversionary attacks in the north in order to hold American forces in place and discourage the transfer of more American and French forces southward.[416] These plans went nowhere however until Benedict Arnold arrived back in New York to organize and conduct an operation in his usual, aggressive manor. What resulted was an action that found a place in infamy. Arnold's invasion of New London and Groton was infamous because he was a native son of Norwich just a few miles upstream and because of the massacre of defenders that took place at Fort Griswold on Groton Heights.

The diversionary nature of General Arnold's operation has been generally accepted as the motivation but why was New London selected as the target? Again, the commonly accepted reason was to punish New London and its harbor for its relentless success as a major base of privateering action and its support of the American Continental Navy. This was indeed a valid reason as was amply illustrated by the career of Dudley Saltonstall of New London. During the early years of the war, he commanded Continental Navy ships *Alfred*, *Trumbull*, and *Warren* in succession. After leaving the Navy, Saltonstall turned to privateering and took command of the sixteen gun brig, *Minerva*. He is credited with capture of the British, sixteen gun, *Hannah* in the summer of 1781. This was the richest prize taken by Long Island Sound privateers during the Revolutionary War. Its cargo was valued at more than £80,000 sterling and included supplies and personal affects bound for British officers stationed in New York.[417] This capture profoundly angered British military leaders and, occurring shortly before General Arnold's operation, was used as one of their justifications.

General Arnold may have had personal reasons as well for the target selection. He may have planned it to make a grand statement of his malice and to snub the area of his birth and boyhood home. He may have been upset as well over unsatisfactory financial dealings with New London merchants. In one such deal in 1778, he was offered a one sixteenth share of the privateering vessel *Putnam* which was being built for an estimated £20,000. When he was ready to consummate the deal, Arnold was told the actual building and fitting costs were £48,000. His one sixteenth share would have cost him £3,000 and he had to pass on the deal.[418] In another 1778 case, Arnold took a one sixteenth share of the sloop *John* for £800. This ship made at least one successful voyage but two years later Arnold had not received any payment for his share of profits. He was forced to request arbitration of the dispute.[419]

Whatever the reason, thirty British ships with 1,700 troops departed Huntington Harbor, Long Island on the evening of September 5 and appeared outside New London Harbor at daybreak the next morning. They proceeded to disembark 800 troops on the New London side and 900 troops on the Groton side of the harbor entrance. General Arnold's goal was to destroy the ships in the harbor and burn the town and warehouses along the river. In order to destroy the vessels he had to capture the forts on each side so he could move his ships into the harbor.

The few defenders at Fort Griswold on Groton Heights sounded a prearranged alarm signal of two canon blasts calling all militia to immediately assemble at the fort. Unfortunately, Benedict Arnold also knew the assembly signal and was able to thwart its intended purpose by firing a third blast every time the signal was given.[420] This effectively converted the alarm to a three gun victory salute which was traditionally used by New London privateers announcing their success upon returning to New London Harbor. As a result of the confusing signals and past false alarms, fewer militiamen reached the fort in time to repulse the invaders and sealed the fate of those who did arrive in time.

General Arnold advanced up the New London side of the river and captured Fort Trumbull, an unfinished blockhouse, after a brief skirmish. The defenders withdrew and attempted to cross the river in small boats. Several were killed or wounded in the attempt, one vessel was captured, but the others made it into Fort Griswold on Groton Heights.

At first, both the British fleet and the ships in the harbor were stuck in place with insufficient wind but a slowly developing onshore breeze enabled some movement on both sides by late morning. General Arnold, traveling northward on the west bank of the river, still saw the opportunity to destroy the whole American fleet if he could hasten his troops on the other side to capture Fort Griswold. The defenders' canon could be turned on their own ships and would have an excellent field of fire from the heights of Groton.[421] The race was on but sixteen of the American ships managed to slip out of range before the battle began and escape upriver to safety at Norwich, taking some of their booty from the warehouses with them. The remaining ships were destroyed.

As the British moved through New London they torched 143 buildings and homes including those of Tory sympathizers.[422] One of these was the home of James Tilley, a friend of Benedict Arnold. Tilley invited Arnold to a repast of food and wine. While they ate, Tilley's house began to burn. When Tilley protested, Arnold told him this was necessary to protect him from the outrage of townspeople if his house was spared. He facetiously exclaimed that the King would reimburse Tilley for his loss.[423]

The British at first tried to salvage the captured *Hannah* and its cargo which was stored in one of the warehouses. They abandoned this effort as the wharfs were consumed by flames and then they put their torch to the *Hannah* and sent the burning ship out into the harbor.

Ironically, one of the few houses to survive was that of Nathaniel Shaw, Jr., the most important person directing Connecticut's naval and privateering efforts. This home also served as Connecticut's Naval War Office during the Revolutionary War. The fire was extinguished before much damage could be done. This is probably due to its construction of stone which can be attributed to work done by French Acadian refugees, years earlier.

Meanwhile, roughly 150 defenders inside Fort Griswold faced 900 seasoned British soldiers. Colonel Ledyard refused to accept two separate surrender demands, in spite of their threat to give no quarter, and prepared for the inevitable assault. The first furious attack was repelled with heavy casualties to the British, including their commander, Colonel Eyre who was mortally wounded. During their second assault, a stray shot cut the defenders' flagpole halyards causing the flag to fall. This was mistakenly taken by the British as a signal of surrender even though the flag was quickly remounted on a pike. This unfortunate, chance occurrence may have set the stage for a most brutal conclusion to the battle.

The attackers rallied a third time and resumed their advance. Additional casualties were taken including Major Montgomery, second in command, who was killed by stab wounds from two long pikes as he came over the top of the rampart. These were administered simultaneously by Captain Shapely and Jordan Freeman, a freed black slave. After about forty-five minutes of intense fighting with heavy redcoat casualties, the British forced their way into the fort and further defense became untenable. Colonel Ledyard issued a cease fire order, told his troops to throw down their arms and surrendered the fort.

In an effort to stop continued British aggression, Colonel Ledyard hastened to the nearest British officer to present his sword. This officer demanded to know who commanded the fort. Colonel Ledyard replied "I did sir, but you do now."[424] His sword, presented hilt first, was accepted by the officer who took it and angrily thrust it through Ledyard's body. A vicious massacre of the defenders ensued with over eighty slain and others wounded despite cries for mercy. The wounded and dead were bayoneted repeatedly until British officers finally stopped the slaughter.

Total American casualties were 133 most of which occurred after the fort surrendered. Eighty-eight were killed and forty-five wounded.

Dreadful losses touched many families. Descendants of original settler, James Avery, were the most affected with nine dead, three wounded and two taken prisoner. Among the casualties were two black men and one Pequot Indian. Lambo Latham, a slave, and freed slave, Jordan Freeman, were killed. Lambo was the recipient of thirty-three bayonet wounds. The wounded Pequot Indian was Tom Wansuc.

British casualties of 193 were even greater than the Americans with fifty-one killed, including the commander and second in command of the attacking forces, and 142 wounded. The invaders did not remain long, fearing retribution by arriving militia reinforcements. Before departing however, they burned nineteen homes in Groton near the fort in addition to the 143 New London structures.

After withdrawing from New London following the Battle of Groton Heights, General Arnold crossed the Sound and plundered supplies at Southold even though this was part of British occupied and controlled territory. The houses of Nicoll Havens and James Havens on Shelter Island were both ransacked.[425]

As with previous raids on Connecticut, this one also failed to accomplish its main objective as a diversionary effort. The troops of General Washington and Rochambeau continued on to Yorktown and victory. While the British won The Battle of Groton Heights they lost the war. On a punitive basis, the British invasion was successful although a number of American ships did escape destruction. On a personal basis for Benedict Arnold, the results were probably mixed. The heavy casualties were not something he wanted. Fort Griswold was a far stronger fortification than he expected it to be. As he first viewed the fort through a telescope from the other side of the river he tried to stop the attack, fearing another Bunker Hill, but it was too late. He also played no role in the massacre of American defenders and probably would not have condoned that action had he been on the scene. The invasion of New London did help to enhance his reputation as a villain in the American mind and this probably pleased him.

After Washington and Rochambeau moved their forces to Yorktown, Brigadier General David Waterbury's Connecticut militia established a small garrison and modest fortification in Stamford.

Constructed between October and December 1781, this fortification was needed to fill the void and also protect the area between Greenwich and New Haven. The war was beginning to wind down however. The one big opportunity presented to Fort Stamford occurred in February 1782, but its role was minimal. The day was saved instead by Jabez Fitch and a small group of whaleboat men. Fitch was commander of three whaleboats that were frozen in the Mianus River and he had seventeen crewmen stationed nearby to protect the boats from attack. That attack came at daybreak on February 15, 1782 when about 100 mounted British soldiers came into view.[426] Their objective however, was primarily to obtain food supplies and plunder rather than destroy his boats.

Fitch and his men were forced to retreat until the raiders split into smaller groups to plunder the area. Fitch then made a stand and began to force one group after another to retreat. Meanwhile, the Patriot garrison commanded by Brigadier General Waterbury at nearby Fort Stamford was aroused but their efforts to organize were delayed while trying to locate the quartermaster who held the keys to the powder room. As Fitch began to pursue the retreating enemy, he finally received assistance from the garrison troops. They managed to kill a number of invaders, recover most of the stolen livestock and liberate several people who had been taken prisoner.

General Washington's victory at Yorktown dealt a devastating blow to the British war effort. As a result, during the winter of 1782, Great Britain initiated major changes to bring the war to an end. British Parliament called a cessation to offensive military action and the British began withdrawing troops from the southern theater of operations. In March, Parliament authorized peace negotiations. General Washington's Army returned to New York and went into winter quarters. He was initially intent on resuming his effort to take back New York City but little was done in that regard.

Although the war was winding down, privateering, as well as illicit trade, continued at a high level. David Hawley concluded his long and varied Connecticut naval responsibilities and turned his efforts to privateering. He became part owner of the sloop *Seaflower* and operated under a privateer commission issued by Massachusetts in May of 1782.

The Whaleboat War declined significantly but by no means, ended. The final raid endured by Guilford, Connecticut took place on May 19, 1782 near East Wharf in what is now Madison. Although little is known about this affair, fighting took place on the landing beach. Leading the defenders, seventy-three-year-old Phineas Meigs died when he was struck in the head by a musket ball.[427] The attackers left one dead on the beach and escaped with several wounded.

By the end of 1782, only one significant military operation was planned for the Long Island Sound area and that ended up being aborted. Colonel Benjamin Tallmadge organized one last whaleboat raid and it would be the largest one yet attempted. The British Army had established a winter camp at Huntington for 600 men of the Seventeenth Light Dragoons which Major Tallmadge proposed to attack. General Washington approved the plan but wanted to coordinate it with movements of his own along the North (Hudson) River.[428] At Shippan Point in Stamford, Tallmadge collected whaleboats and a force of over 700 men which included his own company of Continental troops, Caleb Brewster's small force of Continental whaleboat men and a large contingent of Connecticut militia.

General Washington dictated a departure date after sunset on December 5, 1782. During embarkation the weather turned violent with rain, snow and high winds. Snow squalls marched across the area and the wind whipped sea turned to angry foam. Departure was repeatedly postponed as the stormy weather continued for three days. For three nights the troops slept on the shore underneath their overturned whaleboats making the best of a miserable situation. The mission was finally cancelled on the fourth day. Mortified, Major Tallmadge reported his failure to General Washington and was relieved to learn that Washington's other plans were also abandoned when British ships moved up the Hudson River preventing the passage of his forces downriver.

This event would probably be lost to history had it not been for the boat fight that took place on the second day. Pitched battles between opposing whaleboat forces were relatively rare, however this was a bloody confrontation in the middle of Long Island Sound on December 7, 1782 that nearly cost Captain Caleb Brewster his life. The episode began after Loyalists in Stamford and Norwalk sent word across to Long Island warning them about the large number of troops and boats assembling in Stamford.

Three Loyalist whaleboats came across the Sound to investigate. They were under command of Captain Hoyt but resources do not identify his first name.[429] Due to the violent weather, Hoyt's three whaleboats were forced to take shelter overnight on one of the Norwalk islands. Tallmadge learned about these lurking whaleboats and, when the wind abated somewhat, ordered Captain Brewster to intercept them with six of his best whaleboats that were equipped with sails. Three of the six boats turned back under the horrendous conditions but Brewster and two others doggedly pursued the fleeing Loyalists. Hoyt's boat was the first to open fire while Brewster waited until he was within fifty yards. The ensuing battle lasted only twenty minutes but many were killed or wounded. Brewster suffered a potentially mortal wound with a rifle ball through the chest. Every man but one in Hoyt's whaleboat was killed or wounded.

Reportedly, Hoyt was one of those killed but this has not been confirmed. It is known that there were at least seventeen committed Loyalists with the Hoyt name and the one involved here was considered to be a notorious opportunist alternately plundering and trading with each side. The previous year Colonel Tallmadge confronted this individual onboard his ship in Norwalk Harbor. When Tallmadge inspected the ship he found it contained illicit British trade goods. Hoyt angrily detained Tallmadge on his ship and made sail for Long Island. After stern warnings from Tallmadge that his kidnapping would result in a death sentence, Hoyt finally relented and returned to Norwalk.[430] Hoyt then fled the ship and made his way to Long Island.

Brewster's determined force captured two of the three Long Island whaleboats and returned with them to Black Rock Harbor. Brewster survived his serious wound and, while still recuperating, participated in the capture of two more British ships in the five months of war that remained.[431] He would live to be almost eighty years old.

A tentative peace treaty between England and America was signed on November 30, 1782 but had to be transmitted to America and ratified by Congress. A separate treaty between France and England also had to be concluded before the war could be officially ended. In the next few months, both sides agreed to end hostilities pending ratification but some maritime action continued nevertheless.

Colonel Tallmadge increased his efforts to control illicit trade and he captured several boats involved in this trade. The most significant action involved the armed British privateering vessel, *Three Brothers*, which not only harassed American ships but was frequently seen off Stratford Point exchanging goods with other illegal traders. Tallmadge went to Bridgeport and contracted with Amos Hubbell for the use of his fast sailing ship, the seventy ton *Julius Caesar*, to take on the enemy vessel.[432] A highly disciplined military contingent was placed in readiness to act as boarding party. They included forty-five of Tallmadge's own men plus Captain Brewster's Continental whaleboat men. Brewster, although still recuperating from his chest wound, was placed in charge of the combined military unit.

The *Three Brothers* was strongly armed with eleven carriage guns, four swivel guns and twenty-five men with small arms plus a crew of twenty-one. This ship was spotted cruising in the Sound on February 20, 1783 by lookouts at Stratford Point. Captain Brewster's military unit quickly assembled and boarded the *Julius Caesar*. Captain Hubbell maneuvered his ship out of the harbor at two o'clock in the afternoon and overtook the *Three Brothers* by four o'clock.

Hubbell intended to ram the *Three Brothers*. He instructed the boarding party and most of his crew to stay hidden until their ship struck the enemy vessel.[433] As the ships approached, the British privateer commenced firing with a full broadside and musket discharge which damaged the hull, spars and rigging of the *Julius Caesar* but didn't diminish the ship's momentum as it closed the gap. Upon contact, Hubbell's troops jumped up, fired their one shot weapons and swarmed across to the enemy vessel with fixed bayonets. The assault was overwhelming. Captain Johnstone was killed and three or four of his crew were wounded, two mortally. There were no American casualties.

The war officially ended when Congress ratified the treaty on April 15, 1783. Norwalk was probably typical of most towns when it celebrated the end of the war with a huge community bonfire. The log pile was twenty feet high topped with barrels of tar. At first, bitter feelings prevented any reconciliation with Loyalists but eventually moderate or passive Loyalists who had not joined military units or harmed patriot causes were allowed to return based on discretion of a committee that was formed to review these cases and make recommendations to the town selectmen.[434] People like Gould Hoyt, a moderate Loyalist who remained in Connecticut, were allowed to return to Norwalk. Most of the other Hoyt individuals and families who had left Connecticut to live on Long Island were not welcome and departed for New Brunswick, Canada.

The Richard Smith family was allowed to return to Connecticut in February of 1783 when the family agreed to take an oath of allegiance and become loyal citizens of the new country. It was previously noted that Smith was the owner of the Salisbury Iron Works. The family fled to Boston and then to England in 1775. They sailed to New York City in 1779. Governor Trumbull gave them a permit to enter New London in the sloop *Polly*. In spite of this they were captured by the *Hampton Packet*, a privateer out of New London commanded by Thomas Wickham.[435] Instead of bringing the *Polly* into New London however, Wickham, motivated by shameless profiteering, proceeded to Rhode Island where his chances of claiming the ship as a legitimate prize were better. On the way, they were overtaken by the *Minerva*, another privateer out of New London, in a successful attempt to rescue the *Polly*. The resulting court battle in New London was won by Richard Smith.

British troops continued to occupy New York City while they evacuated from their other posts in America. Along with New York Loyalists already there, the city became a collecting point for many Loyalists driven out of other areas. In the spring, summer and fall of 1783 more than 50,000 departed from New York City on British ships with the majority headed to Nova Scotia or New Brunswick which was not yet a separate province.

William and Sarah Frost, formerly of Stamford left in May for St. John, New Brunswick.[436] They had two children and Sarah was pregnant. The property they were given was twenty-five miles north of St. John. Fyler Dibble also relocated to New Brunswick with his family. Conditions were harsh and making a living was difficult.

In 1784, deeply in debt, Fyler committed suicide by cutting his throat.[437]

Approximately 3,500 black Loyalists joined the exodus to Nova Scotia and New Brunswick.[438] During the war, Great Britain offered freedom to any slave who joined their cause. Many living in British occupied areas took advantage of this opportunity and were augmented by escapees from outside. As many as 1,500 black Loyalists settled in the Shelburne area, mostly at Birchtown. An attempt was made to make Shelburne a major refugee community. The population swelled from almost nothing to over 10,000 in one year. Black Loyalists however, were not given equal consideration for land or other benefits and were expected to serve primarily as a labor supply or in household service.

Initially, labor was in great demand for housing construction and infrastructure development but this need collapsed in less than a year for two reasons. First, a large number of Loyalist militia soldiers arrived. They had been the last to leave New York after all the other remaining Loyalists had left. These soldiers felt entitled to the jobs held by black laborers.[439] A riot ensued in 1784 and all of the black Loyalists were forced to remove to Birchtown. The second reason was that Shelburne could not support its large population because the soil was too poor for farming. Most of the settlers were forced to move elsewhere. Black Loyalists petitioned the British government to relocate them to Sierra Leone, Africa and about 1,200 were resettled there in 1792.

Most, but not all, of the Long Island Patriots who fled to Connecticut returned home as the war ended. Anna and Sellah Strong were reunited after the war. Anna had remained on Long Island as a Patriot spy while Sellah was exiled to Connecticut. She died in 1812 and he in 1815. Colonel Benjamin Tallmadge married Mary Floyd of Mastic, Long Island in 1784 and moved to Litchfield Connecticut where he represented the state in Congress for sixteen years. Lieutenant Caleb Brewster settled at Black Rock Harbor where he married Anne Lewis.

George Washington triumphantly entered New York City on November 25, 1783 on the heals of the last departing British troops. Amidst the parades and ceremonies, Washington made a point of visiting several people who had been spies during British occupation of the city. He publicly acknowledged their service so that they wouldn't be mistakenly persecuted as Loyalists. Among those he acknowledged were Hercules Mulligan and James Rivington.

Part III

The Burden of Independence

Chapter Eleven

The Struggle Between Wars

Along with hard won independence, maritime America looked forward to unfettered trade prosperity. At first, it appeared that these hopes would be realized but unfortunately, harsh political realities would not let that happen. Instead, America's shipping interests were oppressed and then literally crushed by a series of events over the next thirty-two years. The initial blow fell after the war when England, exasperated by the loss of its American colonies, banned all trade between the British Empire and the United States except for certain enumerated items carried in British-built vessels. Before normal trade was restored twelve years later, Britain and France declared war against each other and both began to capture any American ship caught trading with the other side. At the same time, Great Britain greatly increased the impressment of American sailors into the British Navy. By 1797, France started capturing every American ship it could stop which resulted in a two year, undeclared war between France and America. This was followed a few years later by a U.S. embargo initiated by President Jefferson on all foreign trade and subsequently replaced by various Non-Intercourse Acts. The chain of depressing events continued and only culminated when America finally asserted her rights in a second war for independence—The War of 1812.

The challenge to America's maritime trade began gradually and, in fact, wasn't immediately apparent. For a couple of years, England did not enforce its ban on American trade with Nova Scotia and the British West Indies. After eight years of war, both provinces were desperately short of supplies and England knew that only America could quickly provide the provisions and necessities required to build back those economies. In addition, Nova Scotia was struggling with a tremendous influx of Loyalist refugees who needed food and livestock just to survive until they could become self sufficient.

Nova Scotians anxiously awaited further information in the early spring of 1783 about the pending cessation of hostilities. In Liverpool, just about every arriving ship brought news and information regarding preliminary peace agreements but the people needed official confirmation from England via Halifax.[440] Meanwhile, Liverpool privateers continued to capture ships. The *Dreadnaught* arrived in port on April 20 with two captured Connecticut sloops, one out of Wethersfield and the other out of Hartford. The *Dreadnaught* also brought word that the peace treaty had been signed and was in effect.

With war ending, the owners of the privateer *Dreadnaught* decided to immediately sell their vessel at an auction which garnered them £175. The crews of both captured Connecticut ships petitioned for their freedom. After spending three days in jail, Simeon Perkins agreed and ordered their release.[441] Two days later, on April 25, Liverpool finally received official confirmation from Halifax that the King had issued a Proclamation for a Cessation of Arms.

Trade between New England and Nova Scotia began immediately. The first ship from Long Island Sound to arrive in Liverpool was a schooner from Stratford on May 18 loaded with flour, corn and pork. The captain sold his goods and contracted for a cargo of alewives to carry to the West Indies.[442] Captain Jabez Perkins of Norwich arrived on June 24 with a cargo of forty-eight barrels of pork but found the Liverpool market temporarily saturated. Upon the advice of Simeon, Jabez sold his pork in Halifax and used the proceeds to acquire a return cargo of beaver pelts and old cordage.[443]

Trade with Nova Scotia continued at a brisk pace for another two years before England began to enforce its trade ban. Simeon Perkins' diary occasionally mentioned the influx of Loyalist refugees and problems related to their absorption. His entry for July 29, 1784 reported information received from a fishing schooner. "They report that an extraordinary mob or riot has happened at Shelburne. Some thousands of people assembled with clubs and drove the Negroes out of the town and threatened some people."[444]

Use of apprentices on seagoing vessels was reduced during the Revolutionary War due to the risks involved and the need to utilize only experienced mariners. The process of training new mariners resumed after the war. Simeon's nephew, sixteen-year-old Zebulon Perkins of Norwich, arrived in Liverpool in 1785 to learn all he could about shop keeping, lumber harvesting and sailing. Simeon's help was critical to Zebulon's future since the boy's father, Daniel Perkins, had died of smallpox in 1777.[445]

Zebulon completed navigation training the evening of February 1, 1787. This probably involved navigating by stars in the winter sky. The following year Zebulon was sent on his first long journey; a trip to Barbados. Simeon was very careful to provide as much protection as he could for Zebulon. He provided the boy with a "Letter of Consignment" which would protect him from being seized and impressed onto British naval ships. He also provided a "Letter of Credit for 100 dollars in case of war & he should fall into the enemy's hands & be distressed."[446]

In 1785, British officials began enforcing trade ban restrictions with America more strenuously. Liverpool officials, including Simeon Perkins, took a more relaxed position at first and Simeon's diary reflects numerous trading voyages between Liverpool and New London or New York continuing through 1787 and beyond.[447] This laxity in trade restriction enforcement resulted in disciplinary action directed at Liverpool by British officials. For a period of time, Liverpool's Collector of Customs was recalled and Liverpool was put under the jurisdiction of Halifax so that they would be more tightly controlled.

The temporary resumption of trade with the British West Indies did not generate the same degree of drama as that with Nova Scotia. Long Island Sound merchants had developed trade connections with French, Dutch and Spanish islands in the years leading up to the Revolution and these ties were strengthened during eight long years of war. Merchants had no compelling need to trade with the British islands even though profits, for a time, might be higher.

To Americans, opportunities appeared boundless and they began to develop direct trade with European countries, something that was prohibited by England prior to the Revolutionary War. When Great Britain began enforcing its trade ban in 1785, the blow was not catastrophic to American enterprise. Although American ships were squeezed out of all trade with the British Empire, there were other sufficient opportunities. In spite of the ban, Long Island Sound merchants enjoyed maritime trade prosperity from 1785 to 1793.

The majority of trade from Norwich and New London during these years was with the French, Spanish and Dutch West Indies islands. In 1785, 215 ships cleared outbound through the port of New London. Clearing New London in 1791 were fifty-seven sloops, thirty-two schooners, sixty-five brigs, two miscellaneous category vessels and nine larger ships.[448] There were 7,403 horses, mules and cattle among the exports that year.

Norwich alone had thirty-one major ships in 1788. They included twenty sloops averaging forty-seven tons, five schooners averaging 65 tons, five brigs averaging 109 tons and one ship of 200 tons. By 1795, there were forty-two ships operating out of Norwich. Nineteen different trade items were listed in the 1788 time period. By value, the top commodities from Norwich were 549 horses worth £6,588, 1,744 barrels of pork worth £5,322, 1,903 barrels of beef worth £3,806, 205 mules worth £3,075 and 586 barrels of potash worth £2,880.[449]

In New Haven, Joseph Hull purchased a sixty ton sloop in 1785 called the *Hawk*. He made numerous trips from that port to the West Indies in the next few years principally to French ports in St. Domingue (Haiti) and Martinique. A typical cargo was one he carried in June of 1787. Onboard were six thousand feet of lumber, twenty-eight horses, six oxen, and twenty sheep or swine.[450]

Despite general prosperity, there were many merchant failures mostly due to bad luck or the perils of ocean travel and disease that claimed the lives of many seamen in the tropics. At least twenty-two New London ship captains and countless seamen lost their lives during the twelve year period following the end of the Revolutionary War.[451]

Long Island Sound merchants began to develop new maritime enterprise opportunities after the war. These involved the seal trade, whaling and direct trade with ports of other nations of the world.

These places or ports included Cadiz, Lisbon, Bordeaux, Le Havre, Amsterdam, Suriname and Madeira.

The seal trade, also known as the China trade, developed in the 1780s after a great demand for these pelts was identified in China. Word spread throughout Long Island Sound and before long, fleets of ships were engaged in the business. New Haven merchants entered the trade in 1790 when two ships were sent to the Falkland Islands to catch seals. After skinning them, one of the two ships carried the pelts to Canton, China and traded for tea, porcelain, spice and silk. Stonington would soon become a major player in this trade as well.

Sag Harbor initiated long distance whaling in 1785 when merchants copied Nantucket's innovation of carrying a furnace and try-pots onboard ship. This freed the vessels from having to return to port after each whale was caught and made journeys lasting several years possible. By 1795 there were three whaling companies operating out of this port. In 1805, four vessels returned to Sag Harbor with a total of 4,150 barrels of oil.

The ascendancy of shrewd Yankee traders and entrepreneurs came to an end on February 1, 1793 when France and her allies went to war against Great Britain, Spain and the Netherlands. At first, the war appeared to work in America's favor. Immediate supply shortages in the British West Indies islands prompted island governors to reopen trade with America under a plea of necessity.[452] America declared its neutrality in the war but France and then Great Britain declared their intent to capture American ships that traded with any of their enemies.

The potential of additional trade opportunity was more than offset by the added risk of capture on every trip. Trading with the French consortium risked capture by British ships and trading with the British consortium risked capture by French ships. Under neutrality, American ships could not retaliate or readily defend themselves and privateering was not authorized by Congress.

Caught in a squeeze, Long Island Sound merchants suffered greatly. By April, 1794, for example, eleven New Haven vessels were being held by the British in the West Indies for trial by the Court of Admiralty and eight others in the French islands of Martinique and

Guadeloupe for a decision by the French Marine court.[453] Despite the risks, potential profits were enormous for successful journeys. Long Island Sound merchants pressed on but the situation continued to deteriorate.

Great Britain and America did manage to formally end the British trade ban but it only made matters worse. In 1794, Special Envoy, John Jay concluded a commercial treaty with Great Britain. It did address some of the trade difficulties that festered since the Revolutionary War. Most importantly, it opened all British Empire ports to American trade on a most-favored-nation basis and created joint commissions to review and compensate cases of illegal ship seizures by the British. It failed to address the issue of British impressment of American crewmen. The Senate ratified the treaty by a narrow margin in June, 1795 and President Washington signed it in August.

Great Britain was undoubtedly motivated to approve the commercial treaty with America because it was at war and found America's trading power to their advantage. They had already relaxed the ban on West Indies trade so it wasn't that much of an additional concession. On the other hand, the United States was concerned about how the commercial treaty would be received in France. The reaction from France was far worse than expected. In February 1796, they proceeded to denounce the agreement and nullified all previous treaties with the United States. In effect, France, without actually saying it, declared war on America's international interests.

Later in the year, France suspended diplomatic relations with the United States and authorized the capture of every American ship encountered. By June, 1797, Secretary of State Timothy Pickering reported that 300 American vessels had been captured by the French. The worsening crisis descended into undeclared war between the two countries which lasted until September of 1800. In May of 1798, American naval warships were authorized to seize French ships interfering with American trade, convoys were organized and American privateers were commissioned.

The fortunes of several merchant entrepreneurs are detailed to illustrate how the complex international situation affected maritime trade during the years between the Revolutionary War and The War of 1812. Some failed, some barely survived, and some diversified into trade with lesser risk involved. The most successful entrepreneurs shifted much of the fortunes they accumulated during good years of maritime trade into other businesses altogether.

One example of failure was that of Isaac Hull of Derby. Joseph, his father, had been a successful privateer and Whaleboat War veteran during the Revolutionary War and made profitable trading voyages to the West Indies prior to 1793. Isaac began his maritime career in 1792 as second mate on a brig bound for Europe. In 1794 he made his first voyage as commander of a ship. His voyages were all successful until 1797. Then, in two successive trips, his ships were seized by French privateers. A third trip was successful but the profits were insufficient to cover his previous losses and his business partnership had to be dissolved.[454] Hull vowed that he would never again be a helpless victim. He quit the merchant business and accepted a naval commission as lieutenant on the nearly completed *Constitution* in Boston. He would later become commander of this vessel during The War of 1812 and defeat the British frigate, *Guerriere* which earned his ship the nickname "Old Ironsides."

A number of prominent New London merchant families failed to survive the post Revolutionary War years. After a thirty year merchant career, General Gurdon Saltonstall was forced to declare bankruptcy in 1785. He had lost fifteen ships during the Revolutionary War and found it impossible to recover financially. His sons struggled to make a go of it independently but death from diseases contracted in the West Indies trade put an end to the family aspirations.[455] Saltonstall's sons, Thomas died in 1795, Dudley in 1796 and Winthrop in 1802. Winthrop was even pre-deceased by one of his own sons, Gurdon, who died in the West Indies in 1795. After this, the Saltonstall name ceased to be prominent in New London maritime circles.

Samuel Driggs is an example of one who eked out only a marginal existence from West Indies trade. Son of a seafaring father, Samuel was born in Middletown in 1763. He and at least one brother went to sea at a young age and learned their seamanship skills as apprentices. At twenty-six, Samuel purchased a quarter share of the schooner *Lark* and followed that up the next year (1790) with a half share of the schooner *Marlbury*, a new ship built in Wethersfield. He also owned a half share in a rum distillery and spent much time in Nassau where he married Sarah Brown who may have been a planter's daughter. His rising fortunes ended abruptly in 1806 with sudden bankruptcy after several ships in which he was part owner were seized by the French, Spanish and British.[456] This apparently forced him to hire on as a paid ship captain in 1808 working for Stephen Clay, his one time business partner in the rum distillery. He died in 1814 in Nassau at age 51.

Joseph Williams of Norwich began his merchant career by selling supplies to soldiers encamped around New York in 1776. After Congress authorized privateering, he purchased and outfitted a number of vessels for this purpose as well as for trade with the West Indies. He continued to prosper after the war and, by 1793, was a wealthy merchant. He owned a shipyard, two warehouses and all or part of more than twenty vessels.[457] During the last seven years of the eighteenth century however, Williams suffered serious financial losses in ships captured. When he died in 1800 at the age of forty-seven, much of his fortune had vanished.

The Joseph Williams Collection of documents held by Mystic Seaport contains information on four of William's ships that were captured by the French during the Undeclared War.[458] The *Esther and Eliza*, homeward bound from Tobago with a cargo worth $17,000 was captured in April 1797. The *Hope*, bound to Suriname with a cargo worth (illegible amount) was captured in November 1797. The *Speculator*, homeward bound from St. Bartholomew with a cargo worth $18,000 was captured in April, 1798. The *Prosperity*, bound to St. Vincent with a cargo worth $15,500 was also captured in 1798. Williams' heirs struggled for more than eighty years to obtain some compensation for damages and still had petitions filed with the United States Court of Claims in 1887.

Many of the merchants who survived the vagaries of West Indies trade did so by diversifying. Over a forty-five year span, John Caldwell owned at least a portion of twenty-five vessels operating out of the Connecticut River. He made and lost money in the West Indies trade and eventually shifted some of his funds when he was on the plus side to invest in banking where he founded the Hartford National Bank.

Another person who successfully diversified was Jeremiah Wadsworth of Hartford. As with most mariners, Jeremiah began his career onboard ship as an apprentice to gain experience. He was a ship captain in his twenties and owned at least one brig by the time he reached thirty years of age. During the Revolutionary War, Jeremiah held the enormously important position of Commissary General, charged with the responsibility of purchasing supplies for both General Washington's Continental Army and the allied French forces. He was aided in this effort through a silent partnership he maintained with the brothers, Silas and Barnabas Deane of Wethersfield.[459] It was Silas Deane who negotiated with the French for military supplies during the Revolutionary War and was instrumental in obtaining a Treaty with France for friendship, commerce and alliance. The Deanes were also merchants who provided many supplies to the army and operated several distilleries along the Connecticut River. It is perhaps no surprise that Connecticut became known as "the provision state" during the Revolutionary War and that Wadsworth became one of the wealthiest men in the state.

Some of Wadsworth's wealth was used to start the first bank in Hartford and provide capital to build the first woolen mill in Connecticut. England had long suppressed American industry in order to protect its own interests so this was an important step to help Americans develop an industrial base that could compete directly with England.

The Hubbell family of Stratford was important during the years between wars. As previously noted, Amos Hubbell was commander of the seventy ton *Julius Caesar* that captured the British privateer, *Three Brothers* in one of the last actions of the war in Long Island Sound. Captain Wilson Hubbell was killed in 1799 when a French privateer captured his ship. In 1798, Ezekial Hubbell's ship *Citizen* was seized and brought into Halifax by the British. The ship was soon released however, when the British examined its papers and determined that it had not traded with the French.

In October 1799, Ezekial Hubbell began his first voyage to China in command of the 250 ton *Enterprise* out of New York, of which he was a part owner. The owners, fed up with the constant threat to their livelihood, mutually agreed to engage in safer trade by avoiding both French and British interests.[460] Ezekial obtained furs on the northern Pacific Coast of North America and on the Kamchatka Peninsula which he traded in Canton, China. He was the first captain from the New York area to circumnavigate the globe. He made several more trips to China before the War of 1812.

The fur seal trade (a.k.a. China trade) represented a significant financial opportunity and also a way to substantially reduce risks by avoiding British and French interests. Except during the Undeclared War, seizure of American ships engaged in the China trade were not considered legitimate seizures since the trade did not involve France, England or the allies of either country. Thus, if seized, they could not be successfully prosecuted for condemnation. During the Undeclared War with France, American ships engaged in the China trade were still fairly safe since they operated in areas where there were few French ships to bother them. Although the heyday of this trade was only between 1795 and 1807, it continued into the 1820s at which time the supply of seals was finally exhausted.

The seal trade involved two types of vessels. The "sealers" were fleets of small ships. These ships and their crews landed in remote locations to slaughter seals and prepare the pelts. The pelts were then transferred to large vessels for the long trip to China and then back to America with trade goods obtained. The full roundtrip generally took one year but many trade voyages lasted considerably longer. A typical cargo returned from China might have included tea, cloth, silk, cinnamon and chinaware. Typical compensation for crew members was $50 per month and twelve tons of personal trade for the captain; $35 per month and three tons of personal trade for the first mate; $30 per month and two tons of personal trade for the second mate and for the ship's physician; and $25 per month for the third mate.[461]

Many New Haven merchants scrambled to get into the China trade. From 1790 to 1815 the New Haven fleet numbered as many as twenty ships profitably engaged in this long haul trade. Perhaps the most successful voyage out of New Haven was made by Captain Daniel Greene in the 360 ton *Neptune* whose principal owner was Ebenezer Townsend, Sr. This ship departed in 1796 on a three year voyage where it collected 80,000 pelts, ultimately trading them in China and returning in 1799. After paying duties and wages of $74,000, the ship owners split the remaining $220,000 profit according to their share percentages.[462] By 1815 however, seal populations in the easier to reach South Pacific rookeries were decimated and New Haven merchants largely withdrew from the trade.

Edmund Fanning of Stonington entered the China Trade in 1797. His initial outfitting, insurance and supply costs were $7,867. The seal skins he obtained were sold for $120,467 in Canton, China and his total additional expenses were $67,349 leaving a profit of $45,251.[463] Fanning made another China voyage in 1801 as master of the *Aspasia*. He obtained 57,000 skins in the South Georgia Islands and traded them in Canton.

The China trade spurred the building of progressively larger ships and encouraged the trend to concentrate these vessels in large ports such as New York City. In 1798, the commercial maritime shipping out of the Port of New York was double that of Boston and was equal to the commerce of all Massachusetts Bay ports combined.[464] Many Long Island Sound merchants, sea captains and seamen began migrating into New York City where they would become the core of this port's maritime industry. Curtiss Blakeman of Stratford was an example of this growing trend. Born in Stratford in 1777, Curtiss went to sea at a young age and was a ship captain by the time he was twenty-two. In 1804 he stepped up to command the 320 ton *Triton* out of New York City and departed for Canton, China.[465] Just two years later he stepped up again taking the 501 ton, 111 feet long, *Trident* on its maiden voyage to China.

There was considerable growth in maritime industry around Long Island Sound from 1783 until the United States initiated a trade embargo in 1807. This growth continued in spite of heavy losses suffered by many merchants at the hands of British and French ships. Shipbuilding in particular thrived under these conditions due to the need to replace captured vessels. This process began to transfer the wealth that had been accumulated by merchant ship owners during good times to the ship building industry and the brokers who arranged contracts for building these vessels. This trend could not be sustained indefinitely, however.

Beside shipbuilding, there was strong advancement in coastal trade which was immune to capture and seizure during this turbulent period of time. Improvements were also made in the area of navigation aids. As of 1795, the only lighthouse within the Sound guarded the entrance to New London Harbor. Nine more were built in the next thirteen years.

The port of Bridgeport (Newfield) grew dramatically after the Revolutionary War fueled by both direct West Indies trade and coastal trade. Between 1783 and 1793 there was a five fold increase in population, stores, wharves and maritime commerce.[466] During the 1790s however, merchants suffered the loss of twenty-nine vessels captured by British or French ships. These losses crippled the port's economy but Bridgeport struggled back. In 1799, it was homeport to fifteen major vessels. Large quantities of farm produce from the Connecticut hinterlands were shipped out. Other products shipped out that year included 14,900 pounds of iron, 2,791 pairs of shoes and 1,800 hats.[467]

The Connecticut River was a particularly vibrant area with numerous seaports and shipyards. At Windsor, the river's farthest navigable limit, ship building began prior to the Revolutionary War. This was initiated by Ebenezer Grant, a Yale graduate, with a shipyard at the mouth of the Scantic River. Between 1800 and 1816, forty-nine of the 315 ships built in the Connecticut River Valley were built in the Windsor area. Just to the south, Hartford became a bustling port after a deeper channel was dredged between there and Middletown which was maintained by tolls collected. In 1790, about sixty vessels could be seen in the port of Hartford.[468]

Altogether, Glastonbury shipyards produced 270 ships after 1784. The most active Glastonbury families in this business were the Welles and Hollister families. Most of the vessels were small, designed for costal trading but some were considerably larger. The *Confederacy*, commissioned in 1794, was a square rigger rated at 459 tons.

In the Wethersfield and Rocky Hill area, approximately 111 ships were launched between 1784 and 1865. Cromwell, known as Upper Middletown or the Upper Houses, had six shipyards with the Savage family being the most prominent. By 1807, Middletown had become the largest port between New York City and Cape Cod in terms of registered and enrolled tonnage.[469]

Across the river in Portland, the Gildersleeve family became the most successful ship builders. Obadiah Gildersleeve was a patriot refugee who had fled to Portland from Sag Harbor, Long Island in 1776. His son, Philip, built the U.S. Navy frigate *Connecticut* in 1798. His grandson, Sylvester carried on the work. During the War of 1812, Sylvester supervised the construction of many ships on Lake Erie for Admiral Perry, utilizing a contingent of Connecticut workers.[470]

Jesse Hurd established a ship yard in Middle Haddam. Much of the lumber he used was hauled by oxen from nearby communities of East Hampton, Marlborough, Hebron and Westchester. Most of the ships he built were purchased by New York owners and were docked at South Street.[471] In 1800, he opened a large store in the village and sent two or three ships per year to New York City to obtain a wide variety of merchandise. His store also received a retail liquor license in 1816.

Six large shipyards operated in Essex and Deep River where they supported seven saw mills and five blacksmith shops. Quite a few ships were also built in Lyme near the mouth of the Connecticut River. Most of these vessels were constructed on the Lieutenant River, a tributary of the Connecticut River.

Perhaps Lyme's greatest contribution to the maritime merchant industry was made by four members of the Griswold family. George, an outgoing, gregarious individual, moved from East Lyme to New York in 1794 and Nathaniel, quiet and introverted, moved in 1796. Their initial enterprise involved ship brokering, importing and exporting. By 1810, the Griswold brothers had established a major shipping line utilizing a blue and white checkered pennant as identification. Their cousins, John and Charles, would later establish the even more famous Black X line operating out of New York Harbor.[472] These were clear harbingers of the future of Long Island Sound. By the early 1800s, American maritime trade was starting the transition to larger ships, bigger shipping companies and large deep water ports.

The Griswold brothers continued to maintain strong ties with Long Island Sound. They employed many Connecticut River mariners as ship captains and crew for their ships based in New York. An example was Captain Henry Champlin of Essex, whose wife was Amelia, daughter of shipyard owner, Uriah Hayden. He became the pioneer shipmaster of the Black X Line and was the Line's Senior Captain and Marine Superintendent. The Griswold brothers were also major brokers for ship builders on the Connecticut River and other locations. They identified buyers for ships being built in Connecticut and made recommendations on ship construction to facilitate these sales.

A typical brokering situation involved a ship being built in 1804 by Jesse Hurd in Middle Haddam. On July 31, the Griswolds wrote to Hurd relative to this ship which had lines similar to another ship called the *Connecticut* which they noted to be a fast sailor. They advised that if the new ship proved to be as fast when calculated for carrying guns, it would make a desirable vessel for the St. Domingo trade.[473] The Griswolds told Hurd that they had a buyer who wanted to see the ship and was likely to make an offer. They also made specific recommendations about the work of the joiners and caulkers to insure quality acceptable to the prospective buyer and to insure a good price.

New Haven Harbor still struggled with several deficiencies. While the harbor was large, it was shallow, not well protected and prone to silting. In the early nineteenth century, a long wharf was built which projected a half mile outward to reach deeper water. This was a first step towards remedying the problems of this harbor but breakwater construction and dredging would not come until later. The Long Wharf itself was a bustling place lined with various commercial enterprises such as shops, taverns and warehouses. In 1811, New Haven boasted of having four ship chandlery stores, three rope walks, two sail lofts but only one shipyard which was a reduction from three that existed just prior to the Revolutionary War.[474]

Although the first ship built in Milford was a substantial 150 tons, most were less than fifty tons. There were three shipyards in Milford that produced about fifty vessels between 1784 and 1824. After this period, all three ship building companies went out of business. By 1803, Black Rock Harbor had six stores, five wharves and four ships. There were about nineteen families, fifty-four inhabitants and an additional twenty boarders who most likely worked as seamen or in some other maritime related capacity.

The Long Island side of the Sound lagged significantly behind Connecticut in maritime enterprise. Oyster Bay, Cold Springs Harbor and Huntington Bay were slow to develop although there had been considerable privateering and Whaleboat War action emanating from these harbors during the Revolutionary War. Still, Cold Spring Harbor and the Port Jefferson area began to grow in shipping volume during the 1790s and Congress declared both ports to be Ports of Delivery in 1799. Significant shipbuilding began around 1812 at a shipyard owned by John H. Jones but whaling did not commence until 1836. Coastal trade of fruits, vegetables and cord wood were the primary products with New York City being the primary destination.

Port Jefferson and Setauket Harbor occupied different arms of the same bay. Ship building began in 1797 but less than one a year were being completed before the War of 1812 temporarily halted construction altogether. After the war 500 vessels were built here totaling about 100,000 tons.[475] About sixty percent of this was built in Port Jefferson and forty percent in Setauket. Builders John Wilsie, Richard Mather and Thomas Bell produced ships that were mostly coasting vessels carrying cordwood.

Shipbuilding on Shelter Island in Gardiners Bay began near the end of the eighteenth century when a descendant of Thomas and Dorothy Lord moved to the island from Lyme, Connecticut. The Lord family had come to America in 1635 and settled in Hartford. Forests around Lyme had become depleted so the move to Shelter Island was made to acquire virgin woodland, the prime resource for ship building. Lord established a shipyard on West Neck Creek, also called Shipyard Creek.[476] Many vessels were built in the shipyard and Lord's three sons also helped in the business and sailed many of the ships that were launched.

In order to promote maritime trade along the east coast, the United States Government recognized a need to address safety issues and improve navigation aids. Congress authorized the construction of nine Lighthouses around Long Island Sound between 1796 and 1809. These were positioned to mark hazards along shipping routes and to mark entrances to harbors.

The first of these lighthouses was activated in 1796 on Montauk Point at the eastern tip of Long Island. This point had taken a heavy toll on ships that approached New York City from the north and east entering through Long Island Sound. During the Revolutionary War, the Royal Navy kept fires lit on Montauk Point to act as a beacon for their vessels especially when they were providing guard duty or were operating a blockade of the Sound. The most famous shipwreck near Montauk Point was that of the HMS *Culloden*, a seventy-four gun, third rate ship-of-the-line. This vessel went aground during a snowstorm in January 1781 while maintaining surveillance on the French fleet in Newport. The crew was saved but the *Culloden* was a total loss. The following summer, Joseph Woodbridge of Groton salvaged sixteen of the thirty-two pounder cannons and offered them to General Washington.

Eaton's Neck Lighthouse at the head of Huntington Bay was next in 1799. The rocks around this point were the cause of more shipwrecks than any other place along the north shore of Long Island. Even a lighthouse did not put an end to ship losses at this location during the age of sail. In one particularly ferocious storm in December 1811, more than sixty ships were driven onto the rocks with great loss of life.

A lighthouse on Faulkner's Island, three and one half miles off the coast of Guilford Connecticut, was activated in 1802. This beacon warned of hazardous reefs and shallows around the island. During the War of 1812, British troops landed on the island but did no harm, apparently deciding the lighthouse was an important service to the safety of their own ships as well as their enemy.

The first lighthouse marking the entrance to the Connecticut River was constructed on Lynde Point, Old Saybrook in 1803. The Connecticut River was the largest in New England. The many ships built or based in the river relied on this beacon when navigating the shallows and swift tides at the river's mouth.

A lighthouse was constructed on the east side of New Haven Harbor in 1805. It was placed on Five Mile Point (today Lighthouse Point Park). When entering New Haven Harbor, mariners knew they should chart a course which kept them at least two miles off the shore from where the lighthouse stood in order to avoid a dangerous ledge. It was here during the Revolutionary War invasion of New Haven that half of the British forces landed. In the lead landing barge, Ensign Watkins yelled out to demand that the rebels disperse from the shoreline but was killed in the brief skirmish that followed. He was buried near the lighthouse.

The primary entrance to Long Island Sound was a passage about five miles wide lying between Little Gull Island and Fishers Island to the northeast. This area was known initially as the "horse race," but then simply as the "race" due to strong tidal currents flowing back and forth through this funnel. Depending on weather and tide, conditions in the race could be fierce with breaking waves and rip tides. Little Gull Island Lighthouse was activated in 1806. The island, with only one acre of land, was extremely remote. During the War of 1812 however, it had a front row seat overlooking British fleet movements at the mouth of the Sound making it a strategic site. When the British Navy extended their blockade to the eastern end of the Sound, they landed on the island and put the lighthouse out of commission by removing the lamps and reflectors. They didn't want this facility to be capable of signaling warnings about British ship movements or assisting blockade running American ships.

The lighthouse on Fayerweather Island, guarding the entrance to Black Rock Harbor in Bridgeport, was activated in 1808. In 1819, twenty-four-year-old Catherine Moore effectively took charge of this lighthouse when her father was injured.[477] She continued as caretaker until her retirement in 1878 at the age of eighty-three. The last seven years of her service were officially credited in her name after the death of her father at age 100. Catherine died at age 105. She is also credited with saving twenty-one lives. She stated that "Sometimes there were more than two hundred sailing vessels in here at night, and some nights there were as many as three or four wrecks, so you may judge how essential it was that they should see our light."[478] There were eight oil lamps which consumed a total of four gallons of oil each night. On windy nights it was impossible to keep them all burning.[479]

A lighthouse at Watch Hill, Rhode Island was also activated in 1808. This beacon warned mariners who were entering Fishers Island Sound of dangerous nearby shoals. A tower was originally situated on Watch Hill in the 1740s to serve as a lookout for French ships during King George's War and during the French and Indian War but was destroyed by a storm in 1781.

Finally, Sands Point Lighthouse near Port Washington was erected in 1809 to warn of a dangerous reef near the harbor entrance which was also hazardous to ships approaching the East River and Hell Gate Narrows. Many more lighthouses were constructed after this but they are outside of the time frame covered by this book.

The hostilities between Great Britain, France and their allies continued but there were two events that gave hope for a reduction in the economic risk faced by American merchants on the high seas. First, the undeclared naval war between France and the United States ended in September of 1800 and the two countries re-established diplomatic relations. The issue of French compensation for seizure of American ships was left to future negotiations. Second, there was a temporary cessation in hostilities between France and England from the spring of 1802 until the fall of 1803. While brief, it did offer a temporary respite and encouraged American merchants to persevere in an attempt to reverse their previous losses. Unfortunately, America's good fortune was fleeting and the very success of its entrepreneurs conspired against them.

By 1804, the trade of Nova Scotia with the British West Indies was depressed due to competition from the United States. Great Britain had continued to apply its restrictive colonial trade policies to Nova Scotia, something that America was now free of. Nova Scotia merchants complained that their costs were much higher partly because of the war with France and partly because of duties they had to pay that American merchants did not have to pay.[480] They further complained that Americans were underselling them on just about everything and they were particularly upset that Americans could purchase dried or salted fish from Nova Scotia and then re-ship and sell it cheaper in the West Indies than Nova Scotians could do trading directly. They urged Great Britain to either eliminate the trade tariffs they had to pay or re-institute the ban on American trade with their West Indies Islands.[481] Great Britain decided to ban American trade and instructed their West Indies Governors to close their ports to Americans except under conditions of great necessity.

After the resumption of hostilities between France and England, threats to American maritime interests steadily increased and became severe enough to cripple the shipping industry. Few ship owners or captains were willing to risk a trade mission to Europe. One captain who did was Sam Lord of Shelter Island but his voyage did not start out that way. One of the ships built at the Lord shipyard on Shelter Island was the 176 ton schooner, *Paragon*. This was a fast ship under the command of Lord's eldest son, Samuel with a nine man crew, all Shelter Islanders.[482]

In 1804, Samuel Lord set out on a coastal trade mission which took him to Norfolk, Virginia. While in port, the brokerage firm of Gouveneur and Suydam offered a cargo of 1,000 barrels of flour to anyone who would take it to Liverpool, England. This presented an opportunity for significant profit but it would be accompanied by great peril. Napoleon had just crowned himself Emperor of France and his Navy had established a blockade of English ports with picket ships patrolling the Atlantic approaches to Ireland and England. Due to the hazardous international situation, trade was depressed and many ships were idle, yet in the circle of ship captains who gathered to hear the offer, only Samuel Lord stepped forward.[483] He was a hard headed Yankee who felt the cargo value of 1,000 guineas in gold was too good to pass up (a guinea was equal to one pound, one shilling).

Just fifteen days after clearing Norfolk Harbor, the *Paragon* approached the coast of England. The dash through the French blockade began at nightfall, favored by a gale force wind and double reefed sails. Through the black of night, Captain Lord had only one close encounter. The *Paragon* careened past a ship looming out of the darkness directly in its path but it quickly passed from view before the picket line ship could react. By dawn they were safely inside the Irish Sea and proudly coasted into Liverpool.

A large crowd quickly gathered to express their awed congratulations and ask questions about the blockade and sentiments in the United States. The Mayor of Liverpool sent a message to the dock with a proclamation of respect and good will and an invitation for Captain Lord to attend a dinner in his honor the next evening at Town Hall. Lord had no suitable clothing for the occasion but that presented no problem in light of the large payment he had just received for delivery of his cargo.

Captain Lord hastened to the best tailor in town who put aside all other work to dedicate himself to the task. "The coat was a light blue satin, trimmed with gold lace; the waistcoat and knee-breeches of white satin; there were white silk stockings and polished shoes adorned with high red heels and big silver buckles."[484] As Captain Lord departed for dinner, he portrayed an image of refined, high society. The crew was delighted and greatly amused by the sight of their rough hewn captain so far out of his natural environment. Their stories back on Shelter Island would not be believed.

Two days later the *Paragon* got underway for the journey home and again passed through the blockade like a ghost in the night. However, three days out a large warship was spotted without identification flag. Taking no chances, Captain Lord loaded on all sail. In a fresh breeze, the swift sailing *Paragon* easily put distance between herself and the man-of-war. Later in the day the wind slowed and became unreliable. Under these conditions the huge, square rigged sails of the warship had an advantage.

As the gap between the ships steadily shortened, Captain Lord hid the sacks of gold guineas in the ship's bilge area and then surrendered his ship. Only then did the warship make its identity known; it was British. That alone wouldn't save him unless he could prove his destination had been trade in a British port. The British Captain was not easily convinced and was incredulous that an American had chanced to run the French blockade.[485] The matter was easily resolved after Samuel Lord showed the British Captain a Liverpool newspaper printed on the date of his sailing.

The seizure of ships was not the only hazard faced by American merchants and seamen. There was one other issue that would inflame the American conscience and lead to a declaration of war with England. It involved the very independence and sovereignty of the new nation and the rights of its people. The issue was impressment of American seamen into the British Navy. England had been doing so for over a hundred years but the prolonged war between France and England made matters infinitely worse as England struggled to maintain its sizeable navy. Also, the United States was now an independent nation and its rights were being trampled by many nations.

Between the Revolutionary War and War of 1812, matters became more complex and the issue of impressments more odious to Americans. Royal Navy desertion rates peaked during the Napoleonic Wars at about 2,500 sailors each year.[486] England did not recognize naturalized U.S. citizenship which could be granted after two years of residency. She pursued the concept of unchangeable allegiance which meant that citizenship of a native born Englishman superseded any other acquired in later life.

Many deserters from the British Navy did, in fact, melt into American merchant society. Not only did England feel entitled to seize and impress these people, she took thousands of American seamen who were not deserters. Even though most seamen carried proof of residency and citizenship papers and other documentation, British naval captains often ignored these proofs which they felt could easily be faked.[487] At least 10,000 Americans were seized in this manner when, in reality, only ten percent were proved to be deserters.

The convoluted maritime adventures of Jeremiah Holmes of Stonington included a period of almost three years where he was forced to serve on British warships. He initially shipped out on an American trading vessel, spent several months imprisoned in Brazil under the Portuguese government and then signed on to an English whaling vessel for the next two and a half years.

In 1804, his ship was captured by a French privateer near the South Atlantic Island of St. Helena. Cast adrift in a small boat, Jeremiah, with some of the crew, rowed to the island. Before he could ship out on another merchant vessel, he was forcibly impressed onto the British seventy gun warship, *Trident*. When examined by the ship's first lieutenant, Jeremiah protested by declaring "I am an American." The British officer responded: "Well, we will make an Englishman of you." Jeremiah responded: "No sir; you will never do that."[488]

By now, Jeremiah had lost his American protection papers and had to write to his family and friends back in Stonington for new documentation. Even after receiving his new documentation proving American nativity, the British continually refused to release him. Transferred to the seventy-four gun *Saturn*, Jeremiah just missed out on participating in the bloody naval engagement off Trafalgar October 21, 1805. His ship was delayed by strong headwinds.

Nevertheless, he did participate in an engagement near the Straights of Gibraltar where he served as a lower deck gun captain.

Jeremiah made two unsuccessful escape attempts but his third was successful. He then made his way to the American consulate in London where he obtained his cherished protection certificate.

> "I now had the hand and seal of liberty. It was an hour of inexpressible relief and I stood up in the pride and dignity of an attested American citizen. But the more I rejoiced in my liberty and my endorsed rights the more I scorned and hated the English that had so wronged me of my time and strength. And I was glad, too, that for my liberty I owed the haughty crown no thanks."[489]

Jeremiah finally reached home in March, 1807. He married Anne Denison Gallup and, after a trade embargo was lifted, returned to sea. After one transatlantic voyage, he engaged in coastal trading as a part owner of the schooner *Sally Ann*. In just eight months he more than recovered the cost of his investment in the ship. War with England was fast approaching and Jeremiah would have an opportunity for revenge and to pay back the British for impressing him.

Americans were not the only ones to suffer the sting of British impressments. In January 1800, a Nova Scotia privateer, partially owned by Simeon Perkins of Liverpool, was stopped in the West Indies by Captain John Beresford of H.M.S. *Unite*. Nine of the privateer crew were forcibly taken off their ship and impressed into the British Navy.[490]

The mere arrival of a British warship in a generally non-military port would cause apprehension about its intentions. When a Royal Navy schooner arrived in Liverpool on June 29, 1805, the residents were convinced it was there to impress townspeople. A shore party landed causing some commotion in the village. Three black men took shelter in Simeon Perkins home who said they had been chased by sailors from the schooner.[491] That evening, the sailors onshore were insulted and a scuffle ensued with villagers. Next day, the commanding officer complained to Simeon and declared that he had no intention of impressing anyone. Simeon was forced to apologize for the incident. The mission of the navy schooner was to search for and seize deserters. Three men were subsequently hauled onboard and taken away.[492] Apparently, the schooner was also mandated to identify and seize indigent or unconnected black men to place in a black military unit being formed in Halifax.

Americans reacted bitterly to the increasingly heavy handed British impressment tactics but all efforts to reason with Great Britain or to find a diplomatic solution failed utterly. President Jefferson chose a non-confrontational approach to avoid escalation of the crisis. He urged Congress to enact a trade embargo which it did on December 22, 1807. Trade with all foreign countries was banned. Only coastal trading was allowable but merchants were required to post a substantial bond guaranteeing they would not violate the embargo. The amount of the bond was double the cost of the ship and its cargo. The embargo did not prompt Great Britain to change its impressment policies and did more to hurt American maritime interests.

The Embargo Act was enormously unpopular along the eastern seaboard and especially in New England. It nearly destroyed the American shipping industry and depressed the New England economy. The embargo was not well received in Fairfield in spite of all the difficulties their merchants had previously encountered. People felt it would have fatal consequences.[493] Governor Trumbull of Connecticut declared the embargo to be unconstitutional and an infringement of Federal power. The other New England states concurred and resolved not to provide any funds or militia that would be used to enforce the embargo.

Due to the groundswell of opposition, the total embargo was rescinded in March of 1809 but replaced only a few months later by non-intercourse acts prohibiting trade with France and England. The situation at this time within Long Island Sound was disastrous. Upon the termination of the total trade embargo, William Wheeler of Fairfield commented that the effect had been to paralyze local business and shipping.[494] Jonathan Buckley, also of Fairfield, noted in his diary on July 7, 1809 that the continuing non-intercourse policies could have fatal consequences and could jeopardize the hard won liberty recently gained from England.[495]

Connecticut River Valley exports dropped from $1.6 million to $414,000 and in Middletown alone from $85,000 to $49,000.[496] Customs records at New London reflect that duties paid dropped from $214,940 in 1806 to less than $100,000 in 1808. By 1811, duties further declined to a mere $22,343.[497] While the total embargo on trade was no longer in effect, trade with England and France was still prohibited most of the time prior to the War of 1812. Ships had to run a gauntlet to avoid American Navy patrol vessels (if smuggling was the intent) plus a British blockade that was established along the eastern seaboard to stop, search and seize American ships or impress sailors.

The blockade was extended to almost all American ports with the objective of stopping every ship trying to depart or enter an American harbor in order to scrutinize the crewmen onboard. Using these tactics, the British Navy arrogantly increased their impressment of American sailors. Captain Charles Pond of Milford, Connecticut was embroiled in one of these situations and his crew victimized while outward bound on a voyage to Lisbon, Portugal. British and Portuguese troops were heavily engaged in the Peninsular War against France at this time. In violation of the Non-Intercourse Acts, many merchants found excellent profit in selling beef, grain and flour to the British Army fighting in Spain under the command of the Duke of Wellington.[498] Captain Pond's vessel was stopped by a British ship shortly after its departure and four sailors were taken from him. Upon arrival in Lisbon, Captain Pond stormed into the British military commander's office and angrily complained to him that ... "a continuation of those offenses would inevitably lead to a declaration of war by my country."[499] The year was 1812.

The extent of illegal trade is unknown during this period but there were other merchants who also ignored the non-intercourse laws and risked trade with France or England. Not only were they subject to seizure by one of these two countries, they also risked enforcement by ships of the U.S. Navy. The Federal Government established a patrol base on Block Island. The ships were under the direction of Commodore Isaac Chauncey and their task was to patrol the shipping lanes approaching Narragansett Bay, Long Island Sound and New York Harbor.

In April, 1812, just prior to the United States declaration of war with Great Britain, the Griswold brothers sent the *Cornelia* on a trade mission to England under the command of Hezekiah Smith of Middle Haddam, Connecticut. Arrangements had been made to deliver a cargo to Cropper, Benson and Co. of Liverpool.[500] On April 6, the *Cornelia* was ordered to sail twelve miles offshore, outside the limits of territorial waters, and wait for delivery of additional crew members, required shipping certificates and instructions. This was accomplished by April 7 using several small ships with secret identification signals. The *Cornelia* then set sail for Liverpool and arrived there on May 12.

The *Cornelia* returned to U.S. waters on September 14 with a rich cargo of English wool, cotton goods and hardware but the Griswold brothers would receive nothing for their effort. Their ship was seized by a U.S. Navy gunboat under Commodore Chauncey operating out of Block Island and brought into New York for libel proceedings.[501]

Long Island Sound merchants, captains and seamen were continually frustrated by the harassment of their ships from all quarters and the disrespect for America's sovereign rights. The difficulties facing American vessels trying to engage in foreign trade is shown by the experiences of Captain Richard Law, Jr. in just one voyage. In command of the *Egeria,* he departed from New London in 1810 bound for St. Petersburg, Russia. It would be almost three years before he returned home—without his ship.

The Treaty of Tilsit in 1807 had brought Russia within the sphere of Napoleon's continental system but she soon began to disengage from France's control. In 1810, Russia opened its ports to neutral shipping and effectively declared its neutrality. Captain Law took immediate advantage of this opportunity. Under these circumstances, trade with Russia at this time did not violate the restrictions of any country and Law's voyage should have proceeded unimpeded. It did not. The *Egeria* was seized and taken into Denmark by a Norwegian privateer, presuming it to be a British ship.[502] It was common practice for privateers to simply take ships and let the courts decide if the seizure was legal or not.

After many months of legal maneuvering, the *Egeria* was released in January, 1811. Law had barely set sail before he was stopped again; this time by a French privateer. It didn't matter that he was inside Danish territorial waters and still had a pilot onboard. Back in Copenhagen, it was December before the *Egeria* was released again.

All hope of making a profit on the voyage had now evaporated so Captain Law decided to make no further attempt to reach St. Petersburg.

He sold his cargo in Copenhagen and sent the ship back to America with a new cargo while he remained to settle accounts. The *Egeria* never arrived. It was seized by a British privateer just after America declared war with Britain in June of 1812. The ill fated *Egeria* was then directed to Halifax, Nova Scotia with a prize crew onboard but, again, never arrived. The ship hit rocks and sank.

Meanwhile, Captain Law settled his accounts and took passage on a small ship headed to America. Bad luck continued to hound him when his voyage ended in a shipwreck on the North Carolina coast. It was early 1813 before he finally made it back to New London. The final blow fell when no insurance money was payable for loss of the *Egeria* or its cargo. This was probably due to a war clause exclusion in the policy. While America was not at war when the *Egeria* departed, it was seized by the British after war was declared.

In Liverpool, Nova Scotia, Simeon Perkins' diary fell silent in April, 1812. He died on May 9. He would not bear witness to the War of 1812. His beloved Liverpool had come a long way since the early years of the American Revolution when his village was completely defenseless. He would not know of the fame Liverpool would garner as a privateering center in the approaching war through the courage of its seafaring population. Still, Simeon had witnessed the vagaries of maritime trade over a long and important time in history including war, peace and embargo. He had seen the affects on his family, his town and his relatives and business associates back in Connecticut. Nova Scotians would continue to persevere and the new war would also pass.

Chapter Twelve

The War of 1812: America's Second War of Independence

The War of 1812 was a direct result of Great Britain's prolonged war with France which prompted the Royal Navy to impress increasing numbers of American sailors using less discretion in the selection process. Once seized, impressed sailors would not be released even when proven to be native born Americans. Most appeals were simply ignored or denied even in high profile cases.[503] These sailors became prisoners, often not allowed off ship for years at a time.

The relentless humiliation finally became unbearable and frustration over the continuing violation of American sovereign rights tipped the scales towards a declaration of war. The United States however, was too weak to seriously challenge Great Britain on the high seas. An alternative rationale had to be developed in order to garner support for a declaration of war. The principle strategy was a threat to attack Canada in hopes of pressuring England to change its impressment policies.

New England States and New York were uniformly opposed to the war, fearing a complete destruction of their maritime enterprise. The Congressional vote however supported a declaration of war. The Senate vote was nineteen for and thirteen against and the House vote was seventy-nine for and forty-nine against. War was declared on June 19, 1812. Ironically, states with less maritime involvement provided the staunchest support for war. There were a number of reasons for this. First, British use of its awesome sea power would have fewer negative consequences for territories that were away from the seashore. Second, the armies of Great Britain were tied up fighting Napoleon and would not likely be available for an inland invasion of America. Third, these states championed two issues that could benefit from war. These were the seizure of Florida from Spain and an invasion of Canada to put an end to British support of continuing Indian attacks along the frontier.

The declaration of war idled many ships in harbors around Long Island Sound. William Wheeler of Fairfield called the war foolish and unnecessary. He noted in his diary on August 14, 1812 that there were eight inactive vessels in Black Rock Harbor.[504] At the outbreak of war the total tonnage of ships harbored in Middletown was 6,000. By the end of the war it was down to 3,537.[505] Surprisingly, sentiment in Norwalk was contrary to the rest of Connecticut. While the people had been less enthusiastic to endorse the rebellion, this time they staunchly supported the War of 1812.[506] Possibly, this was because a larger percentage of Norwalk's commerce involved coastal trade. Regularly scheduled market boats took farmer's produce to New York City, Albany and Troy. This trade was little affected by the vicissitudes of England and France and would continue whether there was war or not.

Great Britain, now at war with America, still needed American trade while the Napoleonic Wars continued. They were especially dependent on New England which provided the bulk of the food supplies supporting Wellington's Army in Spain. They also did not wish to curtail New England's trade with their West Indies islands. These islands had always been dependent on food and supplies from the American colonies or states. British policy even encouraged this trade by advising American merchant ships how to circumvent efforts of the U.S. Navy to prevent it.[507] The British recommended that ships either sail under a foreign flag or use a certificate declaring the destination to be a neutral port such as the Swedish island of St. Bartholomew. This island had been sold to Sweden by France in 1784.[508] The ship could then either divert to its real destination or make arrangements for transfer of goods in the neutral port.

One of the first actions of the war involved Captain Isaac Hull of Derby, Connecticut. When war was declared, he was already a veteran naval officer with fourteen years experience. He began his career as a lieutenant on the *Constitution* where he participated in the Undeclared War with France during a cruise off the coast of Hispaniola. He then served as commander on several other vessels which included a mission in the Mediterranean against the Barbary States. By 1811, he was back onboard the *Constitution*, this time as its commander. In July of 1812, Captain Hull was ordered from the Chesapeake to join up with Commodore Rodgers' squadron already making its way into the North Atlantic. At Boston, Hull's orders were changed holding him in port until further notice. It was too late. Captain Hull, fearing this might happen, hurriedly departed two days before his new orders arrived.

Cruising southeast of Nova Scotia, in the vicinity of the Grand Banks, Hull captured several merchant ships before the looming sails of the British frigate *Guerriere* came into view. Both ships began maneuvering for position as they approached each other.

The *Guerriere* opened fire at long distance and kept up a continuous fire while approaching. The shots caused little damage and several even bounced off the *Constitution's* solid oak construction, instantly garnering it the nickname of "Old Ironsides."[509] The guns of the *Constitution* remained silent. At point blank range, Captain Hull finally gave the order to fire. In a matter of minutes the *Guerriere* was shredded. Its sails, masts and rigging were all down and water poured in from hull damage. Boarding parties from each ship tried to cross over but were prevented from doing so by a violent sea, wildly pitching decks and deadly musket and pistol fire from the opposing sides. The *Constitution* eased away from the *Guerriere*, which was now just a hulk, and accepted its surrender. Unable to tow or salvage the badly damaged ship, the British crew was transferred and the *Guerriere* was sent to the bottom.

British losses were fifteen dead and sixty-two wounded. There were also about twenty-four missing British crewmen who were probably hurled overboard and drowned when the masts and rigging came down. American losses were seven killed and seven wounded.

Back in Long Island Sound, ship owners were uncertain about their prospects. In the Fairfield and Westport area many ships took shelter within Southport Harbor on the Mill River. The harbor had no defenses however, and was vulnerable to enemy raid. Most Revolutionary War fortifications were in poor condition and abandoned. In October, the British took advantage of this vulnerability to strike at Southport, capturing several ships and destroying one. Two ships in the harbor did manage to fight off their attackers and escape.[510] The next year, volunteers raised an earthen fort at the mouth of the harbor but Governor Smith failed to deliver a field piece as promised. The resourceful residents however, found a buried twelve pounder in Black Rock and a six pounder in Westport.

British warships also ventured across the Sound to strike Port Jefferson. The *Indemnity* and *Parmoon* managed to slip into the harbor unnoticed and came away with seven merchant ships. One of the merchant ships ran aground and was burned while the other six were later ransomed back to their owners.[511]

Another famous victory for the United States Navy occurred in 1812 that would have significant impact on Long Island Sound for the remainder of the war. On December 4, the U.S. frigate *United States* arrived in New London with a captured British frigate. In an engagement that lasted only seventeen minutes, Commodore Stephen Decatur had defeated the *Macedonian* at a cost of twelve killed and wounded while the British had 104 casualties. Commodore Decatur was treated as a hero in New London. After some repairs were made, the two ships continued down the Sound into New York. New Londoners would see both ships again and Commodore Decatur would not receive such a warm welcome when he returned the second time.

Great Britain decided on a war strategy emphasizing its naval strength and superiority while its army was fully occupied in Europe. They began with a blockade of the Middle Atlantic States and then began extending it to the south and north. This presented a dynamic situation for merchants who had to decide whether to send their vessels out and what their destination port should be.

Captain Jeremiah Holmes, part owner of the fast sailing sloop *Hero*, prevailed on his partners to approve a coastal trading voyage from Mystic to Charleston, South Carolina. In February 1813, the British were in the process of extending and strengthening their blockade of U.S. ports and the trip would be hazardous. However, a profit of between 200 and 400 percent was possible for rice, wheat and hemp due to the glut of produce in one port and scarcity in another.[512] This was a powerful inducement. The trip to Charleston took six days, every one of which required course changes to dodge enemy vessels.

The return trip to Mystic, Connecticut was just as harrowing. At one point near Martha's Vineyard, the *Hero* became sandwiched between two British frigates and a privateering brig, the *Sir John Sherbrooke* of Liverpool, Nova Scotia. The privateer had the best chance of intercepting them but fortunately, began to veer away when one of the frigates came too close. The Nova Scotia sailors were just as afraid of the British frigate as the Americans because they feared becoming the target of impressment into the Royal Navy.[513]

At four o'clock the next morning, the *Hero* ran past the reefs at Watch Hill and into Long Island Sound where they were shocked to again encounter the *Sherbrooke*. The Nova Scotia privateer had run up the American flag and had picked up a pilot from Edgartown on Martha's Vineyard to guide them along dangerous coastal waters. Local pilots were paid a princely sum of as much as one hundred dollars a day to perform such traitorous service.[514] With full sails flying, Captain Holmes slipped around Fishers Island and into the safety of his home port in the Mystic River.

The voyage had been a considerable personal risk to Jeremiah. As discussed in the previous chapter, he had been impressed into the British Navy in 1804 but managed to escape and return home in 1807. If his ship was captured, the British could classify him as a deserter from the Royal Navy, subject to execution. He decided to stay on land for awhile after this and so he sold his share of the *Hero*.

Adam Pond, commander of the Milford built privateer *Sine qua non*, also had to contend with the changing conditions and modify his itinerary. On one trip in early 1813, he went to Bordeaux, France and traded for a cargo of brandy destined for New York City. On his approach to New York he found the harbor blockaded from Sandy Hook across to Long Island. He simply reversed course and sailed around Montauk Point, Long Island to enter the Sound from the east. His Port of New York destination was then reached by the back door passage through Hell Gate and the East River.

On a later voyage returning from the West Indies, Captain Adam Pond found both entrances blockaded. Undaunted, he devised another scheme to circumvent the blockade. Finding clear sailing into Narragansett Bay, Rhode Island, Pond transferred his cargo of sugar into wagons at Providence. The caravan then proceeded overland to the Connecticut River at Haddam, a distance of about seventy-five miles.[515] There the sugar was transferred to another ship which traveled downriver and into the interior of Long Island Sound and thence to New York City. The additional transportation expenses were easily absorbed by the considerable profit made. The sugar was purchased for six cents a pound and sold for twenty-six cents in New York, an increase of 400 percent.[516]

The blockade was extended to New York Harbor. In March, 1813 Captain Sir Thomas Hardy departed Halifax on the seventy-four gun, man-of-war, *Ramillies*, to rendezvous with his squadron off of New York. Hardy was an experienced commander who had participated in many naval engagements. He was considered a hero in the Battle of Trafalgar where Lord Nelson died in his arms.

In New York Harbor at that time were the U.S. Navy frigates *United States* with forty-four guns and the *Macedonian* with thirty-eight guns as well as the twenty gun schooner, *Hornet*. Repairs had been completed and the ships were now preparing to return to sea. Commodore Decatur needed to find a way to extract his little fleet from the trap this harbor had become. He decided to slip out the back entrance via Long Island Sound although he would have to negotiate the hazardous narrows of Hell Gate.

Also in port was the *Scourge*, a fast sailing, 248 ton privateer schooner commanded by Samuel Nicoll of Stratford, Connecticut. Samuel was the son of General Mathias Nicoll, a merchant with enterprises in both Stratford and New York. His ship carried fifteen guns and a crew of 110 and was owned by a consortium of New York merchants. Captain Nicoll was also ready to embark on a cruise and decided to join up with Commodore Stephen Decatur's ships as they made their way into the open ocean.

The four ships departed on May 24 in a thunderstorm. The *United States* was struck by lightening and scraped bottom while in the narrows, but came through without major damage. The bolt of lightening struck the main mast and the powerful current streaked down through the ship and into the water.[517] Fortunately, it did not touch off the powder magazines and the only damage consisted of several copper plates being blown off the hull. After negotiating the narrows however, Commodore Decatur decided to tarry within the Sound for several days before making his run out the other end. Unfortunately, this gave the British time to gain intelligence on his movements and shift some forces to engage him at the other end of the Sound.[518]

Captain Nicoll could not understand the reason for the delay and decided to separate from the Navy ships and make a speedier departure. As a result, the *Scourge* made it out into the North Atlantic before British warships sealed off the eastern end of the Sound. It would be almost a year before the *Scourge* returned to American waters and her voyage would be a phenomenal success.

Meanwhile, Commodore Decatur took seven days to reach the eastern end of the Sound and then anchored his ships on the Connecticut side of Fishers Island. Anchored on the other side of the island was the *Ramillies*. Commodore Hardy had only just arrived there a few days earlier to participate in a prisoner exchange which had been arranged at New London.[519]

The *United States, Macedonian* and *Hornet* made their attempt to break out on the morning of June 1 and were prepared to do battle with the *Ramillies*. However, as they rounded Fishers Island and prepared their guns for action, Commodore Decatur spotted three more British ships sailing towards them from Montauk Point. They were the seventy-four gun, *Valiant*, forty-eight gun, *Acasta* and thirty-eight gun, *Orpheus*. Decatur's only option was to reverse course and dash into New London Harbor on the Thames River. His ships were now trapped and would remain there for the rest of the war. New Londoners were unhappy about this state of affairs as they believed this would make their city the target of another attack by the British similar to the invasion and destruction they endured during the Revolutionary War.

Over the next several months, Commodore Hardy gradually increased the number of ships he had patrolling the eastern entrance of Long Island Sound. At the same time, Americans were trying to find ways to disrupt British blockades along the east coast. In March of

1813, Congress passed legislation encouraging private enterprise to develop torpedoes, submarine instruments and any other destructive machines which could destroy British ships. The intent was to use these devices to break British blockades. The British would come to label all such devices as "infernal machines."

The first such device was constructed by John Scudder, Jr., a New York entrepreneur. He took an old schooner called the *Eagle* and filled it with gunpowder kegs, stones, a quantity of sulfur and some turpentine. This huge, floating bomb had two flintlock firing devices at the ends of cords attached to two barrels of flour up on deck. Movement of either barrel would set off the explosion. Scudder's goal was to destroy the *Ramillies* which was anchored or cruising just outside the port of New London. His reward would be a prize worth $150,000.

The *Eagle* departed from New York and arrived at Millstone Point in Waterford on June 25 where it anchored within sight of the *Ramillies*. When Captain Hardy sent a boarding party to investigate, the crew of the *Eagle* went ashore and took up firing positions. Once the British sailors were onboard, the *Eagle's* crew commenced firing. Their objective was to force the British boarding party to immediately set sail before they could explore the ship. The scheme worked perfectly and the enemy was forced to cut the anchor cable to make a quick escape.[520] Without an anchor, Scudder knew that Captain Hardy would have to tie the ship up to his own vessel. The *Ramillies* however, had recently captured another ship and Hardy ordered that the *Eagle* be tied to that vessel instead. At two-thirty in the afternoon one of the flour barrels was moved. The explosion obliterated both vessels and shot 900 feet in the air. The British lost ten killed in the affair but the *Ramillies*, almost one mile away, survived.

Two other infernal machines were either ready to go or were under development. Within about a week of the *Eagle* explosion, a man from Norwich (name unknown) attempted to destroy the *Ramillies* using a submarine of the same design as the *Turtle* developed by David Bushnell in 1776. In three separate attacks, the submarine successfully passed underneath the hull of the British warship but the missions failed for the same reason the *Turtle* failed; an inability to attach the explosive device to the hull.[521] The development of torpedoes (actually floating mines) was also in progress in New York City and attempts with these devices would soon be made.

Commodore Hardy, growing increasingly concerned and nervous about these new methods of warfare, moved his anchorage across the Sound to Gardiners Bay. He also ordered that a cable be run under his ship and scraped along the hull every two hours to detect foreign objects that might be attached to it.[522]

British crewmen often went ashore on Fishers, Plum, Gull and Gardiners Islands. Commodore Hardy regularly dined with John Gardiner on his island. This piece of intelligence was noted carefully by Joshua Penny of East Hampton, Long Island. Penny conceived a plan to capture Hardy on one of his visits to Gardiner's home. He took the plan to Commodore Decatur in New London who approved the project and provided additional crewmen for the mission.[523]

Four small boats departed one night in late July and Penny's vessel landed on Gardiners Island to wait for what they hoped would be a visit by Commodore Hardy. Unfortunately, the ship's tender that came ashore was from the frigate *Orpheus* rather than the *Ramillies*. For some reason, Penny chose not to wait for another opportunity and captured the seven men and one boy who came ashore from the tender. He took their signed statements (parole of honor) which could be used for later prisoner exchange, then released them and departed the island.

Commodore Hardy would soon turn the tables on Joshua Penny and succeed where Joshua had failed. In a short time, Hardy had developed an excellent intelligence system and received information from a variety of sources in the New London area, Eastern Long Island and New York City.

It wasn't long before Penny became involved in another developing scheme. New Yorker, Thomas Welling, traveled to New London and met with Commodore Decatur and then with Joshua Penny to discuss his plans to utilize whaleboats filled with explosives. Welling wanted to utilize Penny as a local pilot with expert knowledge of Gardiners Bay. Commodore Hardy soon learned of this scheme and of Penny's role in the attempt to kidnap him on Gardiners Island. On August 21, a Sag Harbor ship captain got word to the Commodore that he had overheard boastful remarks made by Penny about using floating mines.[524]

The perpetrator now became the quarry. Hardy sprang into action and brazenly sent a lieutenant into Sag Harbor to find out where

Penny lived. That night a raiding party went ashore and dragged Penny back to the *Ramillies* where he was held prisoner. The villagers were terrified of the power of the British Navy and its ability to destroy Sag Harbor if it wished. No one made any attempt to interfere and apparently didn't even notify Penny that he was in danger.

Word of Joshua Penny's capture gradually made its way to President James Madison. The President ordered that two British prisoners of war be held as hostages to insure the safe return of Joshua.[525] That fall, Commodore Hardy sailed for Halifax and took Penny with him. There, the British decided to set Penny free rather than risk an incident with uncertain consequences. He returned to Long Island Sound with Commodore Hardy on the *Ramillies* and was released.

The British Navy appeared to be invincible everywhere in or around Long Island Sound during the early days of the blockade. One defensive effort succeeded however. Jeremiah Holmes organized a rescue that prevented capture of the American sloop *Victory* in June. Heading into the Mystic River, this sloop had gone aground at Ram Point on Mason Island and was waiting for high tide to float free. Standing on a hill near his home, Jeremiah spotted two enemy barges making their way towards the stranded vessel. He collected a number of volunteers who boarded the fishing smack *Charleston*. They put a four pounder cannon onboard and sailed out to successfully turn the foe away. Later they built Fort Rachel on the west bank of the Mystic River to deter further incursions. The British nicknamed this fort "The Hornet's Nest."[526]

Another minor British action that did not succeed took place on October 25. The British Brig-of-War, *Bores* gave chase to several American ships near Fairfield and remained in the area all day. Later, it captured a small sloop bound for New York and put a two man crew aboard the prize. A strong south wind blew up which damaged the sloop's foremast and drove the vessel onto the beach. The two British sailors were immediately captured.

The British Navy initially acted with restraint along the northeastern seaboard so as not to turn the people into hardened enemies. They were aware that these states had voted against war, had done little to prepare coastal defenses and did not want their militias used in an aggressive fashion. The New England States even convened a conference to discuss the possibility of secession.

The British government was also acutely aware of the fact that Wellington's army in Spain relied almost entirely on food supplies transported from Connecticut and Massachusetts. Special licenses and protection guarantees were provided to Long Island Sound merchant vessels engaged in provisioning their army. These ships were allowed to pass through the blockade unimpeded and were also protected from seizure anywhere on the high seas.[527] The supplies were unloaded in Lisbon or Cadiz, allies of Great Britain. Technically, trade with Great Britain's allies did not violate trade restrictions although everyone knew the true destination was the British Army. Government officials and customs agents in Massachusetts and Connecticut looked the other way and even the U.S. Congress took no action as long as Wellington's Army remained tied up fighting Napoleon in Spain.

Commodore Hardy's task was difficult and he had to operate within a fine line. He needed to exhibit the awesome power of the British Navy to intimidate the populace yet show restraint in using that force. When learning that whaleboats were being prepared as torpedoes, Hardy sent a threatening letter to the local justice of the peace in Sag Harbor with a copy to Commodore Decatur. In it, he warned the inhabitants of towns along the coast of Long Island that he would destroy every house near the shore if people allowed these devices to remain.

Commodore Hardy maintained excellent intelligence on activities around New London, the Eastern end of Long Island and New York City. Undoubtedly, he had a network of spies who provided a steady stream of both routine and militarily significant information.[528] One of his informants was probably Elizabeth Coles Stewart. She was a native of New London and wife of a British Consulate officer expelled from the city. Although never proven, these espionage efforts probably thwarted two attempts by Commodore Decatur to get his three naval vessels out of the Thames River and Long Island Sound under cover of total darkness. The first came on December 12, 1813 and the second on March 8, 1814. In both cases, blue lights were observed on each side of the mouth of the Thames River. Decatur assumed these were signal lights used by informants to warn the British Navy of the breakouts and he was forced to call off both attempts.

At the same time, Commodore Hardy tried to cultivate good will through public relations schemes. One of these involved the release of an impressed sailor by the name of John Carpenter. He was a native of nearby Norwich, who had been impressed five years previously and was now assigned to the *Ramillies*. Carpenter's father had sent Hardy a letter begging for his son's release. Seeing a good opportunity, the Commodore made sure John Carpenter was paid all back wages and then gave him a ceremonious send off to great acclaim.[529] People tended to overlook the fact there were many other sailors wrongly impressed onto the *Ramillies* who were not local boys.

There weren't many opportunities for British sailors to escape from their ships. Patrol boats were rowed around the fleet anchorage in Gardiners Bay every night. These boats served a dual purpose of guarding against attack by infernal machines and also for detecting escape attempts by crewmen, many of whom had not been off a ship in years.

A successful, fourteen man break out was made from the frigate *Acasta* on the night of September 13, 1813 using one of the very patrol boats that kept the men confined on their floating prison. During a patrol boat crew change just after midnight, two conspirators remained on the launch and twelve additional plotters joined them. When shipboard officers finally understood the scheme to be an escape, the patrol boat was beyond effective musket fire and rockets failed to illuminate their position. The escapees tried to row directly across the Sound but tidal currents drove them in a northeast direction until they heard waves breaking on Fishers Island. At first light, they continued around the eastern end of the island and across an additional three miles of open ocean into the village of Stonington.

The fourteen escapees were warmly received and given breakfast at York's Tavern.[530] They sold their patrol boat, a twelve oared vessel with sails, and traveled to New London where they melted into American society.

Privateering again played an important role although it frequently carried a negative sentiment in the minds of people who thought of it as a mostly mercenary activity. Considering the situation however, it was a necessity. America had almost no Navy and little money to develop one. American privateers made 500 captures during the first seven months of the war and as many as 2,000 during the duration of the conflict.

The *Scourge*, with Captain Nicoll of Stratford in command, was one of the most successful privateers. After escaping through the eastern end of Long Island Sound in late May, just before it was fully blockaded, Captain Nicoll headed across the Atlantic. His hunting grounds would be right on the doorstep of Great Britain. Alone, the Scourge captured twenty-seven vessels and 420 prisoners. Another twenty-three ships were captured while in consort with the *Rattlesnake*.[531] Much of the action took place in the North Sea, Norwegian Sea and Barents Sea with the latter involving British commerce with the Russian port of Archangel.

The *Scourge's* voyage almost ended prematurely when the ship was spotted in July off the North Cape of Norway by the British frigate, *Alexandria* and sloop *Spitfire*. Captain Nicoll had just joined up with the American Navy frigate *President* whom Nicoll initially mistook for the *United States*, the ship he only recently left behind in Long Island Sound. The *President* was actually its sister ship. A running battle commenced but the *Scourge* was easily able to slip away as the British concentrated their fire entirely on the *President*, ignoring the schooner. Eventually the *President* also broke free and lost her pursuers.

At the end of July 1813, the *Scourge* crossed paths with the American privateer *Rattlesnake* and the two captains decided to work together for the rest of the summer. Apparently, the *Rattlesnake's* captain had previously organized a highly efficient system for processing a large volume of captured ships. This is evidenced by the agreement that two thirds of each prize value would go to the *Rattlesnake* while *Scourge* accepted one third despite the relatively equal size of both ships.[532]

The prize ship processing system involved several elements that were put in place with the help of Danish officials at Trondheim, Norway. At the time, Norway was a possession of Denmark. The first element involved establishment of a small fort with one cannon on an island guarding the entrance to Trondheim Fiord. This was built and furnished by Americans but manned by Danes they hired. Second, a compliment of hired Danish sailors was maintained at the fort. When British ships were captured, a prize crew brought the ship to the protected island and transferred it to a Danish crew. The Americans were then free to immediately rejoin their ship while the Danes sailed the prize the rest of the way to Trondheim, deep within the Fiord. There the spoils were libeled and adjudicated by the legal system. In August alone the two ships captured and processed an astounding total of 19 English vessels using this system.

The *Scourge* spent much of the winter in Trondheim and some of the original crew left on another ship for home. In March 1814, Captain Nicoll turned the ship over to Lieutenant Robert Perry for the journey home while he remained behind in Trondheim continuing to oversee the disposition of spoils brought in. Lieutenant Perry finally reached Cape Cod in May. He had captured another fifteen ships on his way home.

Privateers operating out of Liverpool, Nova Scotia were very successful in capturing American ships. Among the ships captured were the *Betsey* of New London and the schooner *George Washington* out of New Haven. This last vessel must have had official business as it was not accepted for condemnation by the Nova Scotia Court of Vice-Admiralty.[533]

The most successful British or American privateer, and perhaps the most successful of all time, was the *Liverpool Packet* out of Liverpool, Nova Scotia. It was a small schooner of only fifty-four tons. It was just fifty-three feet long, nineteen feet wide at the beam and carried only five guns. The *Packet* was a captured slave ship tender which was built for speed. It had slim lines, raked masts and a raked keel which made it exceedingly fast for the purpose of carrying illegal trade.[534] It could also sail closer to the wind than most ships. This ship captured well over one hundred American vessels, fifty of which arrived safely in Nova Scotia for adjudication by the Court of Vice-Admiralty.

The blockade of New York and Long Island Sound continued and was strengthened in 1814. Americans also continued to explore methods of destroying British ships participating in the blockade.

In March, a New York entrepreneur by the name of Ryker developed a torpedo that he attached to floating buoys. The design dictated that the device be released up tide of the target ship and a line paid out as the tide carried it towards the target. When a crossbar on the rope caught on one of the ship's anchor cables, the torpedo would continue to float with the tide but would also be drawn in towards the ship. This movement would also trip a spring causing the firing mechanism to detonate the explosives.[535]

Ryker made arrangements with Jeremiah Holmes to carry out the attack and Commodore Decatur also made plans to use the event for another attempt to get his three vessels out of Long Island Sound. He hoped the attack would cause enough of a diversion to allow his ships to sneak out. Two nighttime missions were run and both were failures. In the first one, the cable line attached to the torpedo fouled on the bottom and had to be cut away. In the second attempt on March 24, Holmes targeted the seventy-four gun *La Hogue* anchored off Fishers Island. They encountered difficulty positioning the device and a sudden strain on the crossbar tripped the detonator prematurely. The explosion was impressive but was a near miss. The perpetrators escaped into the darkness.

The aftermath of this failure was important for two reasons. First, search boats brought in a man who had been in the area on a small skiff. The British named him "Torpedo Jack" and induced him to pilot a retaliatory raid into the Connecticut River in retribution for this latest infernal machine attack.[536] Second, Commodore Decatur determined that any further escape attempts would be futile while a strong blockade was being maintained by the British.

The three navy ships remained in the Thames River at Norwich for the rest of the war. Captain Biddle of the *Hornet* stayed behind as caretaker. Captain Jacob Jones of the *Macedonian* transferred with his crew to the Great Lakes. Commodore Decatur and his crew transferred by land to New York and took over the frigate *President* which had successfully run the blockade returning from a cruise to the West Indies. The *President* remained in port for almost another year and was captured in February 1815 by four British ships while attempting to break out of New York Harbor.

The identity of "Torpedo Jack" is unknown but many suspect his real name was Jeremiah Glover, a resident of Essex (then known as

Potapoug).[537] Using Glover as a guide, the British planned a daring raid on the port and shipyards of Essex located six miles inland from the mouth of the Connecticut River. The harbor was filled with merchant ships and privateering vessels that were idled by the blockade and there were several more vessels nearing completion in the shipyards.

Led by Captain Richard Coote, five barges filled with 136 men were sent off from four British ships at four o'clock in the morning. Rowing with an incoming tide, the raiders quickly arrived in Essex and took control of the village. The surprised residents made no organized resistance and agreed not to contest the operation in return for an agreement to spare the town. Within a few hours, twenty-six ships were on fire but Richard Glover's vessel was spared destruction.

The British departed with two privateers, the *Black Prince* and the *Eagle*, in tow but soon ran into difficulty making progress due to wind and tide. The two privateers had to be cut loose and burned. Local militia forces also began to organize along both banks of the river and fire on the barges. Two of the raiders were killed and one wounded before they reached the river's mouth. Richard Glover was later put ashore on Fishers Island.[538]

The final attempt to destroy a British warship via the use of an infernal machine was made in June. This latest invention actually looked like a turtle and had a slightly arched, ironclad upper surface, only one foot of which was above water line.[539] It maneuvered with the use of a screw propeller operated by nine to twelve men inside the vessel and carried five floating mines that could be towed and released independently.

Built in New York, the vessel made its way along the north shore of Long Island but foundered during a storm and washed ashore near Southold on June 26. As the frigate *Maidstone* and sloop *Sylph* approached to investigate, the crew and local farmers struggled to dismantle and carry away parts of the vessel they wished to keep secret. British officers carefully evaluated the craft taking measurements and making sketches before destroying it with explosives.

Napoleon was finally overthrown in April 1814. After this, England's government decided to put more pressure on the United States.

They placed the aggressive, anti-American, Vice Admiral Alexander Cochrane in charge of their North American Station at Bermuda. There was no longer any reason for the British to use restraint in their dealings with New England. Orders soon came down the line placing Commodore Thomas Hardy in charge of invading Eastport in Passamaquoddy Bay, Maine, supported by an army regiment under command of Lieutenant Colonel Thomas Pilkington. Under threat of destruction, the village and its fort surrendered without a fight on July 11. Shortly after, other British vessels and army forces captured Castine, Belfast, Hamden, Bangor and Machias.

On July 18, Admiral Cochrane issued orders of vengeance and retaliation to commanders of all squadrons along the eastern seaboard under his command. This was in response to an isolated incident of depredation committed by American forces on the Canadian border. Cochrane's unrestricted language stated that "You are hereby required and directed to destroy and lay waste such towns and districts upon the coast as you may find assailable."[540] The direct result of this order was an attack on Stonington, Connecticut. Cochrane would also use it as guidance for his own mission that summer when British forces burned Washington, DC but failed in an attack on Baltimore and Fort McHenry.

In early August, Commodore Hardy's squadron of ships returned to Long Island Sound from Maine. Additional warships arrived along with Rear Admiral Sir Henry Hotham. He brought instructions directly from Admiral Cochrane who wanted to launch a coordinated effort all along the eastern seaboard implementing his orders of mass destruction. Admiral Cochrane would personally oversee the Chesapeake Bay portion of the plan while Admiral Hotham was charged with developing a significant action somewhere along the northern blockade area. By August 7, Gardiners Bay was packed with British warships in addition to those on patrol off of New London. The biggest ships included two of ninety guns, four of seventy-four guns, four frigates and a brig.

For security reasons, British Royal Marines landed on Montauk Point and ordered all of the inhabitants living on ten miles of the outward most portion of the peninsula to immediately vacate the area.[541] The British did not want their enemy to have any view of ship movements around the entrance to Long Island Sound or across to Rhode Island, Block Island or Martha's Vineyard. They had previously put the lighthouse on Gull Island out of commission for this very reason.

Rear Admiral Hotham appointed Captain Hardy to lead the mission and relied on his expertise and local knowledge to select the target. Hardy was probably appalled by this task as it was contrary to his nature. The mission involved no military objective. The goal was pure, wanton destruction. Stonington was selected for no other reason than it was in an exposed location, lightly defended, offered the least risk (or so the British thought) and presented no sensitive political ramification. New York City, New London, Mystic, Sag Harbor and other locations within Long Island Sound were all ruled out for various reasons.

What the British failed to consider, or never really understood, was Stonington's history of fierce independence dating back to 1649. They also may have forgotten their own failed attempt to destroy Stonington in 1775, thirty-nine years previously. In that attack, the villagers refused to give up their town, prevented troops from landing and withstood a day long bombardment.

The first indication of impending danger to the village of Stonington came in the late afternoon of August 9 when several ships were spotted making their way up through Fishers Island Sound. Among them were a frigate, brig and, worst of all, a bomb ship called the *Terror*. Bomb ships were designed to destroy land targets and carried mortars which could lob large explosive shells and firebombs over intervening obstructions. These weapons, along with Congreve rockets, could saturate areas that ship cannons could not reach.

As a precaution, the towns two eighteen pounder cannons were taken out of the armory and installed behind a four foot high, previously prepared earthworks. The frigate *Pactolus* anchored off of Stonington Point and sent a barge towards shore under a flag of truce. They were met by a boat carrying Captain Amos Palmer, Dr. William Lord and Lieutenant Hough. By now, nearly the entire population of the village had made their way to the point, anxious to understand the situation.

Captain Palmer was handed a one sentence message signed by Captain Hardy which bluntly stated: "Not wishing to destroy the unoffending Inhabitants residing in the Town of Stonington, one hour is granted them from the receipt of this to remove out of the town."[542] This was an ultimatum and the British officer was instructed to advise that Commodore Hardy was under orders and no further discussion could be granted. The Americans were reported to have replied that "We shall defend this place to the last extremity; should it be destroyed, we shall perish in its ruins."[543]

Back on shore the entire village elected to stand and fight. Messengers were sent to New London appealing for militia troops and any other military assistance that could be provided. Fire brigades were organized and other preparations made. Meanwhile, the British ships moved into bombardment positions. At eight o'clock in the evening, two hours after Hardy's message was delivered, the first rockets lifted skyward, followed by the large and then small mortar on the bomb ship. The initial bombardment ended at midnight and there was reason for optimism in the village. The fire brigades had done a good job of dousing fires and containing damage. Also, a substantial number of militia had already arrived from as far away as Norwich. On the negative side, General Cushing decided to hold all of his U.S. Army forces in New London fearing Stonington was just a feint and that the enemy's real goal was to burn the U.S. Navy vessels still trapped in the Thames River, north of New London.

The bombardment began again before dawn. This time, fire was directed towards the western side of the Stonington peninsula in order to divert attention away from ships moving around the eastern side where ground troops were preparing to land. When rocket fire suddenly erupted from support barges on the eastern side, the danger of British troops transferring to one of the barges was revealed.

The defenders dragged their only six pounder and one of their two eighteen pounders out of the earthworks and down to the shore on the Point where they would have a better chance of repelling the landing. Illuminated by rocket fire, a well aimed shot fired from the eighteen pounder tore into the landing barge.[544] Survivors were picked up by other vessels and the landing attempt was aborted. The brig *Dispatch* then moved to within a half mile of shore to provide covering fire. The exposed position of the eighteen pounder meant that it had to be abandoned and spiked to prevent its use by the British. The defenders were able to take the six pounder and retreat back to the earthworks.

At this point, Jeremiah Holmes arrived at the earthworks and assumed command of the eighteen pounder. Taking aim at the *Dispatch*, his first shot, double loaded, scored a direct hit. Jeremiah learned his skill well as a gun captain during the years he had been impressed in the British Navy. Unfortunately, the defenders soon expended all of their gunpowder. The eighteen pounder fell silent and was spiked.

A desperate search of the town was made to find any gunpowder available. Dickie Loper, a fourteen-year-old boy, finally discovered a six keg supply owned by Thomas Swan who was away from the area at the time.[545] They were being stored for use in the cannons of his privateering vessel *Halka*. After the kegs were transported to the earthworks, Mr. Cobb, the blacksmith, drilled out the spike from the touchhole and the eighteen pounder came alive again.

Fortunately, the British forces were in a state of disarray during the time that the cannons were out of action. Even though the bombardment continued, they couldn't capitalize on the advantage they held. The frigate *Pactolus*, carrying Captain Hardy, had gone aground near Napatree Point, temporarily putting it out of commission. Hardy's flagship *Ramillies* had not yet arrived from Gardiners Bay. The brig *Dispatch* was beginning to take on more water than its pumps could handle due to continuing battle damage. As this vessel began to move out of range, Jeremiah Holmes touched off one last shot which struck the starboard quarter causing additional casualties onboard.

By noon on August 10, all ships were beyond the range of Stonington's eighteen pounder and only the *Terror* continued lobbing occasional shells into the village. General Isham of the Connecticut Militia arrived to take command. He allowed Colonel Isaac Williams and Dr. William Lord to row out under flag of truce to the recently arrived *Ramillies* in order to find out what the British forces intended next.

Commodore Hardy conversed pleasantly with the two village representatives and told them the attack "was not of his own doing, was the most unpleasant expedition he had ever undertaken."[546] Although Hardy knew differently, he declared the reason for the attack was due to Stonington's involvement with torpedoes. The representatives vehemently denied any torpedo involvement by Stonington and this disclaimer was accepted by Hardy.

The conversation then turned to Elizabeth Coles Stewart, the American born wife of James Stewart who had been the British

Vice Consul in New London charged with arranging prisoner exchanges. The previous summer, James had been ordered to leave the country due to alleged espionage activity and for providing (selling) protection documents to merchant vessels allowing them to pass through the blockade and trade unimpeded with Cadiz and Lisbon. Elizabeth was also suspected of espionage activity although her movements had never been restricted. Commodore Hardy demanded that Mrs. Stewart be allowed to embark on the *Ramillies* the next morning in exchange for discontinuing the destruction of Stonington.

Hardy had information that the two village representatives probably did not know. Three days before, Vice Admiral Hotham had sent a message into New London demanding the release of Mrs. Stewart and her children to the custody of her husband who was on the frigate *Forth* anchored off New London. General Cushing, responding on behalf of New London, stated that he had no authority to comply and was transmitting the message to the United States Federal Government. Since the matter involved a diplomat, it fell within federal jurisdiction. General Cushing added that he expected the decision (from Washington) would be favorable.[547]

It is not known exactly what was said onboard the *Ramillies* by Dr. Lord and Colonel Williams. Apparently, they promised to deliver Mrs. Stewart or at least make a concerted effort to do so because that expectation was contained in Commodore Hardy's written response to officials in Stonington.[548] Perhaps Hardy knew they couldn't comply with his request but he could still use their failure to shift the blame onto the town of Stonington when the bombardment resumed. Hardy could thus clear his conscience and absolve himself and the British command from allegations of senseless destruction.

The shelling continued until sunset on August 10 and then Commodore Hardy called a temporary cease fire. Stonington made good use of the time. The eighteen pounder was recovered from the Stonington Point shoreline and the touchhole was drilled out. The three cannons were all useable again. People roamed through the town scavenging for unexploded shells hurled from the bomb ship. Each one carried seven pounds of powder and a significant amount was salvaged. Nearly three regiments of militia were now on hand making any landing by British troops impossible.

During the morning of August 11, messages were sent to Commodore Hardy explaining that the issue of releasing Mrs. Stewart and her children was being referred to the United States Secretary of War. Neither New London or Stonington had any authority to rule on the matter. The *Terror* resumed its bombardment at three o'clock in the afternoon. The next morning, August 12, the *Ramillies* and *Pactouis* also moved in and sent several final broadsides into the village. Most of these round shot shells whistled over the town and landed harmlessly in tidal marshes. Simultaneously, the British ships began departing and by afternoon all had weighed anchor and moved down the coast.

The Battle of Stonington was over but one small incident was yet to play out that day. Many of the British ships temporarily anchored in Fishers Island Sound opposite Groton Long Point. Several squads of American militiamen were shifted from Stonington to this point to keep watch. They concocted a scheme to capture a British barge from the bomb ship *Terror* by luring it across the Sound. The bait was a large fishing vessel which they sailed out of the Mystic River. The British barge with fourteen men aboard attempted to intercept the fishing vessel. Acting surprised, confused and frightened, the American sailors ran their vessel onto the beach at Long Point and escaped over the bank just ahead of the barge. The militiamen hidden behind the bank then rose up and fired on the enemy, killing one and wounding two. Surrender quickly followed. The captives were gracious and, in return, were well taken care of. When later exchanged, the citizens of Mystic took up a collection and gave one hundred dollars to the British Commander, Lieutenant Chambers. The American militiamen shared a reward of $1200 for condemnation of the barge and $1400 for the prisoners.[549]

British casualties during the Battle of Stonington have never been fully revealed or reconciled. Shortly after the battle, the bodies of four men from the destroyed landing barge washed ashore and were buried. Commodore Hardy only admitted two killed and 12 wounded. After the war, officers from the brig *Dispatch* visited Stonington and admitted that total British losses were twenty-one killed and fifty wounded.[550]

The defenders suffered five wounded plus one whose wound was mortal. Nineteen-year-old Frederick Denison was struck in the knee by a fragment of stone blasted off a nearby rock by cannon fire from the *Dispatch*. His wound occurred when he stepped outside of the earthworks in an attempt to re-light the slow match that was used to fire the cannons. Frederick died three months later as a result of complications from his wound.

Damage to Stonington was not severe. Three houses were totally destroyed and about ten others were heavily damaged. Forty other buildings had minor damage.[551] As if the little town had not suffered enough, a little more than a year later an event occurred that did much greater damage than did the British. At the beginning of October 1815, a severe storm, probably a hurricane, ripped every ship in the harbor from their moorings and dashed them against the shore. Fifty homes were destroyed or considerably damaged. During the storm, Benjamin Morrell left his home to help his neighbors. "Soon the seas surrounded his dwelling, and before relief could be given it was swept from its foundations, and its wretched inhabitants, Mrs. Morrill, and child, and a Miss Mott of Block Island, were buried in a watery grave."[552]

The Federal Government quickly approved the departure of Elizabeth Stewart with her seven children and this was accomplished on August 25, 1814. The British settled the family on a farm on nearby Plum Island where James Stewart attempted to implement a smuggling operation that had been previously approved by Admiral Cochrane in Bermuda. The British desperately needed American dollars to buy food for their blockade forces and the smuggling scheme was concocted for that reason.

The Stewart family reunion was short lived. During the night of September 28, a raiding party from Mystic rowed across the Sound, kidnapped James Stewart and imprisoned him on the U.S. Navy ship *United States*. The tables were now turned, to the great amusement of local inhabitants but frustrated outrage of British officials. Admiral Cochrane threatened severe retaliation so the U.S. Government accepted Stewart's parole of honor, defusing the situation.[553]

During the last few months of the war, British naval forces engaged primarily in small scale operations. On Friday, September 30, a British frigate and a brig anchored off Black Rock Harbor in Bridgeport causing great apprehension. Fearing an attack, many residents removed their furniture and sent it away for safe keeping.[554] On Saturday evening, British troops were seen loading into barges and the worst was feared. To the surprise and great relief of everyone, the barges headed away from shore and crossed over to Long Island. They were headed to Setauket Harbor near Port Jefferson where they captured five sloops and burned another one. Upon returning on Sunday, the flotilla beat a hasty retreat eastward to Gardiners Bay.

Two other actions occurred which were surprisingly vicious and the tenacity exhibited by the British could only be ascribed to arrogance and a feeling of entitlement as the greatest sea power on earth. The first episode involved capture of the American privateer brig *General Armstrong* in the Portuguese, Azores Islands. The ship carried seven guns and a crew of ninety men. Earlier in the war it had been commanded by Guy Champlin of New London. In September of 1814, commanded now by Samuel Reid of Norwich, the *General Armstrong* broke through the New York blockade and headed initially to the Azores for supplies. These were neutral waters and accepted as a haven governed by international laws of neutrality.

Within a few hours of Captain Reid's arrival at Faial Island on September 26, a squadron of six British warships also arrived. They were headed to America in support of British plans to invade New Orleans. Commodore Lloyd decided to capture the American brig, even though it was in neutral waters and his actions would violate international law. He would ignore the Portuguese Governor's protest.

Concerned about the situation, Captain Reid cautiously began to move the *General Armstrong* closer to shore. The British brig *Carnation* and four barges went in pursuit forcing Reid to drop anchor and turn broadside to his attackers.[555] When the barges came alongside, the *General Armstrong* opened fire, killing or wounding more than twenty men and forcing them to retreat under cry for quarter (mercy). The Americans had one killed and one wounded.

Captain Reid then resumed his movement of the *General Armstrong* close to the shore, right below a castle, and prepared for the next onslaught. They could have abandoned ship at this point but all chose to stay and fight. The Island Governor and most of the inhabitants now lined the shore. The moon was full and the spectators had a clear view of the unfolding drama which was not long in coming.[556] About midnight, twelve boats carrying 400 men approached. At first, cannon fire was traded but it soon came down to sword, pikes, pistols and muskets as numerous boarding attempts were beaten off in savage fighting. The attackers were slaughtered in about forty minutes of extreme action before the survivors managed to retreat. Three of the boats were captured filled with dead and wounded. In one boat, all but four were dead.

The Governor sent a message to Commodore Lloyd begging him to break off the hostilities. Lloyd, by now in a towering rage, was more determined than ever to have the American privateer and arrogantly threatened to knock down the whole town if necessary.[557] Under these conditions, Captain Reid decided to end the affair and scuttle the ship. The dead and wounded were taken ashore and the crew began removing their personal effects. At dawn, the brig *Carnation* came in close and opened heavy fire but was damaged by return fire from the *General Armstrong*. The remaining crew then went ashore and the vessel was scuttled.

Although the Americans lost their ship, they had put up a brilliant defense. British losses were estimated to have been at least 300 men. The Americans suffered two killed and seven wounded. The enormous British losses for so little gain is hard to understand and can only be attributed to arrogance. Americans were considered inferior and American fighting forces were held in even lower regard. Disciplined British military forces could not fail without severe humiliation to their commanders. The American Consul on the island wrote a dispatch to the United States Secretary of State summarizing the events and outlining the illegal actions taken by the British Navy. In his dispatch he stated that "A few such victories as this, would teach them [the British] better manners."[558]

The second incident occurred in the heart of Long Island Sound when a New Haven packet ship called the *Susan* was captured off of Stratford by a small British sloop-of-war on October 16, 1814. Packet ships were vessels that made trips to certain ports on a regularly scheduled basis. The *Susan* was returning to New Haven from New York with passengers and a valuable cargo.

Word of the capture was swiftly sent via express rider to New Haven where a decision was made to go after the British sloop and its prize. New Haven's coast guard cutter, a fast sailing schooner mounting six guns, was soon manned by Captain John Davis and its usual twenty person crew plus an additional twenty volunteers.[559]

The cutter glided out of the harbor near sundown but their prey was nowhere in sight. Assuming the vessels were headed eastward to the British fleet anchorage in Gardiners Bay, Captain Davis took up a heading to intercept them and maintained that course all night in light wind. The two sloops were spotted at the first grey light of dawn but pleasant thoughts of taking two prize ships were soon extinguished. During the night, an eighteen gun British brig had joined the two vessels. To make matters worse, the cutter's position was sandwiched between Long Island and the enemy vessels. They were trapped.

Intentional grounding was their only option but light wind threatened their chance for escaping. Three whaleboats were then lowered into the water and the schooner was towed to shore. Four of the six guns were removed from the ship and, with the help of local residents, were dragged up a 130 foot sandy bluff.

The British brig and sloop took up position and began a three hour bombardment of the gun battery on top of the bluff and the schooner below. After a three hour break, the bombardment resumed and simultaneously, two barges full of troops were sent shoreward. Captain Davis and three other volunteers rushed down to the cutter and loaded the two remaining cannons with grape shot and canister. After waiting as long as possible, both cannons were fired at relatively short range sending the two barges scurrying back to the brig.

The next morning both ships sailed away. The Americans spent the day patching and pumping water out of the dismasted, heavily damaged cutter and then anchored the disabled vessel off shore for the night. No one suspected the British would care any further about the hulk of a ship, the forty New Haven men and a few Long Island militiamen who had joined them. The following morning however, the British returned in greater force than before. Besides the brig and sloop, they were now accompanied by the frigate *Narcissus*. They must have suffered casualties the previous day to make them so stubborn and determined to save face by turning the defeat into a victory.

The British ships opened with a heavy protecting cannonade and launched seven barges. The defenders fired their muskets and four cannons from the bluff but were unable to prevent the enemy from getting a line on the anchored cutter and towing it away. The British were victorious. The New Haven men walked twenty or twenty-five miles to Port Jefferson where they chartered a sloop to take them home.

There was a paucity of targets for British privateers in 1814 as most American merchant ships remained in port due to the blockade. Only a few enemy ships passed through the blockade and ventured into Long Island Sound to make hit and run raids. They did not remain long.

The famous *Liverpool Packet* from Nova Scotia made one appearance. Earlier in the war this ship had captured the Bridgeport schooner *Little Joe* between Cape Cod and Cape Ann. Now it bore down on two American ships desperately racing for the safety of Bridgeport Harbor. The sloop made it but the schooner *Nancy* grounded on a sandbar at the harbor entrance (Seaside Park).[560] A boarding party from the *Liverpool Packet* clambered onto the *Nancy* but they were within range of a small fort established on Tongue Point. Fire from muskets and a single cannon soon drove off the boarding party and the *Liverpool Packet* sailed away empty handed.

On December 3, 1814, two privateer English Schooners appeared off of Southport Harbor where they lurked all day. They captured two or three small coasting vessels and then vacated the area. A packet ship from New York arrived safely that night without encountering the privateers.

The schooner *Rover* of Liverpool, Nova Scotia passed through the blockade and gave chase to the sloop *Betsey* on January 16, 1815. Unable to escape, the *Betsey* intentionally grounded on a beach at Saybrook, Connecticut allowing its crew to scramble ashore and avoid capture. The *Rover* lowered a barge and sent Lieutenant Siphorus Cole and five men to retrieve the sloop. Meanwhile, residents of Saybrook mustered with surprising speed and rushed to the beach. They were in time to recapture the *Betsey*. In the melee, Lieutenant Cole was killed and the other five Nova Scotia crewmen were captured.[561] Unbeknownst to the combatants, the war had ended two weeks previously.

Benjamin Palmer of Stonington decided to sign onto a privateer late in the war. Because of the blockade, he traveled by land to Newport, Rhode Island and shipped out on the schooner *Rolla* on December 10. Only one day out his ship was chased by the British frigate, *Loire*. The faster sailing *Rolla* almost got away but was captured after its foremast was shot away. Benjamin ended up in Dartmoor Prison, England.

After months of wrangling, the treaty of Ghent was signed on December 24, 1814. The British were broke and tired of war after many years fighting the French. Both sides wanted an end to it and agreed to a return to the status quo as matters stood prior to the war. None of the underlying problems were addressed in the treaty so the war accomplished little. However, the most serious contention, that of impressment, gradually disappeared as a natural consequence of peace itself. After the Battle of Waterloo, Great Britain could reduce the size of its fleet and no longer needed to impress Americans.

Rumors of peace began circulating in early January. Official word of the treaty was carried by express riders making their way along the Post Road to Boston. It was received in Fairfield on February 12 and a major, day long celebration was held there on February 24. The festivities started with an eighteen shot salute fired from a cannon on the parapet which was answered by another cannon on the village green. Following this were parades and military maneuvers, prayer services in the meeting house, speeches and singing accompanied by instruments. Heavy snow began to fall around mid-day as a lavish feast featuring roast oxen was served. About 150 men dined in the Fairfield Academy Building and several hundred women were served in the Court House.[562]

As darkness fell on the Fairfield Green, another eighteen shot salute was fired (one blast for each state). Eighteen tar pots on poles arranged in a cone shape were then lit as the snow continued to fall. The evening concluded with a ball held in Knapp's Tavern on the north corner of the Green. The happy townspeople departed in the snow, cheered by their gaily illuminated homes and the burning tar pots on the Green. They were anxious to move on and face a brighter future.

After peace was announced in New London, British officers from the blockading fleet came ashore and were welcomed. The British released Commodore Decatur and Lieutenant Shubrick who had been captured only a week or two earlier when the U.S. frigate *President* tried to run the blockade out of New York Harbor. The culmination of celebrations in New London was a huge "peace ball" held in the new courthouse that was built to replace the one burned by the British in 1781.[563] Officers on British ships who had been blockading the eastern entrance to Long Island Sound were invited to attend.

Unfortunately, a joyous end to the war was spoiled by a tragic event that occurred at Dartmoor Prison in England. Long after the war ended, there were still large numbers of prisoners waiting for release and transportation home. There were about 10,000 French and American prisoners in Dartmoor and most were still there in April, 1815. These included many from Long Island Sound communities including Pulaski Benjamin of Stratford and Benjamin Palmer of Stonington.

Conditions at Dartmoor, bad to begin with, deteriorated even more when rations were reduced and moldy bread was served. The prisoners demonstrated to demand fresh bread but this only angered Captain Shortland, the jail commandant, who vowed to get even. On April 6, he created an incident to initiate bloody revenge. During sports activity, whenever balls were accidentally knocked over the prison yard wall, the guards would always throw them back inside. On this day the guards did not return the ball. One of the American prisoners thereupon made a hole in the wall and went to retrieve the ball. An alarm was sounded and Captain Shortland organized his troops to fire into the prison yard where there were about 7,000 prisoners gathered to see what all the fuss was about.[564] Seven people were killed immediately and more than thirty wounded, some dying later of their wounds. Pulaski Benjamin reported that the death toll would have been much higher if it had not been for the fact that many of the guards disobeyed the order and fired their guns high over the heads of the prisoners.

Chapter Thirteen

Free at Last

Long Island Sound merchants began immediate preparations to resume full maritime activities after learning in February, 1815 about the Treaty of Ghent, ending the War of 1812. It was a glittering opportunity to re-start failed businesses, earn money to pay off debts that had been suspended or simply to start a new enterprise. Moreover, the treaty and America's spectacular victory at New Orleans sparked the soul of a frustrated, depressed and demoralized people. Action would replace idleness. An upwelling of energy coursed through every shoreline community and navigable waterway leading to the Sound. The lure of the sea and boundless adventure would again stir the imagination. Seamen would return to the sea.

Americans, for the first time, were free to conduct unrestricted maritime trade. This exuberance, enhanced by the shrewdness of a Yankee trader culture forged by nearly 175 years of suppression, would propel America to the forefront of worldwide commercial maritime enterprise. Similarly, a renewed burst of energy thrust Long Island Sound entrepreneurs into a new surge of activity through whaling and sealing enterprises, exploration, shipbuilding and shipping line development. It was a time of rapid change however, and, within a few years, this same driving force would bring the golden age of Long Island Sound to an end.

The saga of the brig, *Commerce* of Cromwell, Connecticut is illustrative of the pent up forces propelling maritime enterprise in 1815. The *Commerce* at 220 tons, eighty-six feet long and twenty-six feet wide at the beam, was a substantial and versatile ship. She had two masts with square rigging but the lower part of the forward mast was fitted out with booms carrying fore and aft sails. This feature allowed her to sail better into the wind. The eleven man crew was a mixture of experienced seamen and younger men anxious for an opportunity to enter the seafaring trade.

At thirty-seven years old, Captain James Riley had twenty-two years of experience. Although the Riley name was associated with a great number of Connecticut River mariners, he was born into a poor farming family. He escaped to sea at fifteen and had been a ship captain since the age of twenty.[565] During good times in 1807, Captain Riley bought a house and fifteen acres on Prospect Hill Road in Cromwell. Now, in 1815, he was deeply in debt, had lost his home, was threatened with debtors prison and his wife, Phoebe was expecting their fifth child.[566] The intervening years had been a disaster for many mariners, including James Riley. When he was offered command of the *Commerce*, James jumped at the opportunity for redemption. Principle owners of the vessel were his second cousin Justus Riley and two other relatives.

The *Commerce* departed on May 2 and headed down the Connecticut River with an unlikely cargo consisting of twenty tons of hay and 25,000 bricks. Two days later they glided past Essex and the remains of the twenty-eight ships which had been burned during the British raid just the previous year. On the third day they entered Long Island Sound. Their initial destination was New Orleans but their journey almost ended on Carysfort Reef as they sailed through the Bahamas.[567] The ship scraped bottom three times but was not punctured.

In New Orleans the hay and bricks were sold and a new cargo of tobacco and flour was loaded onboard for transportation to Gibraltar. They did not purchase this produce but were compensated a set price only for hauling the cargo. They did not share in the potential trade profits but the arrangement still made good business sense. The *Commerce's* primary goal was to purchase salt in the Cape Verde Islands. Gibraltar was somewhat out of the way but presented a better sailing route for utilizing favorable trade winds. Receiving compensation for crossing the Atlantic was better than going empty handed.

After a six week crossing, the *Commerce* reached Gibraltar and delivered its cargo. They obtained a quantity of brandy and wine but their primary destination remained the Portuguese, Cape Verde Islands. The salt trade between there and North America had been pretty well shut down by the British during the war. This created both an excess supply and increased demand; perfect conditions for buying low and selling high. A large profit was anticipated but the *Commerce* would never capitalize. It never reached the Cape Verde Islands.

After departing Gibraltar on August 23, poor weather and fog engulfed the ship. Captain Riley was forced to sail by dead reckoning. When a good noontime observation was finally taken, Riley could accurately determine his latitude but not longitude. He was surprised to find he had sailed past the Canary Islands but was unaware that he was 300 miles closer to the coast of Africa than he estimated due to wind and strong currents.[568] Concern over the ship's position mounted and on the evening of August 28, Captain Riley finally ordered a change in direction to bring the ship into the wind. Suddenly, the roar of pounding surf could be heard and it was too late to take further evasive action.

The wreck of the *Commerce* on the barren shore of northwest Africa began an incredible odyssey of capture, enslavement, thirst, starvation and wandering through the Sahara desert at the hands of Arab nomads. Ultimately, seven members of the crew, including Captain Riley, were ransomed while the other six crewmen did not survive their harrowing experiences. Riley's account of the episode was published in 1818 and instantly became a best seller which continued in print for the remainder of the century.[569]

After returning home, Captain Riley temporarily relinquished his seaman's life and moved his family to Ohio. He remained there for more than ten years but the lure of the sea re-claimed Riley's soul. He returned and resumed his sailing career out of Long Island Sound and later, New York. He died in 1840 onboard the brig *William Tell* during a voyage from New York to St. Thomas in the Virgin Islands. Fittingly, Captain Riley was buried at sea.

Dynamic processes were at work between 1815 and 1820 that transformed maritime industry. There were several harbingers of change which included the nature of maritime trade, advancement of transportation technology and the industrial revolution.

First, maritime trade was becoming dominated by larger ships, bigger shipping companies and larger, deep water ports. The small, family owned ships based in Long Island Sound became less important and relegated mostly to coastal trade. Companies in New York, Boston and Baltimore owned fleets of packet ships with regularly scheduled operations. Fast sailing clipper and windjammer ships also sailing from these ports drew international attention.

Second was advancement in transportation technology. In March of 1815, regular steamboat service was initiated between New York and New Haven. Initially, the goal was to improve passenger travel between New York and Boston by eliminating at least one day of stagecoach travel. While Long Island Sound played an important role in the development of steamboat usage, passenger service remained primarily internal with scheduled services between many locations including New York.

In the long run, steamboat usage in Long Island Sound was more beneficial to both Connecticut and the Port of New York for the transportation of cargo. More freight was carried through the Sound than was carried on the Hudson River.[570] This greatly enhanced the Port of New York's shipping volume statistics helping it to forge well ahead of other ports. It also benefited Connecticut by assisting its transition to an industrial state. Connecticut entrepreneurs could now easily transport their products, which were increasingly industrial, to New York for worldwide distribution.

Moses Rogers, a native of New London, is credited with two pioneering landmarks in the development of steamship transportation. He was the first to take a steamship on the open ocean with his route taking him from New York down the New Jersey coast and into Delaware Bay. He then proposed a transatlantic trip and obtained financial backing in the cotton port of Savannah, Georgia. Built in the East River, the 380 ton *Savannah* journeyed down the coast to Georgia and then departed Savannah for Liverpool on May 24, 1819. It arrived twenty-seven days later although steam power was utilized for only eighty hours of the trip.

The most radical impetus for change was the Industrial Revolution coupled with America's maritime trade difficulties of the previous twenty years. For more than 170 years there were few ways to make a living outside of farming. Only maritime merchant operations and ship building enterprises provided a significant number of non-farm opportunities. After 1800, merchants from southern

New England and New York began to invest money they had made in maritime trade into manufacturing opportunities. Factories blossomed along abundant streams and waterways that were capable of water power generation. Long Island Sound communities became far less dependent on maritime industry.

An example of this shift to an industrial society may be seen in the area of Middletown, Connecticut, once a major river seaport of the West Indies trade. At the end of the eighteenth and beginning of the nineteenth century, numerous factories were established. These included factories for the manufacture of swords, pistols, rifles, hats, pewter, buttons, paper goods, ivory combs, woolen cloth (2 factories), cotton cloth (3 factories), nails, gunpowder, rum distillation and ground or lathed wood products.[571]

The pace of maritime commerce transitioning from Connecticut into New York City quickened after the War of 1812. In addition to the shipping line already established by George and Nathanial Griswold, the Black X packet shipping line was established for the London trade in the early 1820s by their cousins, John and Charles Griswold. The Line's pioneer shipmaster was Captain Henry Champlin of Essex, Connecticut. His wife, Amelia, was the daughter of shipyard owner, Uriah Hayden. Champlin became the Line's Senior Captain and then its Marine Superintendent as the company grew.

Many other Long Island Sound merchants and entrepreneurs also moved to New York and established powerful maritime related businesses. Some of these were new enterprises and others were extensions of their businesses back in New England. These leaders recruited other talent from Connecticut; men they knew, trusted and respected. These included businessmen, able bodied seamen and ship captains. Information from Connecticut River ports alone shows that between 1783 and 1820, at least fourteen sea captains moved from there to commanded ships sailing out of New York and an additional forty-three Connecticut River captains moved there to command ships after 1820.[572] Many poor boys from Connecticut also found their way to New York and succeeded on the basis of a strong work ethic enabling them to advance faster than native born workers.[573]

All areas of the Sound were well represented in this astonishing transfer of talent and resources. Another example was George Coggeshall of Milford who made eighty voyages between 1799 and 1844.

He learned his trade in Connecticut and became a ship captain by the age of twenty-five. During the War of 1812 he commanded several privateers including the 200 ton schooner, *David Porter* built at the Pond Shipyard in Milford, Connecticut. After the war, most of his voyages were out of New York.[574]

In his book, *The Rise of New York Port*, Robert Albion convincingly asserts that Connecticut entrepreneurs and maritime talent were the driving forces that made New York, by far, the premier port in the nation. He stated that this port was "swamped by the mighty invasion of business and maritime talent from New England in general and Connecticut in particular."[575] Furthermore, "the New Englanders captured New York port about 1820 and dominated its business until after the Civil War." Albion goes on to state that "It was perhaps natural that Connecticut should be most heavily represented among the invaders from the eastward, since it was the nearest New England state to New York. Yet the even closer New Jersey had made no such contribution."[576] The famous Yankee traders from Connecticut and other New England states had a worldwide reputation for shrewd business arrangements, developing new trade opportunities and beating the competition.

Albion maintains that "New Englanders not only beat the old New Yorkers [Knickerbockers] at the commercial game, but had the effrontery to boast about it."[577] By 1805 they had formed a social organization called the New England Society open only to New England natives or the son of a native. Their annual meetings reeked with self satisfaction and an air of superiority. The organization was so successful that Brooklyn established its own New England Society in 1846.

Nathaniel Palmer of Stonington was on the cusp of this change. He represented the end of an era and beginning of a new one. Born August 8, 1799 in Stonington, he grew up in his father's shipyard. He went to sea at age 14 on his father's schooner, *Gleaner* and became captain of this ship by age 18. After 1815, sealers from Great Britain and America drastically reduced the seal population in the South Pacific and began decimating those in the South Shetland Islands, far south of Cape Horn. In 1819, nineteen-year-old Nathaniel served as second mate on the newly built brig, *Hersilia* which was the first documented American ship to sail into Antarctic waters.[578] The sailors sighted numerous islands now called the Palmer Archipelago. Upon returning to Stonington, immediate plans were made to send another expedition to exploit the seals in the South Shetland Islands and those discovered on the previous trip.

Two brigs, a schooner and one sloop (the *Hero*) were assembled. Palmer, not yet twenty-one was placed in command of the *Hero*. This was the same ship that was commanded by Jeremiah Holmes when he ran the British blockade during The War of 1812. Since Palmer was still a minor, his mother helped him provide a $750 financial stake in the venture and signed the promissory note.[579] The forty-seven foot sloop was twenty years old, the same age as Palmer and carried a crew of only four in addition to himself.

The five ships rendezvoused at President's Harbor on Snow Island in the South Shetlands in mid November, 1820. It was decided to have Captain Palmer explore the area further south. On November 17, 1820 he reached latitude 63-45 south off of Trinity Island where he could view the Antarctic mainland. It was here that Nathaniel Palmer is credited with the discovery of Antarctica. There are two other conflicting claims to this discovery, one by Russian Captain Thaddeus Bellingshausen and the other by British Captain Edward Bransfield.

In January 1821, Palmer returned to the area and sailed along a large portion of the peninsula. On a third exploratory cruise, Palmer encountered several Russian naval vessels near Deception Island that were returning from a cruise around the world. Captain Thaddeus Bellingshausen invited Palmer onboard and the two discussed their respective operations and explorations. Bellingshausen was astounded at the presence of such a small vessel and young captain. He described Palmer's sloop as no bigger than one of the launches from his frigate.[580]

Although Long Island Sound's glory years ended by the early 1820s, a number of important contributions yet remained. Whaling grew steadily in importance and peaked in the 1830s and 1840s with major port locations at New London, Sag Harbor and Cold Spring Harbor. Sag Harbor, for example, sent three whaling ships out to the coast of Brazil in 1815 and by 1819 was home port for six or eight vessels engaged in whaling.

Ship building would also continue to grow on both sides of Long Island Sound. Shipyards along the Mystic River for example, produced their greatest volume in the mid 1800s. The Robert Palmer & Son shipyard in Noank for example, was one of the most important on the east coast and employed about 400 men. Between 1850 and 1860, Mystic shipyards built twenty-one clipper ships and during the Civil War, fifty steamers were built, a total that was more than any other New England port.[581]

Nathaniel Palmer participated in additional seal trade voyages and the South American trade. By 1835 however, he became involved in packet ship services, clipper ships and ship design. He designed and commanded several fast sailing ships operating out of New Orleans that set transatlantic speed records. In the 1840s he began designing more extreme clipper ship models. One of these, the *Oriental*, commanded by his younger brother, Theobald, set a speed record between Canton, China and London of ninety-seven days in 1849.

Today, the Nathaniel Palmer House serves as Headquarters for the Stonington Historical Society. Another connection to Stonington history lies beneath Arctic ice. After participating in the Battle of Stonington in the War of 1812, the British bomb ship *Terror* sailed southward where it participated in the bombardment of Fort McHenry in Baltimore and later, an attack on St. Marys, Georgia. The ship was re-fitted in 1838 and saw service on several Antarctic and Arctic explorations. During the ill fated 1845 Franklin Expedition to the Arctic, the *Terror* became locked in the ice and disappeared.

Today, most people think about Long Island Sound in terms of its recreational opportunity, great beauty and increasingly abundant fish and wildlife. Indeed, many in the Northeast view the Sound as equivalent to a National Park. Its location in the middle of a heavily populated, commercial area makes it even more valuable for these reasons. Still, we must not forget the historical legacies of Long Island Sound.

First, Long Island Sound served as a conduit for commerce and supported a fast growing population. Second, the West Indies trade and other maritime related commerce generated wealth that was used to transform the area, particularly Connecticut, into an industrial society. Third, Long Island Sound nurtured a vast number of versatile merchants and mariners who subsequently were crucial to the growth of New York Port as the nature of ships and maritime commerce changed.

The most enduring legacy of Long Island Sound is its contribution to the maritime and political independence of America. Shrewd Yankee entrepreneurs out-competed Great Britain. They defied British trade restrictions and sought better deals even though that often meant smuggling and other illegal trade (as determined by Great Britain). This conflict of interest was an important cause of the American Revolution. Historically, the volume of commerce from Long Island Sound has been underestimated and, hence, so has its importance. During the Revolutionary War, Long Island Sound played a significant role in thwarting British military goals in the New York area which forced a change in their strategic initiatives. The British were unable to stop privateering from so many small ports just as they could not previously stop trade they deemed illegal. During the War of 1812, produce shipped from Long Island Sound helped sustain Wellington's Army in Europe thus reducing the War's impact in America for two years. Finally, the British attack on Stonington was defeated by a defiant people. This served to raise morale just as the defense of Fort McHenry did several weeks later.

BIBLIOGRAPHY

Primary Resources

Acorn Club. *The Diary of Benjamin F. Palmer, Privateersman.* Connecticut: The Acorn Club, 1914.

Acorn Club. *Letters and Documents of Ezekial Williams of Wethersfield, Connecticut; Deputy Commissary General of Prisoners of War within the State of Connecticut (1777–c. 1783)*, Connecticut: The Acorn Club, 1976.

Bickford, Christopher P. (ed.). *Voices of the New Republic, Connecticut Towns 1800–1832.* Vol. I. New Haven, CT: Connecticut Academy of Arts and Sciences, 2003.

Bontemps, Arna (ed.). *Five Black Lives.* Middletown, CT: Wesleyan University Press, 1971.

Colonial Connecticut Records, 1636–1776. By University of Connecticut Libraries. Vols. 1–15. Digitized copy of "Public Records of the Colony of Connecticut." Hartford, CT: University of Connecticut, 2000–2001.

Dart, Margaret S. *Yankee Traders at Sea and Ashore.* New York: The William-Frederick Press, 1964.

Dudley, William S. (ed.). *The Naval War of 1812, A Documentary History.* Vol. I and II. Washington, DC: Naval Historical Center, Department of the Navy, 1985.

Force, Peter (ed.). *American Archives.* Fifth Series, Vol. 3. Washington: U.S. Congress, 1853.

Huntington Papers. Connecticut Historical Society Collections. Vol. XX. Hartford, CT: Connecticut Historical Society, 1923.

Innis, Harold A. and others (ed.). *The Diary of Simeon Perkins, 1766–1780.* Vol. 29 (1948); *1780–1789.* Vol. 36 (1958); *1790–1796.* Vol. 39

(1961); *1797–1803*. Vol. 43 (1967); and *1804–1812*. Vol. 50 (1978). Toronto: The Champlain Society.

Lathrop, Cornelia Penfield. *Black Rock: Seaport of Old Fairfield, Connecticut 1644–1870*. New Haven, Connecticut: The Tuttle Morehouse & Taylor Company, 1930.

Minor, Sidney H. and George D. Stanton (ed.). *The Diary of Thomas Minor*. New London: The Day Publishing Company, 1899.

Public Records of the State of Connecticut. Vols. 1–17. Hartford: Press of the Case, Lockwood & Brainard Company, 1894.

Rogers, Ernest E. *Connecticut's Naval Office at New London During the War of the American Revolution*. New London, CT: Ernest E. Rogers Publishing Fund, 1933.

Southey, Thomas. Chronological History of the West Indies, Vol. II. London: Frank Cass and Company, Ltd, 1968.

Tallmadge, Benjamin. *Memoir of Colonel Benjamin Tallmadge*. New York: The New York Times and Arno Press, 1968.

Primary Sources (Unpublished)

Fulwar Skipwith Papers. G. W. Blunt White Library, Mystic Seaport, Mystic, CT. Coll. 78, Box 1, Folder 11.

John Palmer Papers. G. W. Blunt White Library, Mystic Seaport, Mystic, CT. Coll. 53, Box 1, Folders 12, 13 and 14.

Joseph Williams Collection. G. W. Blunt White Library, Mystic Seaport, Mystic, CT. Coll. 37, Box 2, Folder 19.

Narrative of Capt. Jeremiah Holmes of Mystic Bridge, Conn. G. W. Blunt White Library, Mystic Seaport, Mystic, CT. VFM 390. Manuscript collections.

Secondary Sources

Albion, Robert Greenhalgh. *The Rise of New York Port, 1815–1860*. New York: Charles Scribner's Sons, 1939.

Allyn, Charles. *Battle of Groton Heights,* New London: by Author, 1882. Reprinted with additions by Norman Boas, M.D., 1999.

Blake, Nelson Manfred. *A History of American Life and Thought*. New York: McGraw Hill, 1963.

Blanchard, Fessenden S. *Long Island Sound*. Princeton, NJ: Van Nostrand, 1958.

Boas, Norman Francis. *Stonington During the American Revolution.* Mystic, CT: Seaport Autographs, 1990.

Brown, Barbara W. and James M. Rose, PhD. *Black Roots in Southeastern Connecticut 1650–1900.* New London, CT: New London County Historical Society, 2001.

Caron, Denis R. *A Century in Captivity.* Hanover, New Hampshire: University Press of New England, 2006.

Carr, J. Revell. *Seeds of Discontent.* New York: Walker and Company, 2008.

Cave, Alfred. *The Pequot War.* Amherst, MA: The University of Massachusetts Press, 1996.

Chidsey, Donald Barr. *The Loyalists.* New York: Crown Publishers, Inc., 1973.

Clark, William Bell. *George Washington's Navy.* Baton Rouge, LA: Louisiana State University Press, 1960.

Coggeshall, George. *History of the American Privateers, and Letters-of-Marque, During Our War with England in the Years 1812, '13 and '14.* Ann Arbor, MI: University of Michigan Library, 2005. Originally published by author in 1856.

Coggins, Jack. *Ships and Seamen of the American Revolution.* Harrisburg, PA: Stackpole Books, 1969.

Crandall, Katherine B. *The Fine Old Town of Stonington.* Westerly, RI: The Utter Company, 1949.

Curtis, Wayne. *And a Bottle of Rum.* New York: Crown Publishers, 2006.

Danenberg, Elsie N. *Naval History of Fairfield County Men in the Revolution.* Fairfield, CT: Fairfield Historical Society, 1977.

De Kay, James Tertius. *The Battle of Stonington.* Annapolis, MD: Naval Institute Press, 1990.

Denison, E. Glenn. *Denison Genealogy.* Baltimore, MD: Gateway Press, Inc., 1978.

Earle, Walter K. *Out of the Wilderness.* Cold Spring Harbor, NY: Whaling Museum Society, Inc., Cold Spring Harbor, 1966.

Farrow, Anne, Joel Lang and Jenifer Frank. *Complicity.* New York: Ballantine Books, 2005.

Feinstein, Estelle S. *Stamford from Puritan to Patriot.* Stamford: Stamford Bicentennial Corporation, 1976.

Ferguson, Henry L. *Fishers Island N.Y. 1614–1925.* Harrison, New York: Harbor Hill Books, 1974 (first printed privately in 1925), 26–27.

Grant, Ellsworth S. *"Thar She Goes."* Lyme, CT: Fenwick Productions, The Connecticut River Museum and Greenwich Publishing Group, 2000.

Hooker, Roland. *The Spanish Ship Case.* Tercentenary Commission of the State of Connecticut, New Haven, CT: Yale University Press, 1934.

Hoyt, David W. *A Genealogical History of the Hoyt, Haight, and Hight Families.* Somersworth, New Hampshire: New England History Press, 1984. First published in 1871.

Ketchum, Richard M. *Divided Loyalties.* New York: Henry Holt ND Company, 2002.

King, Dean. *Skeletons on the Zahara.* New York: Back Bay Books, 2004.

Knapp, Lewis G. *Stratford and the Sea.* Charleston, SC: Arcadia Publishing, 2002.

Kurlansky, Mark. *Salt.* New York: Penguin Books, 2002.

Kurlansky, Mark. *Cod.* New York: Penguin Books, 1997.

Leefe, John. *The Atlantic Privateers.* Queens County, Nova Scotia: Region of Queens Municipality, 1999.

Maloney, Linda M. *The Captain from Connecticut.* Boston: Northeastern University Press, 1986.

Mather, Frederic Gregory. *The Refugees of 1776 from Long Island to Connecticut.* Baltimore: Genealogical Publishing Co., Inc., 1972. First printed in 1913.

McDevitt, Robert. *Connecticut Attacked: A British Viewpoint, Tryon's Raid on Danbury.* Chester, CT: Pequot Press, 1974.

Middlebrook, Louis F. *History of Maritime Connecticut during the American Revolution 1775–1783.* Vol. I and II. Salem, Massachusetts: The Essex Institute, 1925.

Middlebrook, Louis F. *The Last Cruise of the "Oliver Cromwell" 1779.* Vols. I and II. Essex, CT: The Essex Historical Society, 1975. First printed in 1931 by the Marine Historical Association, Inc.

Milkofsky, Brenda (ed.). *A Grande Reliance.* Essex, CT: Connecticut River Museum, 1992. A colloquium and Exhibition.

Moore, Christopher. *The Loyalists.* Toronto, Ontario: McClelland & Stewart, Inc., 1994.

Morison, Samuel Eliot. *The Maritime History of Massachusetts 1783–1860.* Cambridge, MA: The Riverside Press, 1941.

Mullins, Janet E. *Liverpool Privateering 1756–1815.* Nova Scotia: Queens County Historical Society, 1936. Second printing in 1996.

Nelson, Cindy Ellen. "Privateering by Long Islanders in the American Revolution." *Journal of Long Island History.* Volume XI, Number 1, pp. 25–34. Brooklyn, NY: The Long Island Historical Society, 1974.

Overton, Albert G. *Plunderers from Across the Sound.* Florissant, MO: Micro-Records Publishing Company, 1980.

Pares, Richard. *War and Trade in the West Indies 1739–1763.* London: Frank Cass and Co., LTD, 1963.

Perkins, George A., MD. *The Family of John Perkins of Ipswich Massachusetts, Part III.* Salem, MA: By Author, 1889.

Peterson, William N. *Mystic Built.* Mystic Seaport Museum: Mystic, CT, 1989.

Philbrick, Nathaniel. *Sea of Glory.* New York: Penguin Books, 2003.

Piersen, William D. *Black Yankees.* Amherst, MA: The University of Massachusetts Press, 1988.

Radune, Richard A. *Pequot Plantation.* Branford, CT: Research in Time Publications, 2005.

Robotti, Diane Frances and James Vescovi. *The USS Essex and the Birth of the American Navy.* Holbrook, MA: Adams Media Corporation, 1999.

Rogers, Ernest E. Sesquicentennial of the Battle of Groton Heights. New London: Fort Griswold and Groton Monument Commission, 1931.

Rome, Adam Ward. *Connecticut's Cannon: The Salisbury Furnace in the American Revolution.* Hartford, CT: The American Revolution Bicentennial Commission of Connecticut, 1977.

Rose, Alexander. *Washington's Spies.* New York: Bantam Dell, 2006.

Schecter, Barnet. *The Battle for New York.* New York: Walker and Company, 2002.

Schlesinger, Arthur M., Jr. (ed.). *The Almanac of American History.* New York: Barnes & Noble Books, 1993.

Shallops, Sloops and Sharpies. New Haven, CT: The New Haven Colony Historical Society, 1976.

Sisler, Robert and Patricia Hansell. *Those Half Thousand Great Ships Built in Port Jefferson.* Port Jefferson, NY: Port Jefferson and Sissler, 1997.

Spears, John R. *Captain Nathaniel Brown Palmer: An Old-Time Sailor of the Sea.* New York: The Macmillan Company, 1922.

Steiner, Bruce E. *Connecticut Anglicans in the Revolutionary Era.* Hartford, CT: The American Revolution Bicentennial Commission of Connecticut, 1978.

Stevens, Thomas A. *Connecticut River Master Mariners.* Essex, CT: The Connecticut River Foundation at Steamboat Dock, 1979.

Stevens, Thomas A. *Old Sailing Days in Clinton*. Deep River, CT: Deep River Savings Bank, 1963.

The Sound Book. Norwalk, CT: The Long Island Soundkeeper Fund, Inc.

Thomas, Hugh. *The Slave Trade*. New York: Simon & Schuster, 1997.

Truxes, Thomas M. *Defying Empire*. New Haven and London: Yale University Press, 2008.

Van Dusen, Albert E. *Middletown and the American Revolution*. Middletown, CT: The Rockfall Corporation and the Middlesex County Historical Society, 1950.

Weigold, Marilyn E. *The American Mediterranean*. Port Washington, NY: Kennikat Press, 1974.

Wells, James, Louis Hatten and Josiah Briggs (eds.). *The Bronx and its People*. New York: The Lewis Historical Publishing Co., 1927.

Woodruff, Janet, Gerald F. Sawyer and Warren R. Perry. "How Archaeology Exposes the Nature of African Captivity and Freedom in Eighteenth and Nineteenth Century Connecticut." *Connecticut History*, Vol. 46, Number 2. The Association for the Study of Connecticut History, Fall 2007.

Secondary Sources (Unpublished)

Avitable, Dr. Joseph. "Connecting Colonial Connecticut to the Atlantic World Economy, 1690–1776." Research presentation given to The Association for the Study of Connecticut History in Essex, Connecticut at its spring meeting April 28, 2007.

Bumsted, John M. "The Development of the Mystic Clipper Ship." Honors Thesis. Tufts Department of History, 1959.

Decker, Robert Owen. *The New London Merchants: 1645–1909: The Rise and Decline of a Connecticut Port*. Ann Arbor, MI: University Microfilm, 1970. Dissertation.

Jones, Richard M. *Stonington Borough: A Connecticut Seaport in the 19th Century*. G. W. Blunt White Library, Mystic Seaport, Mystic, CT, 1976. Dissertation.

Minuse, William B. *Ship Building in the Setaukets*. 1955. G. W. Blunt White Library, Mystic Seaport, Mystic, CT, 1955. Typed manuscript.

Town and County Histories

Banks, Elizabeth V. H. *This is Fairfield 1639–1940*. New Haven, CT: The Walker-Rackliff Company, 1960.

Barr, Lockwood. *Ancient Town of Pelham*. Pelham Manor, NY: by author, 1946.

Best, Mary Agnes. *The Town that Saved a State*. Westerly, RI: The Utter Company, 1943.

Bolton, Rev. Robert. *History of Westchester County, New York*. Vol. I. (ed. C.W. Bolton), New York: Charles F. Roper, 1881.

Carr, John C. *Early History of Branford*. Branford, CT: The Branford Historical Society, 1985.

Caulkins, Francis Manwaring. *History of New London*. New London, CT: H.D. Utley, 1895.

Caulkins, Francis Manwaring. *History of Norwich*. Norwich, CT: Friends of the Author, 1874.

Cold Spring Harbor Soundings. Cold Spring Harbor, NY: The Cold Spring Harbor Village Improvement Society, 1953.

Decker, Robert Owen. *The Whaling City*. Chester, CT: The Pequot Press, 1976.

Denison, Frederic. *Westerly and its Witnesses*. Providence, RI: J. A. & R. A. Reid, 1878.

Duvall, Ralph G. *The History of Shelter Island*. Shelter Island Heights: by author, 1932.

Federal Writers' Project of the Works Project Administration for the State of Connecticut. *History of Milford Connecticut 1639–1939*. Bridgeport, CT: Work Projects Administration, 1939.

Feinstein, Estelle F. and Joyce S. Pendry. *Stamford*. Woodland Hills, CA: Windsor Publications, Inc., 1984.

Hartley, Rachel M. *The History of Hamden Connecticut*. Hamden, CT: The Shoe String Press, Inc., 1959.

Justinius, Dr. Ivan O. *History of Black Rock*. Bridgeport, Connecticut: Antoniak Printing Service, Inc., 1927.

Klein, Woody. *Westport Connecticut*. Greenwood Press: Westport, CT, 2000.

Osterweis, Rollin G. *Three Centuries of New Haven, 1638–1938*. New Haven and London: Yale University Press, 1953.

Ray, Deborah Wing and Gloria P. Stewart. *Norwalk*. Norwalk, CT: Norwalk Historical Society, 1979.

Shumway, Floyd and Richard Hegel (ed.). *New Haven, An Illustrated History*. Windsor Publications, 1981.

Sisler, Patricia Hansel and Robert Sisler. *The Seven Hills of Port*. RMP Publication Services, 1992.

Smith, Ralph D. *The History of Guilford, Connecticut*. Albany, NY, 1877.

Steiner, Bernard Christian. *History of Guilford and Madison, Connecticut*. Guilford, CT: The Guilford Free Library, 1975. First published in 1897 with the title *A History of the Plantation of Menunkatuck and the Original Town of Guilford, Connecticut* by Christian Bernard, Baltimore, MD.

Wells, Gordon and William Proios. *Port Jefferson, Story of a Village*. Port Jefferson, NY: Historical Society of Greater Port Jefferson, 1977.

Wheeler, Richard. *History of the Town of Stonington*. New York: Noble Offset Printers, 1966.

Whittemore, Henry. *The History of Middlesex County 1635–1885*. New York: J.B. Beers & Company, 1884.

Newspapers and Magazines

Globe and Mail (Toronto).

Hartford Courant, 1764–1922. ICONN, The Connecticut Digital Library: ProQuest Information and Learning Company, 2006.

The Mystic Pioneer (Mystic, CT), 1859–1870.

Rivington's Royal Gazette.

Stevens, Thomas A. "The Discovery of Antarctica." *The Log of Mystic Seaport*, Vol. 28, No. 4, January 1977.

On-line Resources

Allen, Gardiner W. "A Naval History of the Revolution." Chapter VI. Accessible at www.americanrevolution.org.

Batten, Andrew C. "Long Island Loyalists: The Misunderstood Americans." Accessible at www.raynamhallmuseum.org.

Bleyer, Bill. "A Revolutionary Skirmish." From Newsday, 2006. Accessible at www.newsday.com/community/guide/lihistory/ny-past.

D'Entremont, Jeremy. "Fayerweather Island Lighthouse, Bridgeport Connecticut." Accessible at www.lighthouse.cc/fayerweather/index.

Department of the Navy—Naval Historical Center. Washington Navy Yard. Washington DC. Accessible at www.history.navy.mil.

DeWan, George. "Finding Bounty in War Booty." From *Newsday*, 2006. Accessible at www.newsday.com/community/guide/lihistory/ny-past.

Farrow, Anne. "Beyond Complicity." *Hartford Courant*, 2005. Accessible at www.courant.com/slavery.

Great Britain, "Journals of the House of Commons." Session 1745–1746, vol. 25. Accessible at www.bopcris.ac.uk/bob1700.

Hebert, Tim. "Acadian History." Accessible at www.acadian-cajun.com.

Jensen, Oliver. "The Home Front." *American Heritage Magazine*, December 1992, Volume 43, Issue 8. Accessible at www.americanheritage.com/magazine.

Landry, Peter. "History of Nova Scotia." Book 1 and 2. Dartmouth, Nova Scotia, Canada. Accessible at www.blupete.com.

Malcarne, Don. "The British Attack on Potapoug." Accessible at www.essexhistory.org.

McCusker, John J. "The First Continental Flagship." Smithsonian Studies in History and Technology. Accessible at www.sil.si.edu/Smithsonian Contributions/HistoryTechnology.

Schultz, T. J. "Action off Block Island." Accessible at www.members.aol.com.

Stark, Bruce. "The Spanish Ship Case." Connecticut Heritage Gateway. Accessible at www.ctheritage.org.

Turks & Caicos National Museum. "Salt Industry." Accessible at www.tcmu seum.org.

Tyler, Beverly C. "History Close at Hand". The Three Village Historical Society. Accessible at www.threevillagehistoricalsociety.org.

Underhill, Lois Beachy. "Our Town: Sag Harbor's Revolutionary War Patriots." From *The Sag Harbor Express*, September 16, 1999. Accessible at www.sagharboronline.com.

Warren, Israel P. *Chauncey Judd or the Stolen Boy, A Story of the Revolution.* First published in 1874. Scanned and digitalized by town of Oxford Connecticut. Accessible at www.our-oxford.info.

Western Connecticut State University. American Democracy Project. "Connecticut as the Provision State & Danbury's Early Role in Civic Engagement." Accessible at www.wcsu.edu/americandemocracy/.

White, David O. "Roger Wolcott." Connecticut State Library (ed.), 2003. Accessible at www.cslib.org.

U.S. Army Corp of Engineers. "The Conquest of Hell Gate." Accessible at www.nan.usace.army.mil.

Notes

1. Milkofsky (ed.), *A Grande Reliance*, 2.
2. Ray and Stewart, *Norwalk*, 47.
3. Milkofsky (ed.), *A Grande Reliance*, 17.
4. *The Sound Book*, 16.
5. Ferguson, *Fishers Island N.Y. 1614–1925*, 26–27.
6. One resource indicated the payroll was being sent to the British naval base at Newport, Rhode Island but the British abandoned this base in October of 1779. Other resources indicate the payroll was being sent to the British fleet anchorage in Gardiners Bay. This seems more likely.
7. U.S. Army Corp of Engineers, "The Conquest of Hell Gate."
8. Decker, *The Whaling City*, 5.
9. Shumway and Hegel (ed.), *New Haven, An Illustrated History*, 63 and 64. See also *Shallops, Sloops and Sharpies*, 7–9.
10. Milkofsky (ed.), *A Grande Reliance*, 1–2.
11. Carr, *Early History of Branford*, 46.
12. Milkofsky (ed.), *A Grande Reliance*, 8.
13. Caulkins, *History of New London*, 245.
14. Decker, *The Whaling City*, 23–24.
15. Milkofsky (ed.), *A Grande Reliance*, 1.
16. *Shallops, Sloops and Sharpies*, 7–9.
17. Milkofsky (ed.), *A Grande Reliance*, 1.
18. Grant, "*Thar She Goes*," 16–17. See also Milkofsky (ed.), *A Grande Reliance*, 8.
19. Ibid. An example was Richard Alsop who moved from New York City to Middletown, Connecticut.

20. Milkofsky (ed.), *A Grande Reliance*, 1–2.

21. Avitable, "Connecting Colonial Connecticut to the Atlantic World Economy, 1690–1776."

22. Ibid.

23. Curtis, *And a Bottle of Rum*, 102–103.

24. Avitable, "Connecting Colonial Connecticut to the Atlantic World Economy, 1690–1776."

25. Curtis, *And a Bottle of Rum*, 79.

26. Turks & Caicos National Museum, "Salt Industry."

27. Ibid.

28. Kurlansky, *Salt*, 209.

29. *Connecticut Colonial Records*, vol. 4, p. 129.

30. Ibid, 147.

31. Knapp, *Stratford and the Sea*, 26.

32. Minor and Stanton (ed.), *The Diary of Thomas Minor*, 147. There is uncertainty as to when Daniel Stanton moved to Barbados. Although this reference does not specifically identify Barbados as the reason for the prayers, I believe they were exactly for this reason. My assertion is based upon information I found at the Barbados Museum in Bridgetown, Barbados. The Barbados Historic Society has records documenting people who left Barbados. This material included a reference to Daniel Stanton's servant, James Fanning who returned to New England in 1679. This proves that Daniel was in Barbados prior to 1679 and lends credence to a departure in 1678, thus the reason for prayer by the church congregation.

33. Ray and Stewart, *Norwalk*, 36.

34. Best, *The Town that Saved a State*, 186, 187.

35. Ibid.

36. Innis et al. (eds.), *The Diary of Simeon Perkins*, vol. 29, pp. 104–105.

37. The particulars for this entire incident are in several references. These are: White, "Roger Wolcott;" Caulkins, *History of New London*, 462–468; Stark, "The Spanish Ship Case;" *Connecticut Colonial Records*, vol. 10, 235–237; and Hooker, *The Spanish Ship Case*. Caulkins and Hooker identified the British warship as the *Triton* which arrived in New London in 1754. Two factors combined to create the situation which unfolded. First, New Londoners harbored a dislike for the Spanish due to their participation as an enemy during King George's War ending just four years earlier. Second, was an

opportunistic attitude fueled by the rich cargo carried onboard the *St. Joseph and St. Helena*. Upon reaching New London, the pilot told the Spaniards there were no hazards in the line of approach they were taking into the harbor but then promptly ran the vessel onto Bartlet's Reef. Another pilot was brought out from New London who managed to ground the ship a second time incurring more serious damage. One of the masts had to be cut away and half the cargo removed in order to float the ship off the reef. The *St. Joseph and St. Helena* was moved a third time and anchored directly over another reef where it became grounded as the tide went out. Continuously pounded by stormy weather, the ship was a wreck by the time it was towed into the safety of New London Harbor. While never proven, an assertion was made that the pilots deliberately ran the ship aground in order to create salvage rights to the cargo or create the opportunity for theft of cargo. Salvage awards were in fact granted and by next spring a portion of the cargo had also vanished. Several people were arrested for theft but they soon escaped. The Spaniards then chartered the 196 ton *Nebuchadnezzar* from New York merchants Henry Cuyler and Henry Lane to take them and their cargo back to Spain but continued legal issues held the ship in port. Connecticut Governor Wolcott eventually turned control of the cargo over to Lane who promptly absconded with four chests of silver. The Spaniards filed complaints with the Governor of Connecticut and with the King of England prompting England to send the warship *Triton* to New London to investigate the situation. Under intense pressure, the *Nebuchadnezzar* was finally released to sail for Spain in January 1755. Most of the gold was gone along with nine chests of silver and forty bags of indigo.

38. Hooker, *The Spanish Ship Case*, 30–31. The missing merchandise included forty bags of indigo out of 562, nine chests of silver out of thirty-nine and 4,620 pieces of gold out of 5,100. Most of the remaining silver was paid out for salvage awards, ship charter fees and many other expenses.

39. Grant, *"Thar She Goes,"* 21 and 64.

40. Ibid.

41. Ibid, 13.

42. *Connecticut Colonial Records*, vol. 10, pp. 101–102.

43. Piersen, *Black Yankees*, 18, 163 and 166–169. See also Caron, *A Century in Captivity*, 17.

44. Caron, *A Century in Captivity*, 15–17.

45. Ibid.

46. Ibid, various pages. Prince was initially sent to Newgate prison and then transferred in 1827 to a new state prison in Wethersfield.

47. Bontemps (ed.), *Five Black Lives*, 18.

48. Ibid, 20–22.

49. Ibid. See also Brown, *Black Roots in Southeastern Connecticut*, 47.

50. A suggested starting place would be the book *Complicity: How the North Promoted, Prolonged, and Profited from Slavery*. Further resources are indicated in this book's extensive bibliography.

51. Curtis, *And a Bottle of Rum*, 127–129.

52. Ibid. See also Farrow, "Beyond Complicity, Connecticut's Hidden History."

53. Farrow, "Beyond Complicity, Connecticut's Hidden History." These ships included the brig *Pompey* commanded by John Easton (three separate voyages), the sloop *Rainbow* commanded by Captain Waterman, the brig *Hope* commanded by Thomas Goold and the *Africa* commanded by John Easton. Samuel Gould traveled as super-cargo on the *Africa* from New London to Sierra Leone where he transferred to the sloop, *Good Hope* as supercargo with a destination of St. Christopher's (St. Kitts today). The ship carried 169 slaves of whom 150 survived the voyage.

54. Woodruff et al., "How Archaeology Exposes the Nature of African Captivity and Freedom in Eighteenth and Nineteenth Century Connecticut," 157.

55. Carr, *Seeds of Discontent*, 147.

56. Landry, "History of Nova Scotia," Book 1, Part 4, Chapter 5.

57. Ibid.

58. Carr, *Seeds of Discontent*, 212 and 213.

59. Ibid, 253, 259, 263 and 283.

60. *Connecticut Colonial Records*, vol. 9, 306.

61. Ibid, 486–487. In addition to the assault force of 500 men, Connecticut later raised 500 more troops for reinforcement and garrison duty. Many of these died of disease. See also pages 83–84, 128, 144, 148, 155.

62. The first was a John Prentice who was recruited by the new settlement of New London to be its blacksmith in 1652. Around 1670 he gave up his blacksmith profession in favor of maritime ventures as ship captain, ship owner and merchant businessman. His sons and later generations continued in seafaring activities.

63. *Connecticut Colonial Records*, vol. 9, 210, 332.

64. Ibid.

65. Carr, *Seeds of Discontent*, 314.

66. Caulkins, *History of New London*, 392–394.

67. *Connecticut Colonial Records*, vol. 9, pp. 210, 332, 484, 485, 527, 528. See also Caulkins, *History of New London*, 394.

68. Carr, *Seeds of Discontent*, 309–313.

69. Landry, "History of Nova Scotia," Book 1, Part 6, Chapter 15.

70. *Connecticut Colonial Records*, vol. 10, 425, 452–453.

71. Hebert, "Acadian History." The ships were the *Elizabeth* with 277 passengers on Jan. 21, an unnamed sloop with 173 passengers on Jan. 22, the *Dove* with 114 passengers on Jan. 30 and the *Edward* with 180 passengers on May 22. The *Edward* left Nova Scotia on December 8, 1755 but was blown off course by a storm and landed in Antigua before continuing on.

72. *Connecticut Colonial Records*, vol. 10, 453.

73. Hebert, "Acadian History."

74. Rogers, *Connecticut's Naval Office at New London*, 68–69.

75. *Hartford Courant*, September 28, 1767, p. 3, "Extract of a Letter from Peter Preshon."

76. Innis et al. (eds.), *The Diary of Simeon Perkins*, vol. 29, pp. 29–30.

77. *Hartford Courant*, March 26, 1916, p. XI, "The Acadian House In Guilford."

78. Landry, "History of Nova Scotia," Book 2, part 1, Chapter 3.

79. Ibid.

80. Perkins, *The Family of John Perkins of Ipswich Massachusetts, Part III*, 13. See also *The Diary of Simeon Perkins*, vol. 36, p. xx. There is some confusion whether Abigail and Simeon married in 1759 or 1760 but most references indicate 1759.

81. Innis et al. (eds.), *The Diary of Simeon Perkins*, vol. 36, p. xx.

82. Ibid, vol. 29, pp. 4, 35, 47.

83. Landry, "History of Nova Scotia," book 2, part 1, Chapter 7.

84. Innis et al. (eds.), *The Diary of Simeon Perkins*, vol. 29, p. 20.

85. Ibid, 9 and 11.

86. Ibid, 54.

87. Ibid, 19.

88. Ibid, 24–25.

89. Ibid, 12.

90. Lathrop, *Black Rock: Seaport of Old Fairfield*, 5.

91. Ibid.

92. Truxes, *Defying Empire*, 59 and 60.

93. Pares, *War and Trade in the West Indies 1739–1763*, 396, 397.

94. Caulkins, *History of New London*, 245.

95. Ibid.

96. Ibid, 345.

97. Ray and Stewart, *Norwalk*, 47.

98. Ibid.

99. Pares, *War and Trade in the West Indies 1739–1763*, pp. 448, 449.

100. Ibid.

101. Truxes, *Defying Empire*, 84 and 89.

102. Ibid, 72.

103. Ibid, 40 and 41.

104. Ibid, 42.

105. Ibid, 175 and 176.

106. Ibid, 131, 133, 137, 146, 151, 153, 180 and 181.

107. Ibid, 146.

108. Rogers, *Connecticut's Naval Office at New London*, 177–180.

109. Ibid, 264.

110. Ibid, 267.

111. Curtis, *And a Bottle of Rum*, 104.

112. Caulkins, *History of New London*, 478–480.

113. Ibid.

114. Decker, *The Whaling City*, 40.

115. Ibid.

116. *Connecticut Colonial Records*, vol. 7, p. 512.

117. Great Britain, "Journals of the House of Commons." Session 1745–1746, vol. 25.

118. Rome, *Connecticut's Cannon*.

119. Rogers, *Connecticut's Naval Office at New London*, 274.

120. Knapp, *Stratford and the Sea*, 70.

121. Schecter, *The Battle for New York*, 54–55. The British garrison consisted of five companies of soldiers.

122. Moore, *The Loyalists*, 96. See also Hoyt, *A Genealogical History of the Hoyt, Haight, and Hight Families*, 376.

123. Innis et al. (eds.), *The Diary of Simeon Perkins*, vol. 29, pp. 98, 99, 100, 105, 107, 119, 121 and 129.
124. Ibid, 101.
125. Ibid, 134.
126. Ibid, 129 and 138.
127. Caulkins, *History of Norwich*, 390.
128. *Huntington Papers*, Connecticut Historical Society Collections, Vol. XX, p. 282.
129. Middlebrook, *History of Maritime Connecticut during the American Revolution 1775–1783*, vol. 2, p. 6.
130. Bleyer, "A Revolutionary Skirmish."
131. Boas, *Stonington During the American Revolution*, 30.
132. Ibid.
133. Ibid, 32.
134. Ibid, 35.
135. *Connecticut Colonial Records*, vol. 15, pp. 122, 125 and 129. See also Middlebrook, *History of Maritime Connecticut during the American Revolution*, vol. 1, pp. 25–27. This resource indicates that two black men were part of the seventy-two man crew.
136. Clark, *George Washington's Navy*, 19.
137. *Connecticut Colonial Records*, vol. 15, pp. 131 and 176.
138. Ibid, 177 and 201.
139. Clark, *George Washington's Navy*, 3 and 4.
140. Ibid, 39. See also, Middlebrook, *History of Maritime Connecticut during the American Revolution*, 108 and 109.
141. Ibid.
142. Ibid.
143. Ibid, 43 and 44.
144. Ibid, 80.
145. Ibid, 66. Undoubtedly, his real words were something more like "blundering idiot."
146. Ibid, 82.
147. Ibid, 81 and 82.
148. Coggins, *Ships and Seamen of the American Revolution*, 101.
149. Nelson, "Privateering by Long Islanders in the American Revolution," Volume XI, Number 1, pp. 25–34. According to Danenberg's *Naval History of Fairfield County Men in the Revolution*, the orders for the

Montgomery came from the Continental Congress and it was based out of Black Rock Harbor, Connecticut. It is possible that it utilized both Huntington and Black Rock Harbors.

150. Caulkins, *History of New London*, 524.

151. Coggins, *Ships and Seamen of the American Revolution*, 22.

152. Middlebrook, *History of Maritime Connecticut during the American Revolution*, vol. 1, p. 145.

153. Boas, *Stonington During the American Revolution*, 28. See also *Connecticut Colonial Records*, vol. 15, p. 117.

154. *Ibid*, 29. The *Nancy* was taken to Norwich for libel and condemnation procedures.

155. Middlebrook, *History of Maritime Connecticut during the American Revolution*, vol. 1, pp. 43 and 44.

156. Ibid, 46.

157. Whittemore, *The History of Middlesex County*, 79. See also Middlebrook, *History of Maritime Connecticut during the American Revolution*, vol. 1, p. 201 and Decker, *The New London Merchants: 1645–1909*, 19–21.

158. Ibid. See also Middlebrook, *History of Maritime Connecticut during the American Revolution*, vol. 1, pp. 202 and 203.

159. Ibid.

160. Rome, *Connecticut's Cannon*, 10 and 11. See also Overton, *Plunderers from Across the Sound*, 39–42. The family returned to Connecticut in February 1783, near the end of the war, after his petition to the Connecticut General Assembly was approved. He asserted he was never a Loyalist and the family agreed to take an oath of allegiance and become loyal citizens of the new country.

161. Middlebrook, *History of Maritime Connecticut during the American Revolution*, vol. 1, pp. 188, 194, 195, 197 and 198. See also *Connecticut Colonial Records*, vol. 15, pp. 224, 234 and 249.

162. Middlebrook, *History of Maritime Connecticut during the American Revolution*, vol. 1, p. 197.

163. Ibid, vol. II, 6.

164. *Rivington's Royal Gazette*, "Horse Neck," March 3, 1779.

165. Knapp, *Stratford and the Sea*, 76.

166. Rogers, *Connecticut's Naval Office at New London*, 46. See also Middlebrook, *History of Maritime Connecticut during the American Revolution*, vol. II, 150–153 and 163–164.

167. Middlebrook, *History of Maritime Connecticut during the American Revolution*, vol. I, 11 and 12.

168. Knapp, *Stratford and the Sea*, 76 and 77.

169. Schultz, "Action off Block Island." This online resource is taken from the book *John Paul Jones, A Sailor's Biography*. John Paul Jones was an officer on one of the Continental Navy vessels.

170. Naval Historical Center. "Dictionary of American Naval Fighting Ships."

171. Middlebrook, *History of Maritime Connecticut during the American Revolution*, vol. I, 12–14.

172. Ibid, vol. II, 6–9. One of the eighteen ships was the schooner *Little Joe* under command of Captain Giles Latham of New London. In 1780, Latham and the *Little Joe* would be captured on their return from the West Indies by the *Lucy*, a Liverpool, Nova Scotia privateer owned by Simeon Perkins.

173. *Connecticut Colonial Records*, vol. 14, p. 264.

174. Ibid, vol. 15, pp. 119 and 120. New York merchants Isaac Sears and Thomas Ivers loaned sixty-six cannons to Connecticut. These were installed on Connecticut State Navy ships, privateering vessels and a few were mounted into harbor defense fortifications.

175. Ibid, pp. 177, 260 and 262. See also Middlebrook, *History of Maritime Connecticut during the American Revolution*, vol. I, 14.

176. Ray and Stewart, *Norwalk*, 57.

177. Middlebrook, *History of Maritime Connecticut during the American Revolution*, vol. I, pp. 242 and 243. Tashua Hill is located on Merrimac Road in Trumbull.

178. Ketchum, *Divided Loyalties*, 192–196 and 291–293.

179. Ibid, 343.

180. Ibid, 354–356.

181. Ibid.

182. Ray and Stewart, *Norwalk*, 55.

183. Feinstein, *Stamford from Puritan to Patriot*, 201.

184. Decker, *The New London Merchants*, 9 and 10. The tavern was owned by Stephen Ranney and widow Mary Bigelow.

185. Boas, *Stonington During the American Revolution*, 36.

186. Middlebrook, *History of Maritime Connecticut during the American Revolution*, vol. 1, p. 40.

187. Clark, *George Washington's Navy*, 162.

188. Ibid.

189. Ibid, 163.

190. Ibid, 164.

191. Middlebrook, *History of Maritime Connecticut during the American Revolution*, vol. 1, pp. 105–111.

192. *Connecticut Colonial Records*, vol. 15, pp. 473, 481 and 488.

193. Naval Historical Center, "Dictionary of American Naval Fighting Ships."

194. Ibid.

195. *Hartford Courant*, August 12, 1776, p. 2. "Extract of a letter from a Gentleman who was in the engagement dated August 4, 1776."

196. *Hartford Courant*, August 19, 1776, p. 3. "Extract of a letter from a Gentleman off Fort Washington to his friend in this city [New York] dated August 8, 1776."

197. *Hartford Courant*, August 12, 1776, p. 2. "Extract of a letter from a Gentleman who was in the engagement dated August 4, 1776."

198. Ibid.

199. *Public Records of the State of Connecticut*, vol. 1, pp. 85 and 201.

200. Bolton, *History of Westchester County, New York,* Vol. I, 160.

201. Coggins, *Ships and Seamen of the American Revolution*, 60.

202. Ibid, 63.

203. Knapp, *Stratford and the Sea*, 77–80.

204. Ibid.

205. Allen, "A Naval History of the Revolution," Chapter VI.

206. Ibid.

207. Boas, *Stonington During the American Revolution*, 54.

208. Mather, *The Refugees of 1776 from Long Island to Connecticut*, 29.

209. Ibid, 429.

210. Ibid, 239.

211. Underhill, "Our Town: Sag Harbor's Revolutionary War Patriots."

212. Duvall, *The History of Shelter Island*, 68. The ships were *London*— 120 guns, *Bedford*—100 guns, *Centurion*—80 guns, *Robust*—74 guns, *Royal Oak*—100 guns, *Royal George*—100 guns, *Grand Duke*— 120 guns and *Culloden*—74 guns.

213. Duvall, *The History of Shelter Island*, 67 and 70.

214. Sisler, *The Seven Hills of Port* [Jefferson], 11.

215. Rose, *Washington's Spies*, 82.

216. Ibid, 83.

217. Tallmadge, *Memoir of Colonel Benjamin Tallmadge*, 6. In 1773, there were three public school districts in Wethersfield, each with a school, but there was no public high school. Perhaps this was a private institution.

218. Rose, *Washington's Spies*, 82.

219. Schecter, *The Battle for New York*, 212.

220. Chidsey, *The Loyalists*, 131.

221. Schecter, *The Battle for New York*, 350.

222. Bolton, *History of Westchester County, New York,* Vol. I, xiv.

223. Wells, Hatten and Briggs (eds.), *The Bronx and its People*, 210.

224. *Public Records of the State of Connecticut*, vol. 1, p. 508.

225. Ray and Stewart, *Norwalk*, 55.

226. Hoyt, *A Genealogical History of the Hoyt, Haight, and Hight Families*, 638.

227. Ray and Stewart, *Norwalk*, 55. See also Moore, *The Loyalists*, 96 and Hoyt, *A Genealogical History of the Hoyt, Haight, and Hight Families*, 376.

228. Hoyt, *A Genealogical History of the Hoyt, Haight, and Hight Families*, 112.

229. Feinstein, *Stamford from Puritan to Patriot*, 199–200.

230. Batten, "Long Island Loyalists: The Misunderstood Americans."

231. Acorn Club, *Letters and Documents of Ezekial Williams of Wethersfield, Connecticut*, 65.

232. Danenberg, *Naval History of Fairfield County Men in the Revolution*, 70.

233. Schecter, *The Battle for New York*, 274.

234. Federal Writers Project, *History of Milford Connecticut 1639–1939*, 62–63.

235. Ibid.

236. Schecter, *The Battle for New York*, 274.

237. Ibid.

238. Knapp, *Stratford and the Sea*, 71–73.

239. Ibid.

240. *Connecticut Colonial Records*, vol. 15, p. 467.

241. Decker, *The New London Merchants: 1645–1909*, 10.

242. Coggins, *Ships and Seamen of the American Revolution*, 74.

243. Ibid. See also Boas, *Stonington During the American Revolution*, 49.

244. Middlebrook, *History of Maritime Connecticut during the American Revolution*, vol. II, 258.

245. Ibid, 255.

246. Rose, *Washington's Spies*, 104.

247. Decker, *The Whaling City*, 48.

248. Middlebrook, *History of Maritime Connecticut during the American Revolution*, vol. II, 90.

249. Ibid.

250. Ibid, vol. II, 118–119. See also Boas, *Stonington During the American Revolution*, 81. According to Coggins, *Ships and Seamen of the American Revolution*, 106, the *Pigot* was subsequently purchased and commissioned into the Rhode Island Navy for service in 1779 and 1780.

251. The location of an engagement was not always clearly identified and often an assumption or estimation had to be made based on other captures made by the ship involved. Where this couldn't be done, the cruising area was listed as unknown. Often, the same ship made multiple cruises. Where these occurred in different years or in different operational areas they were counted separately.

252. Decker, *The Whaling City*, 48, 49, 340 and 341.

253. Grant, *"Thar She Goes,"* 26. See also, Denison, *Westerly and its Witnesses*, 119–120 and Boas, *Stonington During the American Revolution*, 49, 79, 81, 88, 103, 104 and 117.

254. Ibid, 26. See also Decker, *The New London Merchants: 1645–1909*, p. 21.

255. Middlebrook, *History of Maritime Connecticut during the American Revolution*, vol. II, 62–63. The statistics for privateer activity in this chapter come from studying the records contained in the entire volume II.

256. Innis et al. (eds.), *The Diary of Simeon Perkins*, 238 and 242.

257. Ibid, 257–262.

258. Ibid, 269, 273, 274, 278. The Lucy probably sailed to New England with Backus and Clement under a flag of truce.

259. Middlebrook, *History of Maritime Connecticut during the American Revolution*, vol. II, 62, 84, 85, 108, 109, 119, 139, 143, 148, 149, 160, 165, 186, 232, 246, 264 and 265.

260. Innis et al. (eds.), *The Diary of Simeon Perkins*, vol. 29, p. 189.

261. Ibid, 214.
262. Middlebrook, *History of Maritime Connecticut during the American Revolution*, vol. II, 54–55.
263. Ibid, 72 and 160. See also Caulkins, *History of New London*, 540.
264. Ibid, vol. II, 72.
265. John Palmer Papers, Coll. 53, Box 1, Folder 12, p. 3.
266. Ibid, 4 and 5.
267. Ibid, 4, 5 and 9 and Middlebrook, *History of Maritime Connecticut during the American Revolution*, vol. II, 207 and 208.
268. John Palmer Papers, Coll. 53, Box 1, Folder 12, vol. 5, pp. 21 and 33 and Middlebrook, *History of Maritime Connecticut during the American Revolution*, vol. II, 51.
269. John Palmer Papers, Coll. 53, Box 1, Folder 12, vol. 6, pp. 1–7.
270. Ibid, 8.
271. Ibid, 11.
272. Ibid, 15.
273. Ibid, 19.
274. Boas, *Stonington During the American Revolution*, 49. See also Middlebrook, *History of Maritime Connecticut during the American Revolution*, vol. II, 207–209.
275. Middlebrook, *History of Maritime Connecticut during the American Revolution*, vol. II, 219–224. See also Warren, *Chauncey Judd or the Stolen Boy*, chapter 8.
276. Ibid. It is not clear whether two separate raids were mounted in June 1778 or just one.
277. Southey, *Chronological History of the West Indies*, 423 and 425.
278. Ibid, 428.
279. John Palmer Papers, Coll. 53, Box 1, Folder 14, volume 7, p. 4.
280. Ibid, 9.
281. Ibid, 10.
282. Ibid, 15.
283. Ibid, 21–22.
284. Ibid, 23.
285. Ibid, 27–28.
286. Ibid, 32.
287. Middlebrook, *History of Maritime Connecticut during the American Revolution*, vol. I, 49–51.

288. Ibid, 30–32.

289. Middlebrook, *The Last Cruise of the "Oliver Cromwell" 1779*, 41.

290. Middlebrook, *History of Maritime Connecticut during the American Revolution*, vol. I, 83–84 and 111–116.

291. Knapp, *Stratford and the Sea*, 81. This reference states the eleven captures were made but Louis Middlebrook in his *History of Maritime Connecticut during the American Revolution*, vol. I lists only eight.

292. Ibid. See also Rogers, *Connecticut's Naval Office at New London*, 303.

293. Knapp, *Stratford and the Sea*, 81.

294. Middlebrook, *History of Maritime Connecticut during the American Revolution*, vol. I, 159. See also Coggins, *Ships and Seamen of the American Revolution*, 97.

295. The *Cerberus* was scuttled or destroyed by the British in 1778 to prevent its capture by the French Navy during the siege of Newport. A number of trapped British vessels were destroyed including six frigates (*Grand Duke*, forty guns, *Orpheus*, *Lark*, *Juno*, *Flora*, each thirty-two guns, and *Cerberus*, twenty-eight guns), three corvettes and a bomb ketch taken after the great storm.

296. Coggins, *Ships and Seamen of the American Revolution*, 97.

297. Ibid.

298. Ibid, 64.

299. Middlebrook, *History of Maritime Connecticut during the American Revolution*, vol. I, 52, 98 and 99 and vol. II, 306.

300. Ibid, vol. I, 84 and vol. II, 306–308.

301. Ibid, vol. I, 52–53 and vol. II, 317–318.

302. Ibid, 30–32.

303. Ibid, 32, 33 and 41 and Caulkins, *History of Norwich*, 403.

304. Ibid, vol. I, 143–144.

305. Banks, *This is Fairfield 1639–1940*, 59.

306. Middlebrook, *History of Maritime Connecticut during the American Revolution*, vol. II, 319.

307. Middlebrook, *The Last Cruise of the "Oliver Cromwell" 1779*, 44.

308. Middlebrook, *History of Maritime Connecticut during the American Revolution*, vol. I, 97.

309. Middlebrook, *The Last Cruise of the "Oliver Cromwell" 1779*, 46–50. The British log on page 46 says the battle took place on June 5 but British ship log book dates are all 1 day earlier than American dates.

310. Middlebrook, *History of Maritime Connecticut during the American Revolution*, vol. II, 246.
311. Innis et al. (eds.), *The Diary of Simeon Perkins*, vol. 36, p. 61.
312. Middlebrook, *History of Maritime Connecticut during the American Revolution*, vol. I, 125–130.
313. Carr, *Early History of Branford*, 34.
314. Middlebrook, *History of Maritime Connecticut during the American Revolution*, vol. I, 149–150.
315. Ibid.
316. Naval Historical Center, "Dictionary of American Naval Fighting Ships." See also Force, Peter (ed.), *American Archives*, Fifth Series, Vol. 3.
317. Middlebrook, *History of Maritime Connecticut during the American Revolution*, vol. II, 150–153.
318. McCusker, John J., "The First Continental Flagship." The four other officers who escaped with Hinman were John Welch, Peter Richards of Norwich, Charles Bulkeley of Colchester and William Hambleton.
319. Naval Historical Center, "Dictionary of American Naval Fighting Ships." See also Grant, *"Thar She Goes,"* 35.
320. Caulkins, *History of New London*, 540.
321. Middlebrook, *History of Maritime Connecticut during the American Revolution*, vol. I, 244–245.
322. Innis et al. (eds.), *The Diary of Simeon Perkins*, vol. 29, pp. 193–200.
323. Ibid.
324. Lathrop, *Black Rock: Seaport of Old Fairfield*, 34.
325. Federal Writers Project, *History of Milford Connecticut 1639–1939*, 63.
326. Weigold, *The American Mediterranean*, 25–26.
327. Wells, Hatten and Briggs (eds.), *The Bronx and its People*, 210.
328. It appears the *Schuldham* was subsequently sent on to New London for libel and condemnation proceedings. The crew was saved for future prisoner exchanges.
329. Western Connecticut State University, "Connecticut as the Provision State & Danbury's Early Role in Civic Engagement."
330. McDevitt, *Connecticut Attacked*, 27–29.
331. Ibid, 31–32.
332. Klein, *Westport Connecticut*, 56–56.

333. McDevitt, *Connecticut Attacked*, 61–62.

334. Steiner, *History of Guilford and Madison, Connecticut*, 431–432.

335. Smith, *The History of Guilford*, 49.

336. Ibid. See also Steiner, *History of Guilford and Madison, Connecticut*, 431–432.

337. Danenberg, *Naval History of Fairfield County Men in the Revolution*, 47.

338. Schecter, *The Battle for New York*, 289–291.

339. Rose, *Washington's Spies*, 47–48.

340. Ibid. See also Knapp, *Stratford and the Sea*, 81.

341. Tyler, "History Close at Hand," 4.

342. Ibid, 2–3.

343. Ibid.

344. DeWan, "Finding Bounty in War Booty."

345. Warren, *Chauncey Judd or the Stolen Boy*, chapter 8.

346. Ray and Stewart, *Norwalk*, 53.

347. Schecter, *The Battle for New York*, 307.

348. Ferguson, *Fishers Island N.Y. 1614–1925*, 60 and 61.

349. Rose, *Washington's Spies*, 103 and 125.

350. Ibid, 126.

351. Ibid, 166 and 167.

352. Jensen, "The Home Front." *American Heritage Magazine*.

353. Bolton, *History of Westchester County, New York*, Vol. I, 71–75.

354. *Hartford Courant*, February 22, 1780, p. 1. "Copy of a letter from General Sir Henry Clinton to Lord George Germaine, dated Headquarters, Dobbs Ferry, July 25, 1779." See also *Hartford Courant*, August 20, 1787, p. 1. "From the British Annual Register for 1779."

355. *Hartford Courant*, August 20, 1787, p. 1. "From the British Annual Register for 1779."

356. Schecter, *The Battle for New York*, 325.

357. Middlebrook, *History of Maritime Connecticut during the American Revolution*, Vol. I, p. xi.

358. Hartley, *The History of Hamden Connecticut*, 82.

359. Osterweis, *Three Centuries of New Haven, 1638–1938*, 146–149.

360. Banks, *This is Fairfield 1639–1940*, 62.

361. Ibid. See also Radune, *Pequot Plantation*, 35 and 36 for information on the battle in this swamp during The Pequot War in 1637.

362. Banks, *This is Fairfield 1639–1940*, 64.
363. Ibid.
364. Ibid, 65 and 67.
365. Lathrop, *Black Rock: Seaport of Old Fairfield*, 30 and 31.
366. Banks, *This is Fairfield 1639–1940*, 64 and 66. General Tryon's numbers are reported in the *Hartford Courant*, February 22, 1780, p. 1, "Extract of a letter from Major General Tryon to General Sir Henry Clinton, dated New York, July 20, 1779."
367. Ray and Stewart, *Norwalk*, 59–63.
368. *Hartford Courant*, August 20, 1787, p. 1. "From the British Annual Register for 1779."
369. Banks, *This is Fairfield 1639–1940*, 63.
370. Ibid, 70.
371. Middlebrook, *History of Maritime Connecticut during the American Revolution*, vol. II, 323 and 324.
372. Ibid, 123.
373. Banks, *This is Fairfield 1639–1940*, 79.
374. Ibid, 61.
375. Feinstein and Pendry, *Stamford*, 44.
376. *Cold Spring Harbor Soundings*, 21.
377. Banks, *This is Fairfield 1639–1940*, 60.
378. Ibid.
379. Ibid, 70.
380. Jensen, "The Home Front." *American Heritage Magazine*.
381. Knapp, *Stratford and the Sea*, 83.
382. Danenberg, *Naval History of Fairfield County Men in the Revolution*, 77.
383. Rose, *Washington's Spies*, 159–164.
384. Ibid.
385. Tallmadge, *Memoir of Colonel Benjamin Tallmadge*, 29.
386. Ibid, 32–34.
387. Innis et al. (eds.), *The Diary of Simeon Perkins*, vol. 36, pp. 24, 98, 104, 108 and 111.
388. Ibid, 108.
389. Middlebrook, *History of Maritime Connecticut during the American Revolution 1775–1783*, vol. II, 189 and 190.
390. Innis et al. (eds.), *The Diary of Simeon Perkins*, vol. 36, p. 140.

391. Middlebrook, *History of Maritime Connecticut during the American Revolution*, vol. II, 84, 85 and 160.

392. Ibid, 94–96. Other references are pages 48, 61, 67, 136, 187 and 211. The Armed boat *Betsey* was commanded by Ackley Riley in 1780. In consort with the *Snake*, they captured a ship loaded with supplies from eastern Long Island bound for New York City. The brig *Ranger*, commanded by Ashbel Riley of Wethersfield, carried fourteen guns and a crew of twenty. Apparently returning from a trip to Surinam the *Ranger* was captured on November 14, 1780 near Montauk Point, Long Island and taken into New York City. Justice Riley provided one third bonding for four privateer ships and was half owner of one of these.

393. Ibid, 136, 137, 239 and 240.

394. Lathrop, *Black Rock: Seaport of Old Fairfield*, 32 and 33.

395. Middlebrook, *History of Maritime Connecticut during the American Revolution 1775–1783*, vol. 1, p. 168.

396. Rogers, *Connecticut's Naval Office at New London*, 99.

397. Overton, *Plunderers from Across the Sound*.

398. Banks, *This is Fairfield 1639–1940*, 75.

399. Feinstein and Pendry, *Stamford*, 44.

400. Warren, *Chauncey Judd or the Stolen Boy*, Chapter 9.

401. DeWan, "Finding Bounty in War Booty."

402. Ibid.

403. Warren, *Chauncey Judd or the Stolen Boy*, Chapter 24.

404. Ibid, Chapter 25.

405. Knapp, *Stratford and the Sea*, 71.

406. Ibid.

407. Tallmadge, *Memoir of Colonel Benjamin Tallmadge*, 39–42.

408. Rose, *Washington's Spies*, 239.

409. Feinstein and Pendry, *Stamford*, 44. See also Hoyt, *A Genealogical History of the Hoyt, Haight, and Hight Families*, 360.

410. Banks, *This is Fairfield 1639–1940*, 71.

411. Steiner, *History of Guilford and Madison, Connecticut*, 438 and 439.

412. Tallmadge, *Memoir of Colonel Benjamin Tallmadge*, 43. See also Rose, *Washington's Spies*, 252–254.

413. Ibid.

414. Danenberg, *Naval History of Fairfield County Men in the Revolution*, 51 and 52.

415. Schecter, *The Battle for New York*, 348.

416. Ibid, 352.

417. Middlebrook, *History of Maritime Connecticut during the American Revolution*, Vol. II, 163 and 164.

418. Rogers, *Connecticut's Naval Office at New London*, 122–124.

419. Ibid.

420. Rogers, *Sesquicentennial of the Battle of Grotton Height*, 22.

421. Allyn, *Battle of Groton Height*, 103.

422. Decker, *The Whaling City*, 58.

423. Ibid, 59.

424. Rogers, *Sesquicentennial of the Battle of Groton Height*, 27.

425. Duvall, *The History of Shelter Island*, 68. See also Boas, *Stonington During the American Revolution*, 124.

426. Middlebrook, *History of Maritime Connecticut during the American Revolution*, Vol. II, 256–258.

427. Steiner, *History of Guilford and Madison, Connecticut*, 440.

428. Tallmadge, *Memoir of Colonel Benjamin Tallmadge*, 47–49. See also Rose, *Washington's Spies*, 263 and 264.

429. Rose, *Washington's Spies*, 261 and 262.

430. Ibid. Tallmadge's *Memoir of Colonel Benjamin Tallmadge* and Rose's *Washington's Spies* both identify Hoyt as having been killed and that he was the same one who Tallmadge confronted the year before on the *Shuldham* but no first name is given. A study of Hoyt's book, *A Genealogical History of the Hoyt, Haight, and Hight Families*, does not identify any Tory with the Hoyt name dying in 1782 and does not contain any specific information about this incident.

431. Danenberg, *Naval History of Fairfield County Men in the Revolution*, 54.

432. Tallmadge, *Memoir of Colonel Benjamin Tallmadge*, 51 and 52.

433. Knapp, *Stratford and the Sea*, 70.

434. Ray and Stewart, *Norwalk*, 66 and 67.

435. Overton, *Plunderers from Across the Sound*, 39–42.

436. Moore, *The Loyalists*, 152.

437. Feinstein, *Stamford from Puritan to Patriot*, 199 and 200.

438. *Globe and Mail*, June 17, 2006, p. D13, "Black Loyalists railroaded."

439. Moore, *The Loyalists*, 209.

440. Innis et al. (eds.), *The Diary of Simeon Perkins*, Vol. 36, pp. 181–185.

441. Ibid, 183.

442. Ibid, 187.

443. Ibid, 190 and 191.

444. Ibid, 238.

445. Ibid, 291, 355, 358 and 407. See also Vol. 29, p. 151.

446. Ibid, 496.

447. Ibid, 235, 238, 291, 319, 364 and 368. See page xlv for a listing of the occasions where Liverpool was criticized by government officials for laxity.

448. Caulkins, *History of Norwich*, 478.

449. Ibid, 476 and 477.

450. Maloney, *The Captain from Connecticut*, 5.

451. Decker, *The Whaling City*, 63.

452. Innis et al. (eds.), *The Diary of Simeon Perkins*, Vol. 36, pp. xxxix and xl.

453. *Shallops, Sloops and Sharpies*, 34–36.

454. Maloney, *The Captain from Connecticut*, 7–12.

455. Decker, *The Whaling City*, 63 and 64.

456. Milkofsky (ed.), *A Grande Reliance*, 21.

457. Joseph Williams Collection, Coll. 37.

458. Ibid, Coll. 37, Box 2, Folder 19.

459. Grant, "*Thar She Goes,*" 46 and 47.

460. Knapp, *Stratford and the Sea*, 152.

461. Knapp, *Stratford and the Sea*, 155.

462. Shumway and (eds.), *New Haven, An Illustrated History*, 66. See also *Shallops, Sloops and Sharpies*, 29.

463. Jones, *Stonington Borough: A Connecticut Seaport in the 19th Century*, 85. See Crandall, *The Fine Old Town of Stonington*, 91 for Fanning's 1801 trip.

464. Morison, *The Maritime History of Massachusetts*, 396–398.

465. Knapp, *Stratford and the Sea*, 153–155.

466. Bickford, *Voices of the New Republic*, 32.

467. Ibid.

468. Grant, "*Thar She Goes,*" 46 and 47.

469. Milkofsky (ed.), *A Grande Reliance*, 3.

470. Grant, "*Thar She Goes,*" 98 and 99.

471. Dart, *Yankee Traders at Sea and Ashore*, 16.

472. Albion, *The Rise of New York Port*, 245 and 246. See also Grant, *Thar She Goes*, 140–143.

473. Dart, *Yankee Traders at Sea and Ashore*, 12 and 13.

474. *Shallops, Sloops and Sharpies*, 54.

475. Sisler, *The Seven Hills of Port* [Jefferson], 3.

476. Duvall, *The History of Shelter Island*, 94 and 95.

477. D'Entremont, "Fayerweather Island Lighthouse."

478. Ibid.

479. Ibid.

480. Innis et al. (eds.), *The Diary of Simeon Perkins*, Vol. 50, xxvi–xxx.

481. Ibid.

482. Duvall, *The History of Shelter Island*, 93, 97 and 99.

483. Ibid, 98.

484. Ibid, 102.

485. Ibid, 103–106.

486. Robotti and Vescovi, *The USS Essex*, 124–126.

487. Ibid. See also Schlesinger (ed.), *The Almanac of American History*, 183.

488. Narrative of Capt. Jeremiah Holmes of Mystic Bridge, Conn., 39–41.

489. Ibid, 77 and 78.

490. Innis et al. (eds.), *The Diary of Simeon Perkins*, vol. 43, xlvi.

491. Ibid, vol. 50, 123–124.

492. Ibid.

493. Banks, *This is Fairfield 1639–1940*, 84.

494. Lathrop, *Black Rock: Seaport of Old Fairfield*, 77.

495. Banks, *This is Fairfield 1639–1940*, 84.

496. Grant, *"Thar She Goes,"* 50.

497. Decker, *The Whaling City*, 68.

498. Dart, *Yankee Traders at Sea and Ashore*, 21.

499. Federal Writers Project, *History of Milford Connecticut*, 69.

500. Dart, *Yankee Traders at Sea and Ashore*, 32–35.

501. Ibid.

502. Decker, *The Whaling City*, 68 and 69.

503. De Kay, *The Battle of Stonington*, 6–8. Two of George Washington's nephews were impressed and repeatedly denied release.

504. Lathrop, *Black Rock: Seaport of Old Fairfield*, 79.

505. Bickford, *Voices of the New Republic*, 188.

506. Ray and Stewart, *Norwalk*, 73–75.

507. Dudley, *The Naval War of 1812*, Vol. I, 566–570.

508. France sold the island in exchange for trading rights in the Swedish port of Gothenburg. It was re-purchased by the French in 1878.

509. Maloney, *The Captain from Connecticut*, 185–190.

510. Banks, *This is Fairfield 1639–1940*, 84.

511. Wells and Proios, *Port Jefferson, Story of a Village*, 9.

512. De Kay, *The Battle of Stonington*, 13–15.

513. Ibid, 18–20.

514. Ibid.

515. Federal Writers Project, *History of Milford Connecticut 1639–1939*, pp. 70–71.

516. Ibid.

517. De Kay, *The Battle of Stonington*, 23–27.

518. Knapp, *Stratford and the Sea*, 86.

519. De Kay, *The Battle of Stonington*, 23–37.

520. Ibid, 34–37.

521. Ibid, 54–60.

522. Ibid, 56.

523. Ibid, 44–47.

524. Ibid, 58–61.

525. Ibid.

526. Ibid, 52–54.

527. Ibid, 62–63.

528. Ibid, 81–88 and 102.

529. Ibid, 50–51.

530. Ibid, 67–68.

531. Knapp, *Stratford and the Sea*, 88 and 89. See also Coggeshall, *History of the American Privateers, and Letters-of-Marque*, 219–225.

532. Ibid.

533. Mullins, *Liverpool Privateering 1756–1815*, p. 29.

534. Ibid, 93.

535. De Kay, *The Battle of Stonington*, 103–106.

536. Ibid.

537. Malcarne, "The British Attack on Potapoug."

538. Ibid.

539. De Kay, *The Battle of Stonington*, 128–131.

540. Ibid, 110.

541. Ibid, 135 and 136.

542. Ibid, 147 and 148.

543. Ibid, 152.

544. Ibid, 163 and 164.

545. Ibid, 165–168.

546. Ibid, 170–173.

547. Ibid, 136 and 137.

548. Ibid, 173–177. The written message given by Commodore Hardy to Dr. Lord and Colonel Williams reads as follows: "I have received your letter and representation of the State of your Town, and as you have declared that Torpedoes, never have been harbored by the Inhabitants or ever will be, as far as it lies in their power to prevent—and as you engaged that Mrs. Stewart the wife of the British vice consul late resident at New London, with her family, shall be permitted to embark on board this Ship tomorrow morning, I am induced to waive the attempt of the total destruction of your Town, which I feel confident can be effected by the Squadron under my Orders."

549. *The Mystic Pioneer*, Vol. 1, July 16, 1859. The material for this article was verified by eyewitnesses still alive at the time of publication.

550. Ibid, 183.

551. *Hartford Courant*, August 23, 1814, p. 2, "Record of the extraordinary attack on Stonington."

552. *Hartford Courant*, October 4, 1815, p. 2, "At Stonington."

553. De Kay, *The Battle of Stonington*, 194.

554. Banks, *This is Fairfield 1639–1940*, p. 85.

555. Coggeshall, *History of the American Privateers, and Letters-of-Marque*, 372–382.

556. Ibid.

557. Ibid.

558. Ibid, 377.

559. *Hartford Courant*, April 12, 1860, p. 2, 'The 'Scotch Prize'—An Incident of the Last War."

560. Knapp, *Stratford and the Sea*, 93.

561. Mullins, *Liverpool Privateering 1756–1815*, pp. 38 and 39.

562. Banks, *This is Fairfield 1639–1940*, 87 and 88. The Fairfield Academy was a private preparatory school that was founded in 1802 and first opened in 1804. Today it is owned by the Eunice Dennie Burr DAR Chapter.

563. Decker, *The Whaling City*, 72.

564. Knapp, *Stratford and the Sea*, 159 and 160.

565. King, *Skeletons on the Zahara*, 15.

566. Ibid, 24 and 25.

567. Ibid, 29–32.

568. Ibid, 43 and 44.

569. Ibid, 310 and 311.

570. Albion, *The Rise of New York Port*, 146.

571. Bickford, *Voices of the New Republic*, 188 and 189.

572. Stevens, *Connecticut River Master Mariners*. This is based on a review of the information on all ship captains documented in the book.

573. Albion, *The Rise of New York Port*, 242–245.

574. Ibid, 192 and 416.

575. Ibid, 241.

576. Ibid, 242.

577. Ibid, 250 and 251.

578. Stevens, "The Discovery of Antarctica." *The Log of Mystic Seaport*, 106–109.

579. Ibid.

580. Spears, *Captain Nathaniel Brown Palmer*, 71–75.

581. Peterson, *Mystic Built*, 7, 8 and 123.

INDEX

page numbers in bold indicate illustrations

Abigail, 119
Acadians, 33–35
Acasta, 233, 238
Admiral Keppel, 134, 135
agriculture. *See* farming
Aix-la-Chapelle, Treaty of, 32
Albion, Robert, 261
Alexandria, 239
Alfred, 76, 78, 142, 143, 144, 188
Allen, Thomas, 42–43
Alliance, 142
Amazon, 67
Ambuscade, 131
America, 66
American Indians. *See* Indians
American Revenue, 121, 122
American War of Independence.
   See Revolutionary War
Andrew Doria, 78
Andros, Edmund, 3
Anglican Church, 82, 83–84
Anguilla, 17, 20
Annabella, 88
Annapolis Rover, 124
Antarctica, discovery of, 6, 262
apprentice system, 22
Arctic, Franklin Expedition to, 263
Arnold, Benedict
   Danbury Raid, 150
   New London attack/Battle of
      Groton Heights, 26, 34, 79,
      187–191
   Quebec invasion, 62–63
   Valcour Island battle, 96
Arnold, Benjamin, 39
Asia, HMS, 55–56, 102
Aspasia, 211
Atlantic Ocean seaboard, 114,
   176
Avondale, R. I., 21
Azores Islands, 250–251

Backus, Abigail, 37, 117
Backus, Ebenezer, 36–37, 117

Backus, Erastus, 117
Bahamas, 76, 106
Barbados, 18–19, 40
Barlow, John, 106
Barnstable Harbor, 66
Bartram, Ebenezer, 178
The Battle for New York
   (Schecter), vi
Battle of the Kegs, 134
Beaver, 119, 121
Bedford, Conn., 159
Bell, Thomas, 215
Bellingshausen, Thaddeus,
   262
Bellona, 77
Benjamin, Pulaski, 255
Bennett, Deliverance, 150
Beresford, John, 222
Bethany, Conn., 180
Betsey, 57, 240, 253
Biddle, Captain, 241
Black Joke, 55
black people, 24, 137, 223. *See
   also* slaves
Black Point, 79
Black Prince, 242
Black Rock Harbor, 11, 79,
   162, 164, 183, 214, 217, 228,
   250
Blackstone, John, 14
Black X Line, 213–214, 260
Blakeman, Curtiss, 211
Block Island, 60, 76, 224
Blonde, 145
Blue Point, 124
Board of Associated Loyalists, 11,
   116, 172, 179, 180, 181–182
Bonaire, 17
Bores, 236
Boston, Mass., British withdrawal
   from, 86, 87
Boston Harbor, 15
Bourbon, 23
Branford, Conn., 185

Bransfield, Edward, 262
Brewster, Anne Lewis, 197
Brewster, Caleb, 98–99, 154,
   155, 157, 170, 183,
   193–194, 197
Bridgeport, Conn.
   Black Rock Harbor, 11, 79,
      162, 164, 183, 214, 217, 228,
      250
   port of, 212
   Revolutionary War
      fortifications, 79
Briggen Company, 38
brigs, 5, 68, **69**
British Navy
   desertion, 49, 179, 221
   Fort Louisbourg siege, 30–31
   impressment of American
      sailors, 29, 201, 206,
      220–223, 224, 227, 238, 254
   Revolutionary War, 55–56, 86,
      89, 105–106, 116, 157, 166
   ships, 68–72
   trade restriction enforcement,
      45–46, 47
   War of 1812, 217, 230–238
   See also specific ships
British West Indies, 44,
   203
Bronx, N. Y., 101
Brookhaven, 168
Brooklyn, Conn., 27
Brooklyn, N. Y., 96
Brooks, John, 55–56
Broome, 116
Brown, Governor, 106
Brown, Smith, 26
Brush, Jesse, 168
Buckley, Jonathan, 223
Bunker Hill, Battle of, 55
buoys, 22
Bushnell, David, 72, 93, 132–134,
   234
Bushnell, Ezra, 93

Cabot, 77, 142–143
Caldwell, John, 208
Canada, trade with, 4. *See also specific provinces*
Cannon, John, 44, 46
cannons, 51, 74–75, 79, 117
Cape Breton Island, 28, 30, 31, 32
Cape Verde Islands, 257–258
Carleton, Guy, 94, 181
Carnation, 250, 251
Carpenter, John, 238
Carrington, Elias, 105
cartel ships, 104
Catumb Passage, 7
Cerberus, 124, 132–133
Cerebrus, 72
Champlin, Amelia Hayden, 213–214, 260
Champlin, Guy, 250
Champlin, Henry, 213–214, 260
Champlin, Samuel, 121, 177
Chapel, Frederick, 94
charcoal, 73
Charleston, 236
Charleston, S. C., 166, 171
Chauncey, Isaac, 224
Cheeseboro, Charles, 138
Chesebrough, William, 60
Chew, Joseph, 46, 47, 85, 152, 161
China, trade with, 205, 210–211, 263
Citizen, 209
City Island, 11
Clarke, William, 181
Clay, Stephen, 208
Clement, Peabody, 117
Clinton, Henry, 138, 156–157, 157–158, 159, 165–166, 179, 187
clipper ships, 6, 263
coastal trade, 11, 14–15, 212, 215, 219, 228
Cochrane, Alexander, 243, 249
Coggeshall, George, 260–261
Coit, William, 64–66
Cold Springs Harbor, N. Y., 115, 170, 214–215, 262
Cole, Siphorus, 253
Collier, George, 160
Collins, Banajah, 118
Collins, Darius, 140, 141
Commerce (sloop), 58
Commerce (brig), shipwreck, 256–258
Compo Beach, 149
Compo Hill, 150–151, 186
Confederacy, 143–144, 212
Congress, USS, 92–93
Conkling, Edward, 97, 119–120
Conkling, Joseph, 97, 119, 120–121, 177–178
Connecticut

Acadians in, 33–35
agriculture and livestock production, 4, 13
black population, 24
British raids, 147–152, 156–166, 179–180
illegal trade, 46–47
King George's War support, 29–31, 32
Long Island refugees in, 96–97, 119–124
Loyalists in, 82, 83–84, 101–102
merchants, 14–15
prisoners, 103, 106
privateers from, 108–109, 112–115, 116
Revolutionary War, 6, 79–80, 96–97, 148–149, 209
shipbuilding, 211–214
shipping vessel traffic, 16
timber industry, 23
trade with West Indies, 16
See also Connecticut Navy; Whaleboat War; *specific cities*
Connecticut (Connecticut Navy), 94
Connecticut (U.S. Navy), 213, 214
Connecticut Navy
compensation, 129–130
Defense, 29, 31, 72, 87–88, 130, 131, 134, 135, 136–137
establishment, 62–63
Fort Louisbourg siege, 6
Guilford, 139–141
Mifflin, 132, 136
New Defense, 141–142
Oliver Cromwell, 66, 89–90, 95, 130–131, 134–135, 136, 137–139
Revolutionary War action, 66–67, 86–96
Schuyler, 99, 131, 132
Setauket, Long Island attack attempt, 132
ships, 68–72
Spy, 71–72, 86–87, 130, 132, 135–136
supplies, 74–75
in West Indies, 134–135
whaleboat support, 171–172
Connecticut River, 5, 9, 10, 22, 23, 212, 216
Constitution, USS, 207, 229
Continental Army, supply shortages, 148–149
Continental Congress, 67, 77, 108–109
Continental Navy
Alfred, 76, 78, 142, 143, 144, 188
Alliance, 142

Bourbon, 23
Cabot, 77, 142–143
Confederacy, 143–144
formation of, 55, 62, 63–66
Raleigh, 143
Revolutionary War action, 76, 78, 87–89
Trumbull, 23, 143, 188
Warren, 142, 188
Coote, Richard, 242
Cornelia, 224–225
Cornwallis, Charles, 187
corruption, 173
Couch, Simon, 167–168
"Cowboys," 100–101
Crane, 90, 91, 92, 141
Crowell, Samuel, 39
Culloden, HMS, 216
Culper Ring, 155
Cunningham, William, 105
Curacao, 43
Cushing, Thomas Humphrey, 245, 247
customs, 13–15, 42, 43–44, 46, 48
Cygnet, 48, 49
Cyrus, 134, 135

Danbury, Conn., 149–150
Daphne, 138
Dartmoor Prison, 255
David Porter, 260
Davis, John, 252
Davis, Solomon, 168
Day, James, 135
Dayton, Ebenezer, 114, 123–124, 155–156, 180–181
Dayton, Phebe, 181
Deane, 144
Deane, Barnabas, 209
Deane, Silas, 144–145, 209
Decatur, Stephen, 230, 232–233, 235, 237–238, 241, 255
Deep River, Conn., 213
Defense, 29, 31, 72, 87–88, 130, 131, 134, 135, 136–137
Defying Empire (Truxes), 47
De Lancey, James, 100
Delaware, 138
Delaware Bay, 133
Delaware River, 76, 133
Delight, 18
Denison, Frederick, 248–249
Denison, Robert, 35, 36, 71
Derby, Conn., 181, 182
Dering, Thomas, 97–98
Deshon, John, 115
Diamond, 31
Dibble, Fyler, 102, 168, 196–197
Dimon, 40
diseases, 104–105, 134
Dispatch, 245–246, 248–249
Dodge, Joseph, 127–128

Dolphin, 130, 135
Dominica, 73
Dorchester Heights, Battle of, 76
Dreadnaught, 202
Driggs, Samuel, 207–208
Driggs, Sarah Brown, 208
Duke de Choisel, 144–145
Dutch Trade, 42–43
Dutch West Indies, 16, 17, 42–43, 44, 203–204

Eagle, 93, 97, 119–120, 234, 242
Eastern United States, map of, x
East Granby, Conn., 181
East Haddam, Conn., 90
East River, 8
Eaton's Neck Lighthouse, 216
Egeria, 225–226
Elderkin, Colonel, 74
Elderkin and Wales, 74
Eldred, Peleg, 177
Elliot, Andrew, 82
Embargo Act (1807) (U.S.), 223–224
England. *See* Great Britain
Enterprise, 209–210
espionage. *See* spies
Essex, Conn., 23, 213, 242–243
Estaing, Jean Baptiste Charles Henri Hector d', 121–122
Esther and Eliza, 208
Ewan, Michael, 138
Eyre, Colonel, 190

Fair American, 177
Fairfield, Conn.
  black population, 24
  British raids, 81, 162–164, 166–167
  lookout posts, 81
  Loyalist whaleboat raids, 184
  Revolutionary War fortifications, 79
  War of 1812, 229–230, 254
Fairfield County, Conn., Loyalists in, 84. *See also specific cities*
Fairplay, 126–127
Falcon, 132
Falkland Islands, 205
Fanning, Edmund, 161, 211
Fanning, James, 19
Fanning, Roger, 92
farming
  in Nova Scotia, 35
  port access, 5, 14
  productivity, 4, 13, 16
  in Salem, Conn., 27
  salt production, 75
  trade with British during Revolutionary War, 56, 97, 174
  in West Indies, 15–17

Faulkner's Island, 216
Fayerweather Island lighthouse, 217
Firebrand, 111
Fire Island Inlet, 114, 124
Fishers Island, N. Y., 7, 10, 96, 157, 217
fishing, 28, 37–38
Fitch, Jabez, 192
Five Mile Point lighthouse, 216–217
flag of truce ships, 45, 103–104
Floyd, Benjamin, 168
Floyd, William, 99
Fones, Captain, 30
Fort Franklin, 11, 80, 170, 174, 185, 186
Fort Golgotha, 80
Fort Griswold, 79, 187, 188–191
Forth, 247
Fort Louisbourg, 6, 28–32
Fort McHenry, 263
Fort Montgomery, 92
Fort Rachel, 236
Fort Salonga, 80
Fort Setauket, 80, 153–154
Fort Slongo, 185, 186
Fort Stamford, 191–192
Fort St. George, 80, 172, 183
Fort Ticonderoga, 59, 76, 96, 144
Fort Trumbull, 79, 104, 189
Fort Washington, 92, 100
Fox, George, 7–8
France
  Fort Franklin attack, 11
  French and Indian Wars, 32–34, 40, 45, 46–47, 48
  King George's War, 28–32, 45
  Napoleonic Wars, 219–220, 221, 228, 237
  Queen Anne's War, 28
  Revolutionary War aid/participation, 121–122, 144–145, 185–186
  undeclared war with America (1798–1800), 201, 206, 208, 210, 218
  war with Great Britain (1793–1802), 205, 218
  West Indies, 16, 17, 44, 45, 203–204
Franklin, Fort, 11, 80, 170, 174, 185, 186
Franklin, William, 11, 84, 106–107, 170, 172, 179
Franklin Expedition, 263
Freeman, Jordon, 190
French and Indian Wars, 32–34, 40, 45, 46–47, 48
French West Indies, 16, 17, 44, 45, 203–204

frigates, 68
Frost, Sarah, 196
Frost, William, 184, 196
fur trade, 38–39, 205, 210–211, 263

Galatea, 167
Gamecock, 124
Gardiner, John, 235
Gardiners Bay, 9, 67, 179, 235, 243
Gardiners Island, 8, 60, 235
Gates, 94, 95
Gazetter, 83
General Armstrong, 250–251
General Green, 177
General Schuyler, 67
geology, 6–7
George, 88
George III, 157
George Washington, 240
Gerard, Count de, 144
Ghent, Treaty of (1814), 254
Gibraltar, 257–258
Gilbert, John, 161
Gilbert, Michael, 161
Gildersleeve, Obadiah, 213
Gildersleeve, Philip, 213
Gildersleeve, Sylvester, 213
Glasgow, 77
Glastonbury, Conn., 212
Gleaner, 261
Glover, Jeremiah, 241–242
Golgotha, Fort, 80
Good Hope, 26
Gorham, Nathan, 105–106
Graham, Alexander, 180, 181
Grant, Captain, 94
Grant, Ebenezer, 212
Grasse, Comte de, 173
Graves, Matthew, 85
Great Britain
  French and Indian Wars, 32–34, 40, 45, 46–47, 48
  King George's War, 28–32, 45
  Napoleonic Wars, 219–220, 221, 228, 237
  trade restrictions, 3, 13–15, 16, 42–51
  war with France (1793–1802), 205, 218
  See also British Navy; Revolutionary War; War of 1812
Great Inagua, 17
Great South Bay, 114, 116, 124, 172, 183
Greene, Daniel, 210–211
Greenfield Hill, 146
Greenport, 9
Greenwich, 176–177
Greenwich, Conn., 75, 79, 81

Griswold, Charles, 213, 260
Griswold, Fort, 79, 187, 188–191
Griswold, George, 213–214, 224–225, 260
Griswold, John, 213, 260
Griswold, Nathaniel, 213–214, 224–225, 260
Griswold, William, 62
Groton, Conn.
  Arnold's invasion of, 187–191
  British raids/attacks, 170, 178
  Long Island refugees in, 119
  Groton Heights, Battle of, 79, 188–191
grounding, 88, 111–112, 252, 253
Guerriere, HMS, 207, 229
Guilford, 139–141
Guilford, Conn.
  Long Island refugee evacuation, 96–97
  Loyalist whaleboat raids, 151–152, 184–185, 193
  Revolutionary War, 111–112
Gull Island, 8, 244
gunpowder, 73–74

Hale, Nathan, 99–100
Halifax, 99–100
Halifax, Nova Scotia, 32–33, 43, 57
Halka, 246
Hall, Giles, 63
Hampton Packet, 196
Hancock, 177, 178
Hancock, John, 63
Hancox, Edward, 71
Hannah, 64, 188, 189
Hannah and Elizabeth, 86
harbors, description of, 9–12. *See also specific harbors*
Harding, Seth, 87–89, 130–131, 143–144
Hardy, Thomas, 232, 233–238, 243, 244–248
Harlem Heights, Battle of, 99–100
Harrington, Thomas, 175
Harrison, 64–66
Hartford, Conn., 14, 212
Hashamomuck Beach, 151
Hat Act (1732) (Great Britain), 50
Havens, James, 98, 191
Havens, Nicoll, 97, 98, 191
Havens, William, 97, 119, 121, 178
Hawk, 112, 204
Hawkins, Joel, 153
Hawley, David, 75–77, 94–96, 131, 141, 169, 172, 192–193
Hawley, Samuel, 101
Hayden, Uriah, 23, 260

Hazard, 118, 122, 137
Heer Adams, 167
Hell Gate, 7, 8–9
Hero, 230–231, 262
Hersilia, 261–262
Hessians, 49, 159, 160, 161, 163, 164
Hewlett, Richard, 153–154
Hibernia, 167
Hinman, Elisha, 142–143
Hispaniola, 46, 48, 126
History of Maritime Connecticut during the American Revolution 1775–1783 (Middlebrook), 112
Hoadley, William, 14
Holmes, Anne Denison Gallup, 222
Holmes, Jeremiah, 46, 221–222, 230–231, 236, 241, 262
Hope, 86–87, 208
Hopkins, Esek, 76–77, 78, 106
Hornet, USS, 232, 233, 241
Horse Neck, 157
Hotham, Henry, 243, 244, 247
Hough, Lieutenant, 244
Housatonic River, 10–11
Howe, William, 65–66, 96, 100, 105, 149, 153, 156–157
Hoyt, Captain, 194
Hoyt, Gould, 196
Hoyt, Jesse, 102, 185
Hoyt, Joseph, 102, 184
Hoyt, Stephen, 102, 156
Hubbell, Amos, 195, 209
Hubbell, Ezekial, 209–210
Hubbell, Wilson, 209
Huddy, Joshua, 182
Hudson River, 91–92, 149
Hudson River Highlands, 92, 100, 146, 147, 149, 159, 165
Hull, Isaac, 182, 207, 229
Hull, Joseph, 182–183, 204
Hunt, Samuel, 118
Huntington, Andrew, 58
Huntington, N. Y., 80, 115, 156, 193–194
Huntington Bay, N. Y., 11, 102, 156, 164, 170, 185, 215, 216
Huntington Harbor, 115, 132, 139, 170, 186, 188
Hurd, Jesse, 213, 214
Hurlburt, Titus, 79
Hussar, HMS, 8–9, 167

illicit trade
  categories of, 42–47
  Fishers Island's role, 157
  during Revolutionary War, 147, 174, 192–193, 195
  during War of 1812, 224–226

impressment, 29, 40–41, 201, 206, 220–223, 224, 227, 238, 254
Indemnity, 230
indentured servants, 34
Indians
  British support of attacks by, 228
  in Connecticut Navy, 95, 137
  Groton Heights battle casualties, 191
  Pequot War, 163
  trade with, 39
Industrial Revolution, 259–260
"infernal machines," 234–235, 241–242
Inglesbee, Nicklas, 40
insurance, 21, 58, 124–125, 226
iron, 74
Iron Act (1750) (Great Britain), 50–51
Isham, General, 246

Jabez Perkins & Co., 139, 177
Jamaica, 124
James II, 3
Jane, 31
Jay, 178
Jay, John, 206
Jefferson, Thomas, 223
Jersey, 103, 106, 155, 178
jibing, 125–126
John, 188
John and Joseph, 78
Jolly Fisherman, 38, 39
Jones, Ebenezer, 176–177
Jones, Jacob, 241
Jones, John H., 215
Jones, John Paul, 143
Jones, Thomas, 169–170
Joseph Williams & Company, 167
Judd, Chauncey, 181
Julius Caesar, 195, 209

Keppel, 185
Kerr, John, 136
King-Fisher, 59
King George's War, 28–32, 45
King's Bridge, 100
Kings County, N. Y., 96
King William's War, 29, 40
Kips Bay, 100
Knapp's Tavern, 254
Knowles, John, 39

Lady Washington, 67, 90, 91–92
La Hogue, 241
Lake Champlain, 94–96
Landon, David, 140, 141
Lantern Hill, 80
Lark, 207
Latham, Giles, 117

L'Aurore, 144
Law, Richard, Jr., 225–226
Lawrence, Charles, 33, 35
lead, 72–73
Lebanon, Conn., 27
Ledyard, Colonel, 190
Lee, Charles, 71
Lee, Sergeant, 93–94
Leeds, William, 121, 122
Leete, Ambrose, 185
Leete, Solomon, 140–141, 152
Leffingwell, Richard, 34–35
Leslie, Charles, 49
Lexington and Concord, Battle
    of, 55
Liberty (British Navy), 49–50
Liberty (Perkins), 38, 39
Lieutenant River, 213
lighthouses, 22, 59, 212, 215–218
Lily Ann, 72
Little Gull Lighthouse, 217
Little Joe, 117, 253
Little Rebecca, 127–128
Liverpool, England, 219–220
Liverpool, Nova Scotia, 37–39,
    116–117, 202
Liverpool Harbor, 144–145,
    174–175
Liverpool Packet, 240, 253
Lloyd, Commodore, 250–251
Lloyd, John, 46
Lloyd Harbor, N. Y., 11, 115, 170
Lloyd Neck, 102, 170, 185–186
Loire, 254
Long Island, N. Y.
    agriculture and livestock
        production, 4
    British invasion and
        occupation, 67, 80, 86,
        96–99, 172–173
    patriot refugees from, 97–99,
        119–124, 197
    shipbuilding, 214–215
    See also Whaleboat War
Long Island Sound
    during colonial period, 28–51
    definition of, vii
    geography, 6–7
    historical legacies, 263–264
    map of, xi
    maritime independence, 13–27,
        256–264
    during Revolutionary War (See
        Revolutionary War)
    ship entrances and exits, 7–9
    strategic significance, v, 3–12
    during War of 1812 (See War
        of 1812)
lookout posts, 80–81
Loper, Dickie, 246
Lord, Samuel, 219–220
Lord, William, 244, 246, 247

Lord family, 215
Lord Howe, 89
Lords Passage, 7
Loring, Elizabeth, 105
Loring, Joshua, 105
Lotteryville, R. I., 21
Louisbourg, Fort, 6, 28–32
Lovely Lass, 121
Loyalists
    black people as, 197
    Board of Associated Loyalists,
        11, 116, 172, 179, 180,
        181–182
    British government's treatment
        of, 172–173
    in Connecticut, 82, 83–84, 85,
        101–102, 196
    Lloyd Neck fortification,
        185–186
    Long Island fort establishment,
        11
    in New York, 82–83, 160
    in Nova Scotia, 33, 197, 202
    percentage of population, 81–82
    privateers, 115–116
    after Revolutionary War, 196
    Revolutionary War actions,
        100–101
    from Rhode Island, 103, 172
    weapons supply, 56
    See also Whaleboat War
Lucretia, 115
Lucy, 117, 140, 141
Ludington, Henry, 150
Ludington, Sybil, 150
lumber, 23, 28, 38
Lyme, Conn., 213–214
Lynde Point lighthouse, 216
Lyon, 178

Macedonian, HMS, 230, 232,
    233, 241
Madison, James, 236
Maidstone, 242
Manhattan
    black population, 24
    Loyalists in, 82–83
    during Revolutionary War, 67,
        83, 92, 93, 99
man-of-war ships, 68
Mansfield, Giles, 94
maritime independence elements,
    13–27
    harbors, 9–12
    maritime-related industry
        development, 22–27
    merchant entrepreneurs,
        14–15, 17–22
    trade restrictions and custom
        duties, 3, 13–15
    trade with West Indies, 15–17
    after War of 1812, 256–264

maritime industry, 4–5, 22–27,
    211–215, 258–262, 263
Marlbury, 208
Mars, 140–141
Massachusetts
    British withdrawal from
        Boston, 86, 87
    King George's War support,
        29–30, 32
    state navy, 66
Massachusetts Bay, 87–88
Mastic, N. Y., 80, 103, 172, 183
Mather, Joseph, 26
Mather, Moses, 168, 184
Mather, Richard, 215
Matthews, David, 107
McHenry, Fort, 263
Medway, 135
Meigs, Phineas, 193
Meigs, Return J., 151
Menzies, Major, 88–89
merchants and merchant ships
    captures of, 45, 57–58, 113,
        114, 116, 119, 176
    from Connecticut, 14–15
    expenses, 17–18
    after Revolutionary War,
        206–210
    risks to, 18–22
    during War of 1812, 230–231
    after War on 1812, 256–259
    between wars, 206–210
    See also privateers and
        privateering; trade; specific
        merchants
Mercury, 177
Merwin, Mrs. Miles, 148
Mianus River, 192
Middlebrook, Louis F., 112
Middle Haddam, Conn., 213
Middletown, 119
Middletown, Conn.
    black population, 24
    industries, 260
    lead mine, 72–73
    merchant economy, 14
    patriots in, 84
    rope production, 24–25
    shipbuilding, 23, 212–213
    slave dealers, 27
    trade impacted by Embargo
        Act, 223
Mifflin, 132, 136
Miles, Isaac, 105
Milford, 142
Milford, Conn.
    British foraging raids, 147–148
    during Revolutionary War, 105
    Revolutionary War
        fortifications, 79
    shipbuilding, 214
Milford Harbor, 10, 79, 104

Milford Point, 79
military supply shortages, 72–78
militias, colonial, 29
Mill River, 184
Miner, Nathaniel, 84
Minerva, 62–63, 188, 196
mines, 132–134
molasses, 48
Molasses Act (1733) (Great
    Britain), 43, 49
Montauk Point, 215–215, 243
Montgomery (New York Navy), 67
Montgomery (USS), 67, 92–93
Montgomery, Fort, 92
Montgomery, Major, 190
Montgomery, Richard, 62–63
Moore, Catherine, 217
Morrell, Benjamin, 249
Morris, Robert, 145
Mortimer, Philip, 24–25
Mortimer, Prince, 25
Mulligan, Hercules, 198
Mumford, Thomas, 38, 115
musket balls, 72–73
Mystic, Conn., 9, 248, 263
Mystic River, 236, 263

Nancy, 71
Napoleon Bonaparte, 219, 242
Napoleonic Wars, 219–220, 221,
    228, 237
Narcissus, 252–253
Narragansett Bay, 76–77, 224
Nathaniel Palmer House, 263
navies
    British (*See* British Navy)
    Connecticut (*See* Connecticut
        Navy)
    New York, 66, 67
    state navy establishment, 66
    U.S. (*See* U.S. Navy)
Navigation Acts, 3
Neptune, 210–211
New Brunswick, Canada,
    196–197
New Defense, 141–142
Newgate Prison, 181
New Hampshire
    King George's War support,
        29, 32
    state navy, 66
New Haven, 94
New Haven, Conn.
    British customs site, 15
    British invasion, 140–141
    British raids, 81, 160–161
    lookout posts, 80–81
    Revolutionary War
        fortifications, 79
    seal trade, 205, 210–211
    shipbuilding, 90
    War of 1812, 251–253

New Haven Harbor, 10, 214,
    216–217
New London, Conn.
    Arnold's invasion of, 187–191
    black population, 24
    British raids/attacks, 85, 170,
        178
    customs houses, 43–44
    Long Island refugees in, 119
    lookout posts, 80
    Loyalists in, 85
    privateers from, 115, 177
    Revolutionary War
        fortifications, 78–79
    Shaw Mansion, 34, 190
    slave dealers, 27
    tide, 7
    trade, 204, 223–224
    War of 1812, 233, 255
    whaling, 262
New London, Port of, 14–15,
    17–18
New London Gazette, 49
New London Harbor, 10, 14, 49,
    72, 78, 188, 212
Newport, R. I.
    Battle of Rhode Island, 112
    British trade restriction
        enforcement, 49–50
    during Revolutionary War, 66,
        67, 109, 113, 121, 122, 157,
        166, 171, 184
Newport Harbor, 179
New Providence Island, 76
New Rochelle, N. Y., 7
New York
    Acadians in, 34
    black population, 24
    British occupation, 147, 171,
        172–173
    Connecticut merchants and
        entrepreneurs relocation to,
        260–262
    illegal trade, 47, 48
    Loyalists in, 82–83, 160
    state navy, 66, 67
    See also specific cities
New York, Port of, 211, 259,
    260–262
New York City
    British occupation, 99, 196
    China trade, 211
    patriots' aggressive actions
        against Loyalists, 82–83
    slave trade, 27
    Washington's return after war,
        198
New York Harbor, 11, 86, 114,
    116, 137–138, 176, 224, 232
Nicoll, Samuel, 232, 233, 239–240
Niger, 67
Niles, Robert, 71, 86–87, 136

niter, 73–74
Non-Intercourse Act (1809)
    (U.S.), 223, 224
Northport Harbor, 115, 170
Norwalk, Conn.
    Anglicans in, 84
    British raids, 164–165
    celebrations at end of war,
        195–196
    illicit trade, 46
    Loyalists from, 101–102, 196
    Revolutionary War
        fortifications, 79, 80
    whaleboat raids, 184
Norwalk Harbor, 11–12
Norway, prize ship processing,
    239–240
Norwich, Conn.
    geographical advantages, 10
    merchants from, 34–39, 58,
        208
    privateers from, 115, 117–119,
        175
    shipbuilding, 90, 94
    trade from, 204
Nott, William, 116, 141
Nova Scotia, Canada
    Acadians' expulsion and
        recruitment of New
        Englanders, 33–41
    French and Indian Wars, 32–34
    King George's War, 28–32
    Loyalists in, 33, 197, 202
    privateers, 115, 116–117, 145,
        174–175, 240, 253
    during Revolutionary War,
        56–58
    trade, 5–6, 36–41, 56–58,
        201–202, 218
Noyes, James, 19

Old Man's Beach, 183
Oliver Cromwell, 66, 89–90, 95,
    130–131, 134–135, 136,
    137–139
Oriental, 263
Orient Point, 7
Orpheus, 233, 235
Overton, Albert, 179
Oyster Bay, 7, 115, 170, 185, 214
Oyster Bay Camp, 80
Oyster Ponds, 59

Packwood, William, 47
Pactolus, 244, 246
Palmer, Amos, 244
Palmer, Benjamin, 254, 255
Palmer, John, 121, 122, 126–128
Palmer, Mary, 153
Palmer, Nathaniel, 6, 261–262,
    263
Palmer, Theobald, 263

Palmer, William, 153
Paragon, 219–220
Paris, Treaty of (1783), 195
Parker, Timothy, 87, 131, 134, 135, 137–138
Parmoon, 230
Parsons, Samuel, 165
patriots
  Long Island refugees, 97–99, 119–124, 197
  in New York City, 82–83
  percentage of population, 81
  plundering during Revolutionary War, 100–101
  See also Whaleboat War
Paulus Hook, N. J., 165
Peckham, Stephen, 84
Peekskill, N. Y., 100, 149
Pelham, N. Y., 148
Pendleton, Joseph, 20–21
Pendleton, Joseph, Jr., 20
Pendleton Hill, 80
Peninsular War, 224
Pennsylvania Navy, 66
Penny, Joshua, 235–236
Pequot Hill, 80
Pequot Plantation, 60, 85
Pequot War, 163
Perkins, Elizabeth Headley, 117
Perkins, Hezekiah, 118, 177
Perkins, Jabez, 21, 37, 58, 118, 202
Perkins, Jabez, Jr., 118
Perkins, Jabez, III, 118, 137, 138–139
Perkins, Jacob, 36–37
Perkins, Roger, 37, 175
Perkins, Simeon, 6, 34–35, 37–39, 57, 117–118, 139, 145, 175, 177, 202, 222, 226
Perkins, Zebulon, 203
Perry, Robert, 240
Philadelphia, Penn., 153–154
Phoenix, 65, 91–92
Pickering, Timothy, 206
Pigot, 112
Pintard, John, 44, 46
Pitt, 34
Plaiceway, Robert, 39
Play, 40
Plum Gut, 7, 59–60
Plum Island, 60, 249
Plunderers from across the Sound (Overton), 179
Plymouth Harbor, 64
Polly, 97, 196
Pond, Adam, 231–232
Pond, Charles, 224
Porter, Joshua, 74
port fees, 17–18
Port Jefferson, 215, 230
Portland, Conn., 213

Port of New London, 14–15, 17–18
Port of New York, 211, 259, 260–262
Post, Nathan, 121–123
Potapaug, 23
Prentice, John, 29, 31–32
Prentice, Sarah, 32
President, USS, 239, 241, 255
Prince Edward Island, 28
prisoners
  Revolutionary War, 77, 84, 89, 96, 103–107, 131, 136, 138, 140, 143, 147, 152, 165, 169–170, 184
  War of 1812, 236, 239, 255
prison ships, 87, 104, 178–179
privateers and privateering
  bond requirements, 110
  from Connecticut, 108–109, 112–115, 116, 188
  Continental Congress's authorization of, 67, 77, 108–109
  Duke de Choisel wreck, 145
  in Europe, 225, 239–240
  financial arrangements, 109–110
  Long Island patriot refugees, 119–124
  in Nova Scotia, 115, 116–117, 145, 174–175, 231, 240, 253
  numbers of, 108–109
  after Revolutionary War, 196
  Revolutionary War activity, 115–124, 175–178, 192–193, 195
  ship captures, 45, 57–58, 113, 114, 116, 119, 176
  ship characteristics, 68, 110
  tactics of, 110–112
  War of 1812, 231–232, 238–240, 242, 253–254
  in West Indies, 113–114, 124–128
  See also specific ships
Prosper, 47
Prosperity, 208
Putnam, 188
Putnam, Israel, 132

Quebec, 34, 63
Queen Anne's War, 28

The Race, 7, 8, 217
Racer, 153
Rachel, Fort, 236
Raleigh, 143
Ramillies, HMS, 232, 233, 234, 235, 236, 238, 246, 247, 248
Ranger, 119
Rattlesnake, 177, 239

Raven, 65
Raymond, Thaddeus, 19
Recovery, 167
Reid, Samuel, 250–251
Renommee, 29–30
Restoration, 131, 139
Retaliation, 178–179
Revenge, 120–123, 126
Revolutionary War
  1775–1776, 55–107
  1777–1779, 146–170
  1780–1783, 171–198
  British evacuation of Boston, 86–89
  British invasion and occupation of Long Island, 80, 86, 96–99
  British invasion of New York City, 90–94
  British Lake Champlain advance, 94–96
  British raids/attacks on towns, 59–62, 81, 85, 147–152, 156–167, 178–180
  Bunker Hill, Battle of, 55
  conflicts leading up to, 42–51
  Dorchester Heights, Battle of, 76
  end of, 194–198
  fortifications, 78–80
  Groton Heights, Battle of, 79, 188–191
  Harlem Heights, Battle of, 99–100
  Kegs, Battle of the, 134
  Lexington and Concord, 55
  Long Island Sound's role, 264
  lookout posts, 80–81
  military supply shortages, 72–78
  naval power (*See* navies)
  Norwalk's destruction, 11–12
  prisoners, 77, 84, 89, 96, 103–107, 131, 136, 138, 140, 143, 147, 152, 165, 169–170, 184
  privateers and privateering (*See* privateers and privateering)
  Rhode Island, Battle of, 112
  Ridgefield, Battle of, 150–151
  ships used in, 67–72
  slave soldiers, 26
  start of, 55–56
  trade during, 56–59, 97, 124–128, 147, 174, 192–193, 195
  Valcour Island, Battle of, 95–96
  White Plains, Battle of, 100
  Yorktown, Battle of, 191–192
  See also Whaleboat War
Rhode Island
  illegal trade, 46–47
  King George's War support, 29, 32

Loyalists from, 103, 172
navy, 62, 66
See also specific cities
Rhode Island, Battle of, 112
Richards, Samuel, 156
Ridgefield, Battle of, 150–151
Riley, Ackley, 118–119
Riley, James, 257–258
Riley, Richard, 177
The Rise of New York Port
(Albion), 261
Rivington, James, 83, 173, 198
Robert Palmer & Son shipyard,
263
Rochambeau, Comte de, 11, 184,
186, 187, 191
Rocky Hill, Conn., 118–119, 177,
212
Roe, Austin, 155
Rogers, Moses, 6, 259
Rogers, Samuel, 140
Rogers, William, 67
Rolla, 254
rope making, 24–25
Rose, 59, 61, 84, 91
Rover, 253
row galleys, 70–71, 90, 113
Royal Gazette, 139
Royal Navy. *See* British Navy
The Royal New York Gazette, 173
Royal Savage, 94, 95
rum, 14, 16, 43, 47–48, 135
Russia, trade with, 225–226
Ryker torpedo, 241

Sachem Head, 151
Sage, Giles, 140–141
Sag Harbor, N. Y.
patriot refugees from, 97, 119,
151
privateers from, 177–178
Revolutionary War refugees
from, 213
shipbuilding, 22–23
War of 1812, 235–236
whaleboat raids, 151–152
whaling, 205, 262–263
Sag Harbor Fort, 80, 85, 151–152
sailcloth, 50
Saint Domingue, 47
Salem, Conn., 27
Salisbury, Conn., 74
Salisbury Iron Works, 79, 196
Sally (Hawley), 75, 77
Sally (Shaw), 48
Sally Ann, 222
Salonga, Fort, 80
salt, 16–17, 58, 75, 78, 257–258
Saltonstall, Dudley, 76, 142, 143,
188, 207
Saltonstall, Gurdon, 207
Saltonstall, Thomas, 207

Saltonstall, Winthrop, 207
saltpeter, 73–74
Sands Point Lighthouse, 217–218
Sandy Hook, 114, 116, 138
Sarah, 19, 123
Saratoga, 177
Savannah, 259
Saybrook, 79
Scarborough, HMS, 78, 90
Schecter, Barnet, vi
schooners, 5, 68, **69**, 71–72, 125
Schuldham, 148
Schuyler, 99, 131, 132
Schuyler, Philip, 75
Scourge, 232, 233, 239–240
Scudder, John, Jr., 234
Seabury, Samuel, 83
Seaflower, 192–193
seal trade, 205, 210–211, 261,
263
Sears, Isaac, 83
Setauket, Fort, 80, 153–154
Setauket Harbor, 215, 250
Seton, Andrew, 168
Seven Years' War, 32–34, 40, 45,
46–47, 48
Seymour, Conn., 180
Shark, 90, 92, 141
Shaw, Nathaniel, 16, 34, 47–48,
49, 55, 78
Shaw, Nathaniel, Jr., 34, 115, 120,
121, 190
Sheffield, Joseph, 123
Shelley, Timothy, 152
Shelter Island, 8, 9, 97–98, 191,
215, 219
shipbuilding, 4–5, 22–23,
211–215, 263
Shippan, Peggy, 187
ships
common types of, 6
under flag of truce, 45,
103–104
Long Island Sound entrance
and exit challenges, 7–9
naval ships, 68–72
See also specific ship names
shipwrecks, 8–9, 20–21, 216,
256–258
Shipyard Creek, 215
Shubrick, Lieutenant, 255
Sierra Leone, Africa, 197
Silliman, Gold, 136, 149,
158–159, 163, 168–170
Silliman, Mary, 163, 169, 170
Silliman, William, 158–159, 169
Sine qua non, 231–232
Sir John Sherbrooke, 231
"Skinners," 100–101
slaves
British raid of Fairfield,
163–164

Fort Griswold battle
participation, 190, 191
freedom obtainment, 25–26
Revolutionary War service, 197
rope production, 24–25
trade, 24, 26–27
in West Indies, 16, 26–27, 124
Slongo, Fort, 185, 186
sloops, 5, 68, **70**, 125
smallpox, 104–105, 134
Smedley, Samuel, 130, 134,
136–137, 166–167
Smith, Anna, 98
Smith, Governor, 230
Smith, Hezekiah, 224–225
Smith, Oliver, 61
Smith, Richard, 74, 196
Smith, Venture, 25–26
smuggling, 47–48
Snake, 119
Solomon Leete and Associates,
140–141
South Carolina Navy, 66
Southhampton Fort, 80
Southport, Conn., 230
Spanish West Indies, 203–204
Spaulding, Mrs., 163
Speculator, 208
spies
Revolutionary War, 98,
99–100, 103, 147, 154–155,
173–174, 183, 198
War of 1812, 237–238,
246–247
Spitfire, 90, 92, 177, 239
Spy, 71–72, 86–87, 130, 131,
135–136
Stamford, Conn.
Fort Stamford, 191–192
Loyalists in, 84
privateers from, 176–177
Revolutionary War
fortification, 79, 80
whaleboat raids, 180
Stamford, Fort, 191–192
St. Ann's, Nova Scotia, 31
Stanton, Daniel, 18–19
Stanton, Theophilus, 92
Stanton, Thomas, 138
Starr, George, 25
Starr, Samuel, 35, 36
state navies, 66–67. *See also*
Connecticut Navy
Staten Island, N. Y., 86, 90,
153
St. Bartholomew, 228
steamboats, 6, 259
St. Eustatius, 42–43, 127–128
Stewart, Elizabeth Coles,
237–238, 246–248, 249
Stewart, Howes, 39
Stewart, James, 246–247, 249

St. George, Fort, 80, 172, 183
St. Joseph and St. Helena, 21–22
St. Martins, 17
Stonington, Conn.
  impressed sailor's escape to, 238
  impressment of sailors from, 221–222
  Nathaniel Palmer House, 263
  privateers from, 115
  during Revolutionary War, 60–62, 84
  Revolutionary War fortifications, 79
  seal trade, 205, 211
  vulnerability to enemy attack, 9
  War of 1812, 243–249
Stony Point Fort, 165
storms, 19, 21–22, 121, 249
Stowe, Stephen, 105
Stratford Point, 195
Strong, Anna Smith, 155, 197
Strong, Selah, 98, 155, 197
submarines, 93–94, 234
Suffolk, 114, 123–124, 156
Suffolk County, Conn.
  black population, 24
  Long Island evacuees, 97
  patriots in, 84
  See also specific cities
sugar, 15, 47, 232
Sugar Act (1764) (Great Britain), 43, 48, 49
Sugar Reef Passage, 7
sulfur, 73
Sullivan, John, 121
Susan, 251–252
Susannah, 21–22
Swallow, 124
Swan, 59, 147
Swan, Thomas, 246
Sylph, 242

Talbot, Silas, 112
Tallmadge, Benjamin, 98, 99, 103, 153, 154, 155, 170, 172, 173–174, 183, 185–186, 193, 194, 195, 197
Tallmadge, Mary Floyd, 197
Tartar, 29, 30, 65
Tashua Hill, 81, 149
taxation, 15, 43, 48, 49
Terror, HMS, 244, 246, 248, 263
Thames, 123
Thames River, 9–10
Thatcher, John, 95
Thompson, James, 47
Three Brothers, 195, 209
Throg's Neck, 100, 182
Ticonderoga, Fort, 59, 76, 96, 144
tide ranges, 7
Tilley, James, 189

timber industry, 23, 28, 38
torpedoes, 241
Tortuga, 17
Townsend, Robert, 154–155
trade
  American embargo (1807), 223–224
  British bans after Revolutionary war, 201, 203, 204, 206, 218
  British restrictions of American colonies, 3, 13–15, 16, 42–51
  with Europe, 218–220, 223–226
  fur, 38–39, 205, 210–211, 263
  with Nova Scotia, 5–6, 36–41, 56–58, 201–202, 218
  during Revolutionary War, 56–59, 97, 124–128, 147, 174, 192–193, 195
  after Revolutionary War, 201–211
  slaves, 24, 26–27
  with West Indies, 4, 5, 13–17, 58–59, 124–128, 203–204, 218, 228
  See also illicit trade
Treaty of Aix-la-Chapelle, 32
Treaty of Ghent (1814), 254
Treaty of Paris (1783), 195
Treaty of Utrecht (1713), 28
Trident, 211, 221
Triton, 22
Trowbridge, Anna Sherman, 111
Trowbridge, Caleb, 111
Trumbull, 23, 143, 188
Trumbull, Fort, 79, 104, 189
Trumbull, Jonathan, 59, 74, 87, 106, 107, 131, 134, 137, 138, 168, 223
Trumbull & Company, 38
Truxes, Thomas, 47
Tryon, William, 149–150, 157, 160, 162, 163, 164, 166
Tupper, Benjamin, 91
Turks & Caicos islands, 17
Turtle, 93–94, 234
Two Horse Races, 7–8

Union, 138
Unite, 222
United States, USS, 230, 232–233, 249
U.S. Navy
  Constitution, 207, 229
  Non-Intercourse Act enforcement, 224–225
  War of 1812, 229–230, 232–233
  See also Continental Navy
Utrecht, Treaty of (1713), 28

Valcour Island, Battle of, 95–96
Valiant, 233
Vengeance, 122
Venture, 120
Venus, 178
Victory, 236
Viper, 177
Virginia, 177
Virginia, Acadians in, 33

Wadsworth, Jeremiah, 209
Wahlee, Mel, 95
Wallabout Bay, 178
Wallace, James, 59, 60–61, 84
Wansuc, Tom, 191
warfare
  cannons, 51, 74–75, 79, 117
  "infernal machines," 234–235, 241–242
  musket ball production, 72–73
War of 1812
  British blockade, 230–238, 240–242
  British raid of Essex, 23
  declaration of war, 227–228
  end of, 254–255
  events leading to/causes of, 31–32, 201, 227
  Little Gull Island, 217
  Long Island Sound's role, 264
  naval engagements, 229, 230, 249–253
  privateering during, 231–232, 238–240, 242, 253–254
  Stonington bombardment, 243–249
  support for, 227–228
War of Austrian Succession, 28–32, 45
Warren, 142, 188
Warren, Commodore, 30–31
wars
  French and Indian Wars, 32–34, 40, 45, 46–47, 48
  King George's War, 28–32, 45
  King William's War, 29, 40
  Napoleonic Wars, 219–220, 221, 228, 237
  Peninsular War, 224
  Pequot War, 163
  Queen Anne's War, 28
  Revolutionary War (*See* Revolutionary War)
  War of 1812 (*See* War of 1812)
  War of Austrian Succession, 28–32, 45
warships, 68–72
Washington, 90, 91, 95, 145
Washington, Fort, 92, 100
Washington, George

British supply locations, 149
Continental Navy
   establishment, 55, 62, 63–66
Dorchester Heights battle, 76
espionage network, 154,
   173–174
Fairfield visit during
   presidency, 167
Fort St. George, 183
Huntington whaleboat raid
   plans, 193
Lloyd Neck invasion plan,
   185–186
New London Harbor
   fortification, 78
New York attack plans, 186
New York City entrance after
   war, 198
Silliman kidnapping, 168
Watch Hill Lighthouse, 217
Watch Hill Passage, 7, 21
Waterbury, David, 95, 191–192
Wayne, Anthony, 165
Welling, Thomas, 235
Wellington's army, 224, 228, 237,
   264
Westchester County, N. Y.
   agriculture and livestock
      production, 4
   during Revolutionary War, 83,
      100, 101, 159
   See also specific cities
Westerly, R. I., privateers from,
   115
West Indies
   harbor fees, 18

map of, xii
privateer activity, 113–114,
   124–128
salt production, 16–17
sugar cane production, 15–16
supply shortages during
   Revolutionary War, 124–125
trade, 4, 5, 13–17, 58–59,
   124–128, 203–204, 218, 228
West Neck Creek, 215
Westport, Conn., War of 1812,
   229–230
Wethersfield, Conn., 118–119, 212
whaleboats, 11, 70–71, 235, 237
Whaleboat War
   Brookhaven raids, 168
   Ebenezer Dayton's activities,
      114, 123–124, 155–156,
      180–181
   Fairfield raids, 167–168
   Fort Franklin raids, 170
   Fort Setauket attack, 153–154
   Guilford raids, 193
   Joseph Hull's activities,
      182–183
   Long Island Sound
      confrontation (1782),
      193–194
   Loyalist refugees in Long
      Island, 102–103
   motivations for, 152–153,
      155–156, 179–180
   naval support, 171–172
   Norwalk raids, 168, 184
   outcomes of, 165
   Sag Harbor Fort, 151–152

Silliman kidnapping,
   168–170
Stamford attack, 192
whaling, 205, 262
Wheeler, Thomas, 40–41
Wheeler, William, 146, 180, 223,
   228
Whim, 177–178
Whitby, 104
White, Gideon, 118
White Plains, Battle of, 100
Whiting, 90, 92, 141
Whiting, Colonel, 162
Wickham, Thomas, 196
Wicopesset Passage, 7
William, 120
William and Mary, 38
Williams, Ezekial, 102
Williams, Isaac, 246, 247
Williams, Joseph, 208
William Tell, 258
Wilsie, John, 215
Windsor, Conn., 23, 212
Winslow, Joshua, 71
Winthrop, Robert, 85
Woodbridge, Joseph, 216
Woodhull, Abraham, 155,
   157–158, 173
Wool Act (1699) (Great Britain),
   50
Wooster, David, 59–60, 150
Wright, Obadiah, 156

York, 139
York's Tavern, 238
Yorktown, Battle of, 191–192